THINK
OF
THOSE
DENIED
THE
PRIVILEGE

A well earned Retirement

THINK OF THOSE
DENIED THE PRIVILEGE

MICK RINE

HOODED LION BOOKS
BARTON SEAGRAVE
KETTERING
NORTHAMPTONSHIRE
2014

ISBN 978-0-9537037-4-6

Published by :
Hooded Lion Books
20 Grosvenor Way
Barton Seagrave
Kettering
Northamptonshire NN15 6TG

Hooded Lion Books is an Imprint of Monkshood Publishing

www.monkshood.co.uk

Printed and Bound in Great Britain by

Direct Print On Demand Limited
Denington Estate
Wellingborough
Northamptonshire NN6 9BX

Typeset in Plantin and Raleigh

For my lovely wife
DANUSIA
who supported me
throughout my police career

FOREWORD

This autobiography tells the story of a young boy growing up in the 1950s and 1960s in post war London.

I was born in the borough of Hackney and became one of a family of seven children. My father changed jobs regularly and it was up to my Mum, Rose, to hold the family together. As a young boy, I found work in many different trades and feel that these experiences stood me in good stead, in my adult life.

On leaving school, I did a five year apprenticeship in Mechanical Engineering in Tottenham, North London.

At the age of twenty one years, I met and married my wonderful wife, Danusia, whom I'm proud to say is an Essex girl.

In 1972, after our first two children were born, we moved to Northamptonshire, where, on Danusia's instructions, I joined the Northamptonshire Police.

In hindsight, I can say my upbringing in Hackney prepared me well for what became a thirty year career in the police.

I spent twenty two of those years as a front line Detective Constable and the other eight years in a uniformed role. I had a great career and experienced many really awful incidents along the way.

After retiring, I suffered many nightmares, which always related to the cases that I dealt with, as a front line policeman.

I decided that I should write a book about my experiences with a view to sharing them with potential readers.

On completing my book I have ceased having the nightmares and now sleep quite well at night.

The title *Think of those denied the privilege* relates to persons who lost their lives at a relatively young age, and were therefore denied the privilege of a long life.

I wish to dedicate my book to all of the families involved, in this tragic loss of life.

CONTENTS

page

PART ONE
Early years   1

PART TWO
Work and Marriage   69

PART THREE
Northamptonshire here we come   115

PART FOUR
A Detective at last   203

PART FIVE
Back to uniform - and Retirement   325

Acknowledgements and Thanks   342

Part One
Early years

The Mothers' Hospital

I have had a great life and invite you to journey through it with me, and among other things, meet those denied the privilege of longer life. Those denied the privileges of long life are complete strangers, friends, family and victims. This book is based on my memory of events, and will therefore consist of the truth - but not necessarily the whole truth!

One thing is sure, because I have a birth certificate. I was born in June 1948 at The Mothers' Hospital in Homerton, Hackney, London and my mother Rose played the lead role.

Mum had a brother in law Sidney, whom she was fond of, this culminated in my second name becoming Sidney. I was given the first name of Michael, hence Michael Sidney plus the family name Rine, was recorded on the birth certificate.

Obviously, I inherited the surname from my dad, John Rine who everyone referred to as Jack. To this day I have never really understood why John becomes Jack.

Dad's mum died when I was only knee high to a grasshopper, so I only have a very vague memory of her. Sadly I have no knowledge at all about my Dad's dad, his identity and details remain a mystery to me.

Dad was brought up as an only child in London, served sometime in the army during the Second World War, and then embarked on a life of smoking Woodbine cigarettes, and working mainly in the building and decorating trades. Unfortunately for Mum he wasn't good at keeping a job. On the other hand it could be said, he was good at helping Mum to

1

bring children into the world. He actually felt that he had failed in that arena - he intended to have eleven children, but only managed seven. And I will expand on the seven children along the way.

Well, what a great time to come into the world. The Second World War had ended three years earlier, and people were optimistic about the future.

Our house was in Aspland Grove, Hackney, and my first memories of my early life were of things we all grow up with, namely things forming part of our home life. I recall the building itself, consisting of three floors, and that the top floor was occupied by Jim and Sylvie. Their floor was rather private and generally out of bounds to children. However, I remember them with fondness and recall that Sylvie always smelled of face pack, you know, the stuff women put on their faces. She had pitted facial skin and as a child of maybe four years old, I felt that the face pack smoothed out her skin. She was otherwise a good looking lady, of slim build and always smartly dressed.

Jim was tall and slim with a gaunt face. I formed the opinion that they were nice people to have living above us. I also remember both of them smoked, they used Weights cigarettes, with the smoke billowing from their door, when coming and going from their rooms.

My two brothers David, Alan and I, would sometimes venture up their staircase, to the top landing and suffer their wrath if we were too noisy. As young children we were oblivious to the fact that a combination of three young children playing on wooden, and lino treaded stairs, made an awful din.

Mice could be seen and heard in the shoe cupboard situated in the ground floor backroom, nowadays referred to as the living room. I recall small holes in the floorboards beneath the shoes, and that the mice would appear through these holes.

To the rear of the house, we had a two track railway line, situated at the top of a railway embankment. Steam trains would shunt back and forth with regular monotony. You could taste the coal dust in the air and the 'ratter-to-ta-ratter-to-ta'

2

noise seemed constant. I simply loved the trains and all that went with them!

Because of the constant vibration of the trains, the back wall of the house, bowed outwards approximately two feet from ground level to the roof. The house was over a hundred years old and somewhat spooky for us kids.

Mum had a scullery on the ground floor, at the back of the house, nowadays referred to as a kitchenette. It was simply minute, consisting of a sink with drainer, two small cupboards, and - wait for it - a tap with cold water supply. I would estimate the floor space, in the scullery to be three square metres. This clearly left little room for movement when the family gathered together.

The rear wall of the scullery consisted of a pair of old wooden, single glazed doors. Well, God forbid, in the winter months that little room was certainly avoided by us children at all costs. The wind would whistle through the void of missing putty, around each small pane of glass, in those double doors. Despite these drawbacks, Mum would spend several hours a day in that little room preparing the three meals a day, for the ever increasing family members.

I remember Toad-in-the-Hole particularly, it had a wonderful smell and Mum always made it rise up in the baking tray. It would be accompanied by mashed potatoes, peas, and gravy. Mum also treated us to fish fingers and mash, but not as often as one would like. Then again, very occasionally she would fry cod in batter with chips from the chip pan - very nice too.

My favourite memory would be entering the house when Mum had been baking shortbread in flat trays. I can smell it to this day, delicious to eat. It would be rolled out on the flat tray with the rolling pin, but never seemed to be enough to reach the edges of the tray. The shortbread was therefore thin at the edges, but those pieces were the best in the world to eat, having been slightly burnt.

Mum was very fond of two particular visitors to the house. The first was a man who called to collect overdue rent. He seemed to be a very patient individual, always smiling and speaking nicely to Mum. I feel frustrated not being able to recall his name, I feel as though I have let him down in some way. Mum's worries about rent payment would be regularly coupled with Dad's request to her 'Rose, have you got two shillings for some Woodbines?'

Mum would try to change the subject, which often ended with raised voices, and Dad's next remark 'women always have the last word'. During our younger days, Dad must have repeated that line a thousand times.

Moving on to the second visitor, a nice lady, whose name to my shame I also cannot recall. Mum would turn in her grave if she knew I had forgotten it. I believe she was a welfare lady, who would visit the house initially for a chat and then return about a week later, with new shoes for my brothers and me. This was most welcomed because our shoes would often have holes right through the sole of the shoe. Mum was certainly happier when the lady visited, and of course I now understand why. Clearly one visitor was a provider and the other would take away.

Jim and Sylvie, our top floor residents

Houses in Aspland Grove

The first five children

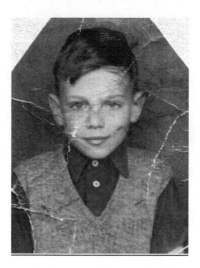

The Author as a young boy

Coronation Day

I suppose my best memory aged five at the time would be the Queen's Coronation day, which fell on or very near my fifth birthday. I didn't fully understand what was happening but I remember very clearly indeed, Mum handing me a wonderful jockey suit, which she had made for me to wear at the celebration. It was made on Mum's sewing machine from silk coat lining material, a perfect fit, together with a peaked cap and riding crop. I believe it was yellow in colour and very proudly worn as I stepped into the street.

My brother David who was a year or so older than me, also had an outfit for the occasion but I'm unable to recall what he wore. My brother Alan who was four years old had an outfit also, and again memory fails me, being unable to describe it.

A large wooden stage had been constructed in the middle of our Street, by my Uncle Harry, Mr Burgess and other neighbours. To a small boy at the time the stage seemed to be huge, and I was amazed at this achievement. Our street, called Aspland Grove, was referred to as a dead-end-street. This reference worried me as a boy, but I later discovered that dead-end referred to the fact that it was closed off at one end. There were approximately sixty houses in the street, and we lived at Number Twelve.

The stage was built directly outside our house on the bend in the road. I was told that the road had been closed for two days, to make it safe for everyone involved in the celebration.

I have vague memories of the stage show, but can recall some of the end of war songs being sung, music being played, and some dancing. Prizes were given for best fancy dress, but sadly I didn't receive any of the prizes.

On a brighter note we were all invited to a children's party which was kindly funded by Gibbons, the local well known furniture store. The store had a rear yard situated at the top of our street, which had a large lean-to style roof, providing a good all weather facility for our party. I believe sixty local children attended, all comfortably seated on trestle style tables and bench seats. Bunting had been strewn above our heads and all along the street. Accompanied by balloons, paper hats, and assorted whistles, the buffet style food was a great treat. Of course the food was washed down with assorted fizzy drinks.

We were also entertained by a magician and assorted games, consisting of pass the parcel and musical chairs. All the kids had a great time, especially when ice-cream, jelly and blancmange was served up at the end of the party. The whole event was then rounded off with all taking part in a rendition of God Save the Queen. This song was a bit of a mystery to most of us kids at the time, but joining in with the song was a small price to pay for such a wonderful time. I formed the view at that early stage in my life that furniture stores were good for kids and have loved the smell they give off ever since.

The Coronation Day street stage

Little girl in Coronation dress

Rams
Infants' School

Aspland Grove in those early days was a great place for kids to play out, in relevant safety. Street games were popular including knock down ginger, where you would knock neighbours street door knockers and run away. We thought that was great fun, until Dad was made aware, then the fun ended in tears.

Tin Tan Tommy was another game, where you would hide in the street, until seen by the one holding the tin can. He or she would then bang the can on the pavement shouting 'Tin Tan Tommy, I see Kenny hiding behind the wall'. Whilst this was being shouted the other persons hiding would try to run back to base, before being seen. Great fun if you made it back to base, but you needed to be very quick.

School began for me at the age of five. The infant school I attended was also situated in Hommerton Road, Hackney, very close to The Mothers' Hospital. I have only three or four clear memories of those school days. I recall arriving there, clinging onto Mum's large wheeled pram. I believe my sister Patricia had arrived as a baby at that time and she remained in the pram, as I reluctantly released my grip on it, and walked into school.

At play time I remember forming a long line with other boys, and all marching across the playground like soldiers. I became friends with a boy called Leslie Chambers who had distinctive front top teeth.

At playtime one day I recall a boy running towards me at great speed. To avoid him crashing into me, I pushed my hands out, in an attempt to push him to the one side. Collision with me was avoided, but the boys head struck the brick work on the corner of the school building, resulting in a large hole being sustained to his right temple. I was shocked at the time because it was the first time I had seen inside someone's head. The boy remained conscious and was taken into reception for treatment. He fortunately later recovered fully and everyone accepted that it was an unfortunate accident.

The walk back from school was fun because we would pass through Hackney graveyard, and whilst Mum was talking to other parents, I would be jumping from one gravestone to the next. I later became a reasonable gymnast, and feel in hindsight that the gravestone jumping was all part of my training. I should point out that the stones were very old, and my understanding of wrong doing was somewhat limited at that time. I now feel a little ashamed of myself despite the fact that I was five years old.

Throughout my childhood Mum worked on a sewing machine in the backroom of our house. I can still hear now that constant noise that the machine made and feel that Mum deserved a medal, for the many years of machining that she achieved.

She formed part of what was called the rag trade, being employed by Jewish people who had a large clothing factory near to where we lived. Mum would acquire what were referred to as linings from the factory, which after machining would form interiors for jackets, coats and skirts. She would receive payment each week relating to the number of linings completed. This is where I first understood the meaning of the words piecework. The more Mum completed, the more she would be paid. I recall despite being young at the time, that Mum would quite often accidentally puncture a finger or thumb, with needles used whilst working on her machine.

There is little doubt in my mind now that the work Mum did, was a sacrifice on her part, which kept our family together. In other words, some of our number would probably have gone into children's homes, without her weekly wage.

As children we would regularly collect and deliver the linings, back and forth to the factory. On those visits to the factory, I would enjoy watching the employees, all working at a frantic pace, to make a living. I was also fascinated by the narrow road which led to the factory doors. It was a very bumpy road surface which had been made with cobble stones. As I grew up I observed that many a road in Hackney, had been made from cobble stones. I assume to this day that cobbles were used due to the fact that they were hard wearing and long-lasting.

❀ ❀

The dreaded Bath

During those early days of my life, Saturdays became a day to dread, why you might ask? Well Saturdays were bath days, and the dreaded tin bath would be brought out and placed in the centre of the scullery floor. The tin bath, for the uninitiated was about five feet in length and fourteen inches deep, with rounded ends.

My parents would heat up several saucepans of water, which were poured into the bath ready for the first child to bathe. David would wash himself first, followed by myself, then Brother Alan, and then Patricia. We all used the same water, which always became somewhat cold and scummy, towards the end of proceedings.

I should point out one luxury during the process, this being to have your hair rinsed with fresh water, before exiting the bath. Of course as time progressed the numbers queuing for this pleasure increased to seven children, as the three remaining children June, Raymond, and John were born.

Little time was spent on drying and dressing oneself after the bath. In winter time the scullery became particularly cold, and goose bumps were never far away. Fortunately as the family grew bigger, Sylvie and Jim moved away to a new home. This had the effect of freeing up two more rooms on the top floor of our house. Sylvie and Jim were sadly missed, but the extra space was much appreciated.

Dad carried out some renovation work and the bedrooms were reallocated. David, Michael, and Alan moved to the top floor front bedroom. My sisters I believe had the top floor back bedroom, and my two remaining brothers had beds below my room. Finally my parents had the bedroom below my sister's. I would imagine that the lady visitor from the Social Department, whom I now recall had the name of Mrs Edwards, would have assisted Mum with the additional rent.

A typical tin bath

Whilst on the subject of bedrooms, my parents' room was always of interest to me, in particular my Dad's tallboy. This was a small wardrobe which dad kept locked with a small key. Occasionally if, the children were well behaved, Dad would allow us to see his wartime black and white photos, mostly pictures taken in Iraq. They were quite interesting but we preferred to see his live ·303 rifle bullet. Dad explained that he kept the tallboy locked because this bullet was potentially dangerous, particularly if touched by nosey kids.

In view of Dad's warning I can honestly say that I personally only touched the bullet once or twice, and I'm pleased that I survived to tell the tale. Dad also had an ornate wooden moneybox in the tallboy, again which he brought back from the war. The moneybox was in the shape of a book, and had a hidden compartment, which consisted of a sliding dovetail joint. I fell in love with that box, particularly the dovetail joint. Sadly despite regular inspection of this moneybox, I never ever found any money in it.

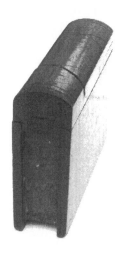

The moneybox...   ...and with it open

13

❀ ❀

The tradesmen

During my younger days in Aspland Grove I was always fascinated by the various tradesmen that would visit to deliver things or to take things away. My favourite had to be the coalman, always as black as the coal that he would deliver. He was clearly a very strong individual, placing a heavy bib on his back, followed by a large bag of coal. Prior to this he would remove round cast iron lids from the pavement and then tip the whole bag of coal through the round hole, in the pavement.

The families living in adjacent houses to the hole in the pavement would then be able to access their delivery of coal via the basement of the house. Several bags of coal were delivered to each house by this method.

We didn't have a coal hole in the pavement, which resulted in the coalman passing through our hallway, and tipping the coal directly into our coal cupboard. This was situated beneath the stair case and would accommodate about six bags of coal. When deliveries were due, one of the children would be given the task of checking the bags in. Given the chance the coalman would deliver a half filled bag! Clearly there are good and bad coalman, as in any occupation.

Next on my list was the milkman, the one we had was always cheerful, and I found the open sided floats interesting. I'm unable to recall his name but I remember him living in Roman Road, Bethnal Green, in a two storey block of flats. He would knock the door of our house on Sundays to collect payment for the week's delivery of milk and would place the cash in a tan coloured leather bag which hung down from a shoulder strap.

My childhood memory of postman is somewhat limited other than to say they were generally dressed in blue.

The dustman sticks in a child's mind, due mainly to the smell of the dust cart. In those early days the interior of the dust cart appeared to be coated in a pink powder, which gave off a very strange chemical smell. It was one of those childhood smells which remain with you whenever you think about the dust cart - can you smell it?

I should also mention the man who would shout out 'rag and bone' repeatedly. It was great to see the Rag and Bone man, because his cart had large rubber wheels and was pulled along by a lovely old horse. If you were really lucky you would see the horse eating hay from a large bag which hung from the horse's neck. I decided at that young age that I preferred the smell of the dung left in the road by the horse, to the smell of the dust cart!

The 1950s in Aspland Grove were great because each individual seemed to know every person residing in the street. Parents could leave the kids playing in the street in the certain knowledge that they were safe! Unfortunately you couldn't do the same in the twenty-first century.

❀ ❀

A brush with the Law

One of my friends in the street told me one day that I could climb over a tall garden wall and scrump some lovely ready to eat apples. I was given a leg up and dropped down into a rather scary overgrown rear garden. I made my way through thorns and God knows what else to arrive eventually at a well laden apple tree.

I very quickly filled my pockets with apples only then to hear a dog barking loudly. The dog seemed to be barking louder and louder, and I formed the view that it was closing in on me. I never actually saw the dog as I left the garden at great speed. I reached the top of the earlier mentioned garden wall without the need for a leg up, only to be met by a tall man dressed in a navy blue uniform.

He had a policeman's helmet on his head and said 'what are you doing young man?' The shock of seeing the policeman left me unable to speak. He then took me home to my parents and together they found the apples in my pockets.

I must have been six or seven years old at the time, and remember Dad giving me a good spanking on my bottom. I can honestly say that I have not taken apples without permission since that day. I actually remember my first encounter with the police that day, with some fondness.

On a brighter note I loved going to the local grocer's shop with Mum when we were small kids. Mum would take her shopping bags with her and make her way up the narrow way to the grocer's shop. In those days you would stand on the customer side of the counter and point out to the grocer which items you wanted from his shelves. The selected items would then be placed on the counter, before being rung up on the till. After paying for the items Mum would place them in her shopping bags and leave the shop.

I can see Mum now, so to speak, carrying those heavy bags of shopping down the street. With luck Mum would tire as we reached the Baker's shop. Mum and her little helper might then be treated to a wonderful jam doughnut. This was a rare treat indeed, only to be enjoyed if Mum had earned a good wage from the Rag Trade that week. Sadly in later life Mum needed surgery on her knee, due I believe to a combination of machining and carrying heavy shopping bags all those years.

During the early days as a young child Guy Fawke's Night was a great night for kids to look forward to. Preparations would begin several weeks before Guy Fawke's Night, particularly the making of the guy. Once made, the guy would be placed on a cart and presented on street corners to the passing public. The shout would be made, namely 'penny for the guy', whereupon passing pedestrians would give you coins to purchase fireworks with later. Alan and I were the main collectors with the guy, standing outside *The Earl of Amhurst* pub at the top of our Street. We were always assured of a good collection at that spot when people known to us returned home

16

from work. Pennies were given in the main, but occasionally a threepence, a sixpence or a shilling would be given.

I realise now that these donations for our Guy Fawke's Night were all part of the community spirit which existed at that time. Under the law I now understand that it was a form of begging, but in our community it was just plain giving to others.

Our second location for collecting was outside the famous Hackney Empire situated in Mare Street, Hackney. I would encourage everyone to visit this building to view the beautiful facade and the interior, both having been built to perfection. The best time to collect with the guy was as people were leaving the theatre, having had a drink and filled their pockets with change.

My Dad always insisted that fish and chips would be purchased with some of the money on bonfire night. Each member of the family would have a portion sprinkled with salt and vinegar which would be eaten out of the chip paper. Dad would make his annual statement that he was not prepared to see all the guy collection go up in smoke. This was always a difficult statement to understand due to the fact that Dad always lit up a Woodbine after eating his fish and chips.

Occasionally my relatives Uncle Harry and Aunt Rene would attend our evening with my cousins Kenny, Gwen, Dennis and Jennifer. The fireworks would be lit by Dad or Harry and we always had enough to last two or three hours.

Despite being a child in a large family a good Guy Fawke's Night was normally assured as a result of the coin collections with the guy. Sadly the guy would then take pride of place on top of the bonfire and go up in a puff of smoke.

The firework display took place in our back gardens and on one such occasion a 'Jumping Jack' made its way into the top of my Wellington boot, resulting in a nasty burn to my ankle. The pain was bad enough but going to hospital whilst the bonfire was still burning was a complete disaster. In hindsight, I'm confident that people, who contributed to our collection, would be happy in the knowledge that fish and chips had been purchased with some of the money.

As a young child I soon became aware of neighbours. Some were very pleasant, for example Mr and Mrs Perrin who were quite elderly and lived next door at Number Thirteen. A Christmas present was always given by them to my family although I now realise they had little wealth to provide such presents. Furthermore birthday presents were also forthcoming. On the other hand The Challis family lived at Number Eleven, and were generally rather miserable. Suffice to say that Christmas presents were not forthcoming from the Challis's. I should remind you that these are a child's perceptions at the time and would not wish to cast aspersions on anyone's character.

The case might be for example that the Challis family suffered greatly during the war years, we shall never know. I suppose the acid test would be to kick a football over the rear garden wall, the Perrins would always politely return the ball, but the Challis's would keep it.

In hindsight I now realise that plants may have been damaged by the ball and the Challis's needed to make a point.

Christmas time

I feel that it's time to be a little more cheerful and talk about my Christmas experiences, in those early days. One thing stands out clearly in my mind namely the making of the paper chains. I found that a very exciting time as it heralded the imminent arrival of Christmas time. We would purchase the various coloured packets of chains from Woolworths, a very large store situated in Mare Street, Hackney.

On returning home the chains would be made by the available children. This was achieved by removing a strand of chain from the pack, followed by a second strand. You would then release the glue by licking the end of the strand. The strand would then be rolled with your fingers into a circle, and both ends would be glued together by applying finger pressure.

The second strand would be passed through the first and then glued as described earlier. Different colours would be used, culminating in a beautiful length of chain. Mum or Dad then fixed our chains to the walls and ceiling with drawing pins, resulting in a beautiful array of decorations.

Balloons were also blown up and pinned to the walls. The most thrilling part of the procedure was the arrival of the Christmas tree, which was decorated and lit up with pretty lights. One must not forget the beautiful fairy dressed in white lace, which witnessed the whole of Christmas from the top of the tree.

I suppose the biggest thrill for all of us kids was waking Christmas morning to the sound of Christmas paper rustling at the foot of our beds. The rule in our house was that the presents should not be unwrapped before 8 am. Well we learnt at an early age that rules were meant to be broken.

My best present ever was a wooden fort that my Dad had made for me. Of course Cowboys and Indians were all the rage at that time. The fort was painted blue/grey in colour, standing about ten inches tall and two feet square. Dad would have spent many hours in his garden shed making and painting the Christmas toys. This was of course a secret place in our garden where kids as I recall were strictly forbidden leading up to Christmas time.

Surprise, surprise, an uncle or an aunt will have purchased and wrapped a number of Cowboys and Indians in order that battle could commence on Christmas morning. What more could a young boy ask for on Christmas Day?

Then there was Mum's stocking tied to the bed end. This was filled with various little gifts that children would enjoy. I recall items like a yoyo, cap bangers, crackers and fruit consisting of a tangerine, an apple, a banana, and assorted nuts. Also sweets and coins were found at the far end of the stocking.

After breakfast kids were allowed out into the street where comparisons would be made of the various presents received. Occasionally kids would be jealous of one another but in the main this would not be the case because kids shared things in those days.

Tommy guns, bikes and scooters were sometimes wished for, but not forthcoming that particular year. I can hear the sound of the Tommy guns being fired in the street to this day.

I can also clearly remember Dad's friend, Charlie, promising to bring chicken for Christmas dinner and Mum being upset because it was twelve midday and Charlie had not arrived. Dad was looking out of the front room window at the time and shouted 'don't worry Rose, here he comes'. As we all looked up the Street we could see Charlie running towards us with a live chicken flapping around in each hand. Well it was the funniest thing I had ever seen. Charlie by the way had a large mop of red hair and I recall the chickens being of a similar colour.

Charlie came in the house and Mum told him in no uncertain terms to take the chickens out to the rear garden. Dad went to his shed and returned carrying a meat cleaver. Charlie held the body of the bird and Dad took hold of its head. The bird's neck was placed over a block of wood, at which point Dad struck the neck with his meat cleaver. Much to our surprise the now headless chicken then ran a complete circuit of our garden.

The second chicken was then dispatched in an identical fashion. The adults then decided that the gutting and plucking of the birds would not be witnessed by us kids. Charlie declined to stop for Christmas dinner and left soon after. I remember him apologising to Mum for arriving so late in the day with Christmas dinner. Having seen the preparations that day, I can say on behalf of the whole family that we all thoroughly enjoyed our Christmas dinner!

Charlie visited our home on four or five occasions and then was never seen again. To this date I'm puzzled as to where and why Dad and Charlie became friends. As a direct result of their friendship I learned that the Christmas chickens were called

'Rhode Island Reds'. Dad was so inspired by them that he subsequently raised chickens in a pen in our rear garden.

Whilst on the subject of gardens I'm reminded of what us kids referred to as the 'tar block adventure'. We were all playing in the street one morning when a strange but not unpleasant smell drifted into Aspland Grove. We followed our noses - so to speak - and on reaching Amhurst Road saw a huge machine breathing fire onto the road surface. The fire melted the tarmac which was then scrapped off by a small army of workmen as the machine made its way along the road. A second group of workmen were then seen to prise large wooden blocks from the road surface with pick axes.

One of the workers said we were welcomed to as many blocks as we could carry for use on our parents' open fires. I ran home where I told Mum about the offer of free tar blocks for the fire. Mum was very pleased and suggested my brothers and I gather up the blocks on our home-made carts. We set to work loading the blocks onto the cart which was then pushed back to our house. We then carried the blocks through the house and stacked them neatly in the back garden.

Over the coming weeks we had gathered in several tons of the blocks, which resulted in a lucrative little business by selling them on to our friends and neighbours. I can smell those blocks in my nostrils to this day and have loved the smell of hot tar ever since. There is of course a downside to all my stories and on this occasion it relates to removing tar oil from your hands with the use of a scrubbing brush.

These tar block roads existed for several miles through the streets of Hackney and surrounding boroughs. To date I have not established why they were placed below the tarmac surface. I do however have a theory that they were placed there in conjunction with the route of trams or trolley buses. It matters not, because many shillings were made as a result of their removal.

One day I remember Dad saying he had a treat in store for me, namely a visit to Hackney Baths. We walked to the baths which were about half a mile from home. On arrival an attendant handed each of us a bar of soap and a clean dry towel. We were then led into separate bath cubicles containing large individual cast iron baths. The attendant then turned large cross handled taps on, resulting in the bath being filled to the brim with lovely hot clean water.

The attendant checked the water temperature before instructing me to get into the bath. Climbing into that bath was a heavenly experience that one would never forget. I'm sorry to tell you that the bathing experience that day was only repeated twice during my upbringing. It was never discussed, but I assume it was relatively expensive. The only downside to the baths trip was a rather musky smell in the air at the time. The smell was due I believe. to the age of the premises and had no reflection on the work of the attendants.

No running!

One fond memory is not always followed by another. Dad was in the habit of sending his kids to buy his Woodbines at Monty's the Barber's shop in Amhurst Road. Brother Alan and I were sent on this occasion and Dad uttered the words 'mind the roads'. We dashed off at break neck speed and as we reached Amhurst Road, I was in the lead. We ran out into the road at which point I was struck firmly by an oncoming car. I was actually struck by the bonnet of the car, which knocked me high into the air with the result that I landed on the road surface to the rear of the car. This left me heavily dazed and somewhat blooded. Monty came to my rescue and carried me into his Barber's shop. The car driver also came into the shop and said 'what on earth do you think you were doing?' I replied 'Shopping'!

Monty cleaned me up and handed me the obligatory Woodbines. Like any true loving Brother Alan then supported me with a sturdy shoulder until I managed to limp back home.

Dad of course said 'what did I tell you?' On a bright note, I had sustained sufficient injuries and Dad chose not to admonish me further.

Monty by the way was a tall stout Jewish gentleman, with a large moustache. I very much appreciated his help that day and became rather fond of him. With regard to the accident, I wish to place on the record that The Green Cross Code did not exist at the time. However I learnt that your parent's advice should always be heeded.

Working life begins early

Shortly after the car accident I started working with my brother Alan at the local fruiterers, known as Jones's. They had a large fruit stall and premises at the disused Hackney Railway Station, situated on the corner of Mare Street and Amhurst Road. This was a great experience for us boys, both aged about nine at the time.

The work consisted of helping to set out the stall in the mornings and packing away in the evenings. Harry Jones was the boss and always had a laugh with everyone connected with the running of the business. The stall had a frontage of about thirty feet which displayed a wonderful selection of fruit and vegetables. This was supported by a large fruit and vegetable storage area, situated inside the old railway station. Alan and I fetched and carried the stock on sack barrows. We were rewarded at the end of the week with two shillings each.

My fondest memories revolved around the smells given off by the various fruits and vegetables. I particularly remember tangerines at Christmas time, but generally celery, beetroot and lemons. Another special time revolved around the arrival at Christmas time of the freshly cut Christmas trees. The wonderful fragrance of pine hung in the air until the last of the trees had been sold. If we were really lucky Alan and I would be given a tree as a Christmas bonus.

23

In addition to the stall, Harry's dad operated a small tobacconist's shop which was known as the dugout. The dugout originally a ticket office was situated between the stall and the stockroom.

Whilst working at the fruit stall one day I was approached by Tommy Herbert, the fishmonger. Tommy had a stall next to the fruit stall, and said he would like me to work for him. I decided to take the new job and began working for Tommy soon after.

I really loved working with the Herberts. Tommy and his wife Elsie sold wet fish on week days and brother Les, together with Reg sold shell fish on weekends. Sometimes despite my age I worked seven days a week on the various types of stall. Monday to Friday, I worked on the wet fish at Old Hackney Station. Saturday, selling shell fish at the same location and Sunday morning selling shell fish at Brick Lane market, Shoreditch.

I started that job whilst still attending Junior School, and continued until I was thirteen years of age. I started work early in the morning which consisted of visiting the railway arches and pulling the stall out. The stall was then pulled about one hundred yards to Mare Street via a cobble stone yard. I can relive that moment to this day, as the contact between steal rimmed wheels and cobbles, juddered through my body. I would then cross Mare Street at my peril, avoiding trolley buses, which apparently had a will of their own.

With my last ounce of strength, the stall would be pulled onto the pavement and positioned on its pitch. Tommy would then appear with his pickup truck loaded with all the different boxes of fish. These were sack barrowed to the rear of the stall and opened with crowbars. A number of trade preparations were then carried out by Tommy and me. Firstly I would smear the golden kippers with oil which gave them a more attractive look. Kippers were very popular and were given pride of place on the front of the stall.

The arches where the fish stall was housed, with Saint John's church in the background

Tommy would cut whole large fresh cod into cutlets, after gutting and removing the heads. I would display the cutlets on trays whilst Tom moved onto removing barbed skins from the skate wings. Herring, Mackerel, Plaice, Haddock, and Sprats were placed in trays and presented without further preparation. One of my favourites came next, namely cod roe. In those days the roes were large, each being a pound or more in weight. They cooked up lovely and were nearly as popular as the kippers.

On school days, I worked on the stall before and after school hours. School holidays were great because I worked all day on the stall, and met and served customers. Tommy referred to me as Siddy and I quickly became known as Siddy to the customers. Tommy had a very ruddy complexion and I often

25

wondered what caused it. Customers said it was caused by his favourite lunchtime tipple, namely several bottles of Mackeson. In fact they said I was the cause of the problem, because I was sent to the pub opposite to fetch the Mackeson.

I'm going to digress a little now to tell you a short story about the pub. It was called *The Railway Tavern,* and had only recently been built. I was about eight years old at the time and during the building process I decided one day to inspect the scaffolding. I climbed three long ladders which led me to the highest point on the building. I walked along the scaffold boards and found the perfect spot for a swing. It consisted of a horizontal scaffold pole which hung high above the Amhurst Road pavement. I grasped the pole with both hands and swung out above the pavement, in what I would describe as monkey style.

It was great fun and just as I was getting into 'full swing' I glanced down towards the ground and saw Dad standing there with his mouth wide open. He shouted very loudly 'Michael get down here now'. I complied quickly with his instruction, and was dragged down the street by the scruff of my neck. Within seconds we were back home and I was placed over Dad's knee. My trousers and pants had been dropped to my ankles and Dad struck my buttocks several times with his leather trouser belt. This was a very painful experience which resulted in a lot of tears.

In retrospect, I feel that without Mum's intervention that day, I would have been visiting the hospital. I realise now that Dad may well have saved my life that day, and feel eternally grateful to him, for his prompt action.

❁ ❁

The cane

Punishment was always close by during my childhood, often received at my senior school, Hackney Free and Parochial.

Admittedly it was often my own fault that led to the use of the cane. However, I would wear my school uniform whilst working at the fish stall in the morning and it occasionally became soiled with fish scales. I was advised by teachers not to arrive at school smelling like a fish. I tried my hardest to arrive at school without a coating of fish scales and the smell of fish. Despite my best efforts, I was caned twice on my hands for the offence of smelling like a fish. I decided that the canings were all part of life's rich tapestry.

On a brighter note Tommy would shout 'time to fetch the tea Siddy'. I would round up the large chipped cream coloured enamel jug and with money in hand, make my way to the cafe. The cafe was situated in Graham Road about a hundred yards from our stall. The proprietor would fill the jug to the brim with lovely hot tea from his chrome tea urn. The tea would be joined by three white crusty cheese rolls, placed in white paper bags. I can taste those rolls to this day as all these years later they were simply lovely to eat.

Yes, you've guessed it, on return to the stall, the tea would be poured into cream coloured enamel mugs and yes they were chipped. As Tommy, Elsie and I tucked in, we all had smiley faces.

The only downside to keeping the stall in the arches was the fact that there was no toilet facility. Most of us used the nearby storm drain set in the cobbles. Tommy had a rather bad habit of urinating under the arch to the side of a beetroot copper. The downside to this was that beetroots were boiling away at the time. I can remember to this day the sound of urine striking the side of the red hot copper, which resulted in a sizzling sound. The beetroots were being cooked by Harry the fruiterer, who on collection could never understand the strange smell, caused by the cooking process. As a young boy, this always made me chuckle.

I'll never forget the day that I crushed my right hand between the stall and the door jamb. It was a very windy day and I arrived at the arches, having pulled the stall back for overnight storage. The procedure was to open and fix back the two large wooden shed doors. You would then pull the stall into the arch by pulling on the round metal pull bar, with both hands. Unfortunately as I gained speed approaching the open doors, the wind dislodged the drop bolt on the right-hand door, which swung open directly in my path. My right hand then became trapped between the door and the pull bar on the stall. The resulting pain to my hand was beyond description.

Fortunately, Tommy had followed me in his pickup that evening and applied first aid. I had in fact collapsed half unconscious with the shock and pain sustained. My hand rapidly became swollen and bruised, requiring a visit to the local German Hospital. An X-ray revealed a fractured bone in the hand which required some bandage and a sling. My hand was throbbing very badly until pain killing tablets relieved the pain. After treatment Tommy took me home, and had the pleasure of explaining what had happened to my parents.

Unfortunately I was unable to work for a couple of weeks. The swelling eventually went down and the fractured bone in my hand has remained slightly curved ever since.

Before I move on from the wet fish work I'd like to tell the reader that my overriding memory was having generally freezing cold hands as a result of constantly rinsing fish in a bucket of ice cold water!

I should also admit an offence although I didn't know it was an offence at the time. On rare occasions I would be taken by Tommy to The Billingsgate fish market, in London, where we would collect the wet fish earlier described. Tommy showed me how to take hold of the tail of a salmon and how the salmon would then be thrown onto the back of his pickup truck. He explained that this should be done whilst the porters were busy fetching the boxes of fish. This seemed great fun to me at the time, because the salmon were quite large, and required some skill to reach the back of the pick up when thrown. It was several years later, before I realised this to be theft.

I should point out that Tommy wasn't all bad, for example each Christmas he would present me with a brand new pair of denim jeans. Also at the end of the week he would give me any remaining unsold kippers. This would be generally one or two pairs of kippers, but occasionally the whole box. These would be carried quickly by me into Aspland Grove, where neighbours would be eagerly waiting for a bargain buy. I remember charging a tanner a pair with the exception of my Mum and Dad who of course got theirs for free. I should explain that a tanner was in fact sixpence in old money.

Tree climbing

It was about this time, I would be ten years old when a group of kids from the street used to go to the cemetery in Hackney and play various games together. The group included my brother Alan, John Burgess, Tony Diamond, my cousin Ken Hawkins and several other children. One of the games involved tree climbing - not a game for the faint hearted. The objective was to see which of our number could climb the highest. One of our friends lived in a street on the far side of the cemetery, I can see him now and his name was Ricky Tivey. He was better known by his nickname 'Ricky Ticky Tivey'. He was a great kid, full of adventure and always great fun to be with. Ricky was also ten years old, of slight build, with a mop of mousey coloured hair.

We would often knock about with Ricky during the school holidays, he would just pop up out of the woodwork, as the saying goes. Then one day, to our shock horror, we heard the awful news that Ricky had died instantly, as a result of a fall from the top of a tree. The location was never explained to us, due, I believe, to the fact that his family were too upset to talk about it. Although this was over fifty years ago, I can see Ricky's face clearly to this day. He had the cheekiest grin you could possibly imagine.

We were all very upset about what had happened to our very dear friend. Needless to say that Ricky is the first person in my life to be denied the privilege of long life. My heart still goes out

29

to his family, to this day. I have named my book in Ricky's memory and who knows, members of his family may one day read it.

Sadly kids in those days were more vulnerable to the likelihood of accidents happening. Largely speaking we were free to do as we wished, due I believe to the fact that our parents, were still coming to terms with the end of the Second World War. I suppose I'm referring to 'The new found freedom'. On my part I particularly remember the bomb damage sustained in London, which had left many properties in a derelict state.

Prior to his sad demise, Ricky and I had been demolishing an old bombed out house in Hackney, when a brick wall collapsed on top of me. I considered myself lucky at the time, having only fractured my right forearm in two places. This stupidity culminated in my second visit to the German Hospital. I was less fortunate on this occasion, and as a result of the injury received a plaster cast, which restricted my movement somewhat, for the next six weeks. Suffice to say, my demolition days were over. Ricky of course, at the time, found the whole event to be hilarious.

At this point I will outline my experience whilst working on the shell fish stall, as a young boy. The stall was owned and run by Lesley Herbert who was Tommy's younger brother. On Saturday the stall would be set up on the same pitch at Hackney Station. The main difference in the set up was that the shell fish would be on an elevated display, when compared with wet fish, which was displayed horizontally.

The elevation was in fact built into the design of the stall. With hygiene in mind large sheets of white greaseproof paper would be spread completely across the elevated area. Empty hessian whelk sacks, being a perfect size for the job, were then rolled up 'jam roly-poly' style to form divisions between the various shell fish. Prior to positioning the divisions, these were also wrapped in white grease proof paper.

The fun part of the job would then be allowed, namely filling the elevated compartments with the beautiful assorted

30

brightly coloured shell fish. Firstly the yellowish whelks had pride of place, due I believe, to the fact that they had given up their sacks. These were followed by the large pink prawns, giving a lovely contrast in colour. Next up were the black winkles, followed by light brown wonderful smelling shrimps.

The next contrast would be achieved with the black shiny mussels, which were followed by the ever popular yellowish cockles. This completed the main elevated display, but - wait for it - there's more to come. I would assist in prising open the scallops, which were beautiful with their bright orange and white contents. These were placed in front. Lovely coloured crabs and lobsters, were also placed on the dividers. The end result was a truly magnificent shell fish display.

Lesley was a nice man, who also had a very ruddy complexion, due partly to the fresh air and partly I believe, due to the consumption of ale. Lesley was always assisted by his brother in law, a man called Reg. He was also a nice man to work for and had a normal complexion, which I found for some reason, comforting,

Purchasing shell fish at the weekend was customary amongst the shoppers in Hackney. We regularly had a steady stream of customers from 8.30 am to 5.30 pm every Saturday. Most would purchase a pint or half pint of shell fish, served up from our trusty pots. The pots consisted of enamelled metal, shaped similar to beer mugs.

The banter between fish mongers and the customers was always enjoyable. One line uttered, I never really understood 'Get these down you, and you'll be all right tonight'. What could they mean? These types of remarks were always followed by plenty of laughter. The women would respond with remarks like 'chance would be a fine thing'. What it all means, will someone please explain.

Reg was a master in the preparation of blackboard and chalked information boards. On the boards he would chalk things like 'Best Cromer crabs and whelks from the south east coast'. The occasional song would be sung 'cockles, and mussels alive, alive oh'.

31

Reg also had black crayon, which he used on the white price markers, to indicate the prices. The figures indicating the price were always elegantly drawn by Reg in bold curvy numerals. The prices were in pounds, shillings and pence in those days, for example, 1s 6d per pint.

Les and Reg always donned smart three quarter length white coats, together with navy blue aprons, worn at waist height. There were zipped pockets in the aprons which secured the cash, consisting of ten bob notes, one pound notes, and five pound notes. Of course two of these notes were later withdrawn from circulation. Many years later, work colleagues would often say that I still had 'ten bob notes in my wallet' what a cheek. What on earth were they trying to say about me?

The traditional visit to the cafe would be made also on Saturdays, for the jug of hot tea, accompanied again by the crusty cheese rolls. I must admit that I would occasionally consume a whole packet of McVities original biscuits, as well, but only when feeling flushed with one's wages.

Les tended to disappear for an hour at lunchtime, normally last seen moving towards *The Railway Tavern* on the other side of the road. It soon became apparent to me that drinking bottled Mackeson ran in the Herbert family.

Working the shell fish stall was not as good a money spinner for me, as most of the stock was sold to the customers. However, Dad was partial to a few winkles, which I managed to take home occasionally for his pleasure.

On Sundays, Les would set up his stall on Petticoat Lane, together with Reg, and my services were only required occasionally. I never complained because this practice allowed me a little time off.

❀ ❀

Trolley Buses

During the late fifties I particularly remember the trolley buses that travelled through Hackney. They were fascinating to most young boys, being powered by heavily built overhead electric cables. The cables were suspended high in the air, from an assortment of road side gantries and wall fixings on adjacent roadside buildings. The power would be received by the bus via two long arms affixed to the roof of the bus. The arms were lifted up above the bus and then hooked onto the overhead cables, thus completing the electric circuit.

All would function normally until the arms became detached, more often than not, at junctions. The detachment caused an almighty bang, with sparks and flashes going in all directions. For most boys of my age, this event was thought to be spectacular.

The first response to this problem would be the arrival of a bus Inspector. He always managed to find a long purpose made pole which he then used to hoist the arms back onto the cables. On rare occasions he would be unable to rectify the problem, resulting in more boyhood excitement as the bus company breakdown vehicle arrived.

This appropriately brings me onto one of my first hobbies, namely bus spotting, and breakdown vehicle spotting. Several of my previously named friends and I became very keen on that particular hobby.

We all acquired a booklet from the local Bus Station which listed all of the London bus serial numbers and also details of the breakdown vehicles. These little books became our bibles, in other words bus number spotting became our religion. Quite a large group of us started recording the numbers in our books. This would be achieved by writing the serial number of the bus down in a note book when seen in the street. Later at home you would compare the noted numbers with the columns of numbers listed in the official booklet. Once a number was identified in the book you would underline it, the objective being eventually to spot every bus listed in the book. I should of course point out that London had thousands of buses.

If you spotted a breakdown vehicle, this would be envied by all your fellow spotters. These vehicles were particularly large and very impressive to young bus spotters. Obviously they needed to be large vehicles, designed for the purpose of towing broken down buses.

The chance of seeing the breakdown vehicles actually operating on the road was rare. This resulted in young bus spotters locating the breakdown vehicles behind locked doors. I'll leave the rest to your imagination. I believe they were kept in what in those days were referred to as engine sheds. I recall one such shed being at a location by the name of Collingdale, which I believe was in north London, this of course was over fifty years ago.

Bus spotters were also in the habit of collecting souvenirs, consisting usually of small items which at some stage had formed part of the bus. Obviously these parts were no longer of use to the bus company at the time, that is, redundant components.

During these early days, I witnessed two further incidents in Hackney, culminating I believe, in the unnecessary loss of life. The first sadly related to a man whose description is still vivid in my memory banks. He was dressed in a full length Crombie type coat and carried a black executive type case. He stepped off the pavement, apparently oblivious to the fact that a van was approaching his position at some speed. He was struck by the vehicle and sadly disappeared beneath it. It was morning rush hour and this man had clearly been making his way to work. He was denied the privilege of long life within one hundred yards of the spot where I had been knocked over by a car, when running for Dad's cigarettes.

The second incident equally shocking, occurred about 6 am on a winter's morning when I was out delivering newspapers in Pembury Road, Hackney. A man on a pedal cycle had been hit by a car. It appeared that he had been crossing the road via a pedestrian island and had been struck by the front of the vehicle. I saw him lying on the road surface with the rim of the car's headlight embedded in his face. He was virtually unconscious at the time and apparently died soon after the accident had occurred.

Both of these deaths were shocking, and to this day my heart goes out to the families. I hope I haven't been too specific with details.

Having mentioned delivering newspapers, this seems a good time to expand on the subject. My older brother David, was the first to work for Wood's Newsagents, whose shop was situated close to Hackney Downs railway station. David arranged for me to meet Noel Woods the proprietor of the shop, who then gave me the job of paperboy. It proved to be very hard work in those days, with very few regulations on hours of work.

We would cycle to the shop in time for 5.30 am deliveries, and the paper rounds were enormous. The bulk of the deliveries were to blocks of flats for example, the Pembury Estate, which consisted of approximately twenty blocks situated either side of Pembury Road. These were five or six storey blocks which were quite poorly lit. Naverino Mansions were another example, built in the early 1900s, again very poorly lit and somewhat spooky. I can ensure the reader that those particular papers were delivered in very quick time. Older paper boys would tell you that others had gone missing on that round, never to be seen again.

In addition to flats there were many street deliveries also stretching from Clapton Pond in one direction to Mare Street in the other. The rounds would take up to three hours on weekdays and Saturdays, and four hours on Sundays. The latter being due to the fact that Sunday papers were much larger, resulting in fewer papers being carried in the paper bag.

We worked seven days a week, which on occasions included marking up the papers with Noel, and also a payment collection round. The marking up consisted of standing behind the shop counter, with one folding the paper as the other wrote addresses in pencil, at the top of it. This would start prior to 5.30 am in readiness for the paper delivery.

The collection round was carried out on Sunday after completion of your paper round. I have fond memories of my collection round based on the following : quite a number of the customers would give cash tips; big band and classical music met you as the street door opened, and I particularly remember Billy Cotton singing out 'Wakie Wakie'.

Sometimes a hot drink would be offered, and sometimes an even warmer drink called alcohol.

My one abiding memory was that wonderful smell of the Sunday roast cooking. That was the best, it beat all the others into a cocked hat.

For the purpose of the collection round you carried a leather cash bag mounted on a shoulder strap. You needed to be very good with arithmetic, and would suffer Noel's wrath if the figures didn't tally. Added to the above there was always a chance that you might be mugged.

All the paper boys were paid on Sundays, and would receive between £3 and £6 depending on their input. Together with tips, I managed to save enough money for things like fishing rods and fishing tackle, which I would use when fresh water fishing.

Noel Woods also had a paper stall which stood underneath the railway bridge at Hackney Downs Station. A man by the name of Stan sold the papers at the stall and always seemed to enjoy his job thoroughly. My memory fails me a little, but I recall standing in for Stan for a two week period. I can clearly remember selling the *Evening Standard*, together with other newspapers and magazines. I recall that period with fondness and really enjoyed the buzz one experienced from the close contact with customers.

At rush hour you could hear the trains arriving at the railway station. The main sound came from the clatter of train doors being slammed shut by the many passengers. This would be followed by a rapid stream of customers at the paper stall. I would shout '*Evening Standard* or '*Standard*. The buzz came from folding the paper in two, receiving the cash payment and giving change when necessary. Time absolutely flew, culminating in a sell-out of all the papers and a full cash box. That wonderful smell of railway stations remains with me to this day. Again a reasonable wage was on offer at the end of the week.

I had a big surprise one Christmas at the paper shop when a raffle ticket I had purchased from Noel, won first prize. The prize consisted of the biggest box of chocolates in the world, measuring three feet long by two feet wide. The chocolates consisted of two layers of both milk and dark varieties. The box was nicely decorated with a daffodil design and tied diagonally with a wide yellow bowed ribbon. I'll never forget the joy on my Mum's face when I arrived home and proudly handed her the box of chocolates.

Whilst at the shop one day I was shocked to find that Noel kept a poodle in his enclosed rear yard. The poodle had been seriously neglected and had long matted hair, which dragged along the ground as the dog attempted to walk. On closer inspection I could see that the dogs hair was actually matted together with its own faeces. The smell from the yard was unbearable and decaying dog faeces lay everywhere. I spoke to Noel about the dog, and told him I was upset about the way the animal had been neglected. He told me to mind my own business and to keep my nose out of his rear yard. I remember being disappointed at his response, but probably out of fear of reprisal, regret to this day not taking further action in the matter.

❀ ❀

Fishing

I feel that it's time for a brighter note, and will now refer to some of my boyhood fishing outings. Prior to becoming interested in the use of rods, I had the pleasure of being taken to Cheshunt in Hertfordshire, by the parents of John Burgess. I would travel with them in their car to a river side meadow, situated beside the River Lea. John and I would then walk a short distance to a small stream which emanated from the river Lea.

Armed with hessian sacks we would then drag the sack along the stream, beneath the border of stream weeds. This culminated in the capture of many small fish consisting of Bull Head, Stickleback, Minnow, Gudgeon and Ruff.

This for young boys in the 1950s, was quite an adventure, although in hindsight we shouldn't have placed the fish in pickle jars for transportation home. Sadly within a couple of days most of the fish would die.

The technique was interesting, with each of us gripping two corners of the sack in each hand and pulling it through the water like a fisherman's net. At the end of the dragging motion, the sack would be lifted to the surface, revealing all the silver fishes flipping from side to side, as the water drained from the net.

In addition to fishing, Jonnie and I would swim in the river, in between the lock gates. This would be rounded off with a wonderful picnic, provided by Mrs Elsie Burgess. What more could two young boys ask for? Well, I suppose an ice cream wouldn't be unreasonable. During the whole of my childhood my parents never had a car, so these adventures with the Burgess family were most welcomed.

In the early days I was introduced to going to Sunday school with my brothers. This was held at Saint John's church in Hackney, a Church of England Church. It was a magnificent building, made in what I describe as a large square format. It was a huge and magnificent building. Much to most people's disbelief I loved singing both in church and at school. On occasions, as a young boy I would sing solo and thoroughly enjoyed doing so.

Then came the calamity, the church was gutted by fire. I recall very little about the actual fire, but was told that several firemen lost their lives whilst tackling the blaze. This was absolutely awful news, leaving the whole community in deep shock. This was even more shocking knowing that Hackney Police Station was situated quite close to the church. I don't know whether foul play was suspected or not. It seemed extraordinary that such a fire might be caused accidentally.

The dirty old man

Saint John's Church was situated in the middle of a small park and cemetery. My friends and I played regularly in that vicinity. I recall boarding up and clean-up work going on for many months after the fire. Tony Diamond, John Burgess, my brother Alan and I were off school, during the summer holidays, playing near to the church. A man approached us and said 'I've built a camp in the burnt out church, would you boys like to see it?' We became quite excited at the thought of seeing a new camp and the man led us into the building.

He then said 'the camp's in this room'. He pointed to a darkened room with a large wooden door. We all peered in through the open door, and could see that the room would make a great camp. It was ready made. After we entered the room the man closed the door and told Johnnie to drop his trousers.

We were all puzzled, because we could see no reason to drop his trousers. The man then grabbed hold of Johnnie and started to pull his trousers down, by force. Johnnie screamed out loudly and began to struggle. I saw the man break Johnnies' trouser belt and tear his trousers at the waist. The remaining three of us shouted loudly for help and ran from the room, followed by Johnnie who had broken free.

Two large workmen appeared at the door and challenged the man in the room. They began to beat the man with their work shovels, at which point we scattered. We were all shaken by the event and made our way home very quickly. Johnnie was then punished by his Mum for tearing his trousers and damaging his belt. The explanation as to what had happened fell on deaf ears. The remaining parents were not told about the incident, because we assumed we had somehow been in the wrong at the time. In hindsight I realise now how close we came to being victims of serious assault.

It was about this time when Dad had a proper bathroom installed in a room on the top floor of our house. It consisted of a large cast iron bath with hot and cold water supplied via a wall mounted Ascot water heater. One winter evening I had a lovely hot bath in the new bath room. Unfortunately I forgot to take a towel into the bathroom. The towels were kept in a cupboard on the landing outside the bathroom door. Standing in the altogether I opened the door and stepped out onto the unlit landing to get a towel. I was very shocked when my younger brother's cat jumped on me from the top of the cupboard. I was in agony as the cats claws sunk deeply into my chest. I tried to pull the cat from my chest but its claws just reactively sunk in deeper.

On impulse I ran screaming down two flights of stairs where Mum came to my rescue and managed after some effort to detach the cat. The attack left me bleeding quite heavily and I have remained very wary of cats ever since. A good lesson was learned by me that day, namely to prepare in advance for any possible eventuality. Sadly my brother's cat was killed a few weeks later when struck by a car. My brother was very upset and clearly loved his cat to bits. We buried the cat in the flower bed, in our rear garden.

On a happier note I'm going to describe the joys of fresh water fishing during the early 1960s. I was introduced to it by my brother David and his friends Terry and Eddie Payton. Firstly I was taken to the tackle shop called Mitchell's where I purchased a wooden Roach pole and appropriate fishing tackle. We would also purchase Hemp seed, which would be boiled during the evening, ready for fishing the next day.

We would rise at 5 am and take the train to Broxbourne in Hertfordshire, where after a half mile walk we arrived at the River Lea. In those days the river contained large shoals of Roach, a beautiful silvery looking fish, which could on occasions grow to several pounds in weight.

On arrival at the river we made our way to the far bank, this being the quieter of the two banks and the opposite side to the tow path. The roach poles would then be assembled by pushing each section into the next, via the bamboo ferrules. I was shown how to tie a short section of line to the tip of the pole. A quill float would then be affixed to the line by means of a small rubber band. A small barbed hook would then be tied to the other end of the line.

A single hemp seed was then pushed onto the hook, after which, the fishing could begin. All of us would then stand on the edge of the river bank, with a spacing of a few feet between each of us. The method of fishing was to throw a small quantity of hemp seed into the river, followed by a cast of the hook bait. My fondest memory was the sight of hundreds of silver flashes, then appearing beneath the surface of water. These flashes were the roach feeding on the hemp seed, which we then began to hook in large numbers. All our dreams from the night before were now coming to fruition.

The fish were removed from the hooks and kept safely in the keep nets, which were mostly submerged at the edge of the river bank. The individual roach measured between four and ten inches in length, and gave each of us a good fight. It was great sport for boys of our age and each of us would catch an average bag of twenty pounds of fish.

Despite the exciting nature of the fishing, young boys soon turned to their lunch boxes. In the summer it would of course be sandwiches followed by diluted type drinks. In the winter a hot lunch was preferable, consisting of Heinz baked beans, which were heated over a small round stove. The fuel was the wonderfully purple coloured methylated spirit, which was quite efficient and economical. The beans were heated in the tin, and when piping hot, were eaten with a spoon directly from the tin. You might then say 'what more could a young man want?' Well, let me tell you the answer - a hot cup of soup from his thermos flask.

These adventures were a great escape from growing up in the centre of London. In the summer at the conclusion of fishing, a further item would be removed from the fishing box. Yes you've guessed it - the swimming trunks.

A swim in the River Lea was invigorating after a hard day's fishing. I recall on one such occasion my cousin Dennis, suffering a serious laceration to the underside of his foot, as he entered the river. It transpired that he had trodden on a broken bottle. The laceration required several stitches at the nearby hospital.

Freshwater fishing continued throughout my younger days into adulthood. Over the years I visited many different venues for the purpose of fishing and made many friends, all of whom were connected to the sport. I feel that fishing gave me an early look at wildlife, a subject not found in abundance in Hackney.

❀ ❀

China stall

Another fascinating part of my early teens related to working on a china stall, at the Waste in Kingsland Road, Dalston, London. The location referred to as the Waste, consisted of a popular street market where a large variety of goods were sold. The owners of the china business had a warehouse in Shoreditch. My role consisted of loading the box van with the assorted china and helping to set the stall up at the market. In those days the majority of the china was transported in old tea chests. Breakfast, tea and dinner services were stored and conveyed in cardboard boxes.

The sales pitch was done by the owner of the business who would stand on a platform, holding a large tray. He would rapidly place plates, cups and saucers on the tray in an attractive manner, thereby presenting a service to the customers. Whilst presenting the service he would shout out a price which became lower and lower. This method attracted large numbers of customers, who were all keen to get a bargain.

My main role in the sales pitch was to throw the earlier described boxes of china to the proprietor, up on his rostrum. The throwing of the boxes was well practised in order to entertain the customers and get them in the mood for buying. The proprietor would purposely drop a box of china, at which point the air would turn blue and I would be loudly admonished. He would then dismiss me from his employ and tell me in no uncertain terms to go away. All of the customers in turn had a good chuckle at my expense.

As a result of this pitch a large number of boxes of china would be sold at a knock down price. I in turn would take a short walk and then return to the stall for the next pitch. I should point out that each dropped box contained previously broken china.

Occasionally the stall was set up in Middlesex Street, another popular market near to Liverpool Street Station. This was normally on Sundays and again proved to be very profitable for the owners. In the main, people dined at home in the 1960s and the dinner service was a well-used household item.

At about this time I remember my brother Raymond had an interesting job working for an elderly Jewish couple who lived in Amhurst Road, Hackney. They were called Reuben and Esther and sold what I believe to be called haberdashery. I'm now told that it wasn't haberdashery, suffice to say they sold household items, for example soap, dishcloths and household cleaning products. Reuben and Esther were real characters whom everybody held in high esteem.

In the early 1960s, my family and I knew very little about Jewish people, but it was generally known that they were good in business and generally prospered well. Raymond certainly enjoyed working for them and I know he was quite fond of them. They ran their market stalls at Ridley Road, in the borough of Dalston, and Brick Lane in Shoreditch.

Secondary School

At the end of the summer of 1959 I started my secondary School education at Hackney Free and Parochial Secondary

Modern School. It was a School which practised The Church of England Religion.

I remember very clearly to this day, donning a brand new school uniform and making my way to school on foot. I felt so conspicuous that I wanted the ground to open up and swallow me. The style of dress for a young barrow boy, did not suit me in the least. The three basic colours of the uniform were red, black and white.

I recall walking up Aspland Grove together with my cousin Kenny who started at the same school as me. We then walked along Amhurst Road where we were joined by other boys all wearing the same uniform. I suddenly felt less conspicuous, as the group of pupils grew ever bigger, as we neared the school, which consisted of a two storey new-ish building with a large assembly room and a large gym.

One of my first teachers was a Mrs Levy, who I would describe as a slightly built Jewish lady who frightened the life out of me. This fact is probably because of my constant bad behaviour in class, resulting in me always suffering her wrath. As the years passed, however, I began to think the world of Mrs Levy and realised what a lovely person she was.

Mrs Levy taught Religious Knowledge, a subject which I grew very fond of. I found the Biblical stories fascinating and although I no longer practise the religion, remember many of them to this date. One story which was dear to my heart was the 'Feeding of the Five Thousand', when Jesus turned two loaves and five fishes into enough food, for the five thousand who had gathered to listen to his sermon.

Other stories included turning water into wine and of course Jesus walking on water. I'm going to stop now, whilst I'm ahead.

Unfortunately I was generally a poor student at school, because of the fact that I would only study subjects that I found interesting. I enjoyed gym classes and became quite good at gymnastics resulting in appearances at the school fete, which was held at the vicarage.

I struggled with English, French and drama. I now believe this was because of a sad lack of confidence. I feel with the benefit of hindsight that the lack of confidence stemmed from being in a large family and not being able to talk one to one with your parents. I was not a natural orator and found I lacked confidence when speaking publicly.

However I was quite confident when it came to more practical subjects like woodwork and metalwork. This particular confidence stemmed from working with my hands as a boy and regularly using my own initiative during those early years.

I also enjoyed Biology which again I felt related to my younger days of fishing and escaping to the countryside. I was helped in this subject also by my experiences on the wet and shell fish stalls.

I absolutely loved Geography, learning about far flung places of interest, like America and Australia. I never imagined that I one of seven children would ever visit such places. I found that I was quite good at arithmetic and consequently enjoyed those lessons with the teacher Mr Crow. He was a very nice quietly spoken West Indian man, who had the patience of a Saint.

Hackney Free was a mixed school and that fact often leads to my downfall. I unfortunately was a bit of a show off and whilst showing off to the girls, would often upset the relevant teacher. More often than not this behaviour would lead to me being caned.

I recall very vividly a particular lesson with the infamous geography teacher, the six feet two inch Mr Lewis. He took a particular dislike to my showing off and caned me twice on both hands, in front of the whole class. He wielded the cane with considerable determination and the pain inflicted by the resulting blows was excruciating. I was left with blue wheel marks across both hands which lasted for a week.

During my early days at the school I took a dislike to a boy in my year named David Everett. He was very tall, probably 6'2" in height, with short ginger hair and wore spectacles. Together with my followers, I would verbally take the 'mickey'

45

out of him at every opportunity. I would call out to him in the school corridor, shouting things like 'you ginger four eyed twit'. A number of other boys referred to as my followers, would join in the name calling. One day at school David Everett snapped back at me and said 'I'll meet you at the library after school and then we will see what you're made of'. I said 'I'll be there four eyes'. At the close of school I made my way to the Library which was situated about fifty yards from the main school gate.

David arrived and I continued to bait him until he landed a solid punch to my nose. The blow from his clenched fist knocked me backwards, as did the next five continuous blows, all of equal strength. I was about to grab hold of him when the school drama teacher came between us and stopped the fight. My nose then bled heavily and we were told to go home and to report to the Headmaster the next morning.

Well what did I learn from this encounter? Firstly that actions speak louder than words. Secondly that the old saying was in fact true, in that 'sticks and stones will break your bones but names will never hurt you'.

David and I reported to the Headmaster the following morning and were both caned for fighting in the street and for damaging the school's good image. I recall very clearly, leaving the Headmaster's office with a sore nose and very sore hands.

Prior to learning how to behave I was caned many times, usually in the Headmaster's office. However, I misbehaved at morning assembly one day and this behaviour resulted in me receiving six of the best on my backside. This punishment was administered on the stage, at assembly in front of the whole school. The humiliation of being bent over a chair and caned in front of the whole school, brought me to my senses and I became a well behaved pupil from that time onwards.

All young boys suffered occasional knocks but I feel that I had more than my fair share. For example, I was out roller skating with my younger brother Alan and a few mates. We were skating on a paved area near to Saint John's church when I collided into Alan and accidentally knocked him to the ground. The other lads all laughed at Alan and after apologising

I carried on skating. One of the lads shouted 'watch out Mick'. I glanced towards Alan and saw he was now holding a large piece of wood, which was four inches square and about four feet long. I sensed danger and tried to skate away from Alan, my effort was in vain. and I received a severe blow to the head as Alan wielded his piece of wood.

The blow knocked me to the ground and the expression 'left seeing stars' springs to mind. Blood began to pour from a wound to the back of my head and flowed down over my face. My shirt was quickly sodden in blood and I felt very queasy indeed. The lads helped me to my feet and Alan was shouting 'I didn't mean it, don't tell Mum'. When we arrived home Mum was shocked at the sight of me and my bloodied clothing. I was taken to hospital and given seven stitches to a deep two inch wound. Suffice to say that I found the process of stitching my head very unpleasant.

In my absence I believe Alan explained that I had started the 'fight' by first knocking him over whilst he was skating. To this date I cannot recall him receiving any punishment for hitting me with what amounted to a weapon. I can recall however that the blow left me lying low for several days.

Head banging

On another occasion we were playing in Marks and Spencer's loading bay which was situated near to the top of our street. The game consisted of being dare devils running in and out of the bay as the large metal drop door came down. These doors were sometimes referred to as roller gates. Well I think you can guess what happened? Yes, you've guessed correctly. The gate came down heavily onto my head. I can only describe the blow as a 'hammer blow' which left me feeling like I had been knocked into the ground.

A further visit to the German Hospital was needed, where severe bruising and concussion were diagnosed. I was beginning to understand the meaning of the phrase 'all part of life's rich tapestry'. I was later told that the roller gate weighed one ton and that I was lucky not to have been killed by the impact. With regard to that incident, I do feel very lucky not to have sustained a long lasting injury. Other individuals have clearly not been so lucky.

They say a cat has nine lives, I wonder how many I have used to date? I will suffer further injury as my story progresses and leave you to guess which part of my body receives the relative blow.

As time passed David Everett and I became good friends, mainly because of the fact that we both became good cross country runners for the school. Most of our training took place at Hackney Marshes when we would run nine miles in a circle around the well-known three hundred football pitches.

For Sports Day purposes, all the school pupils were divided into four large teams. I'm very proud to say that I was selected to be the Villiers team captain and as such had over two hundred pupils in my team. Sadly or some might say on purpose, I cannot recall the names of the other three teams.

The school Sports Day would be held at Eaton Manor and the Villiers team always did well. These events took place many years ago now and although I remember our team colours were red, I am unable to recall specific results. I'm sure all the children who participated in the sports at Eaton Manor, thoroughly enjoyed themselves. For the uneducated, Eaton Manor was a purpose built Field and Track sports venue used by many different schools in and around East London.

My one regret was never to win a prize on Prize Giving Day at the school, despite my considerable efforts in the sports related arena. I feel that the votes never came my way due to my bad behaviour in my early school days. In addition to gymnastics and cross country running I also became quite good at swimming.

Particularly in the school summer holidays, my friends and I spent many hours at that famous institution, the open air swimming pool, otherwise known as The Lido. We had two

48

Lidos within striking distance, namely London Fields and Victoria Park. The sun would shine all day long and we all had a fantastic time. Entrance was quite cheap and we normally had enough money for an ice-cream or a bus ride home, but not both.

My friend John Burgess who was a year below me in school regularly came with us, together with three girls from his class. The girls were Larraine Ewington, Margaret Hall and Margaret Ferris. The friendship with the girls was purely platonic and included visits to the local youth club. It was now the early 1960s and we all thoroughly enjoyed the disco music.

I have now reached the dizzy old age of sixty five years and have considerable difficulty remembering names of my fellow pupils. Three names spring to mind and relate to boys who were in my class at school. Michael Poole was a tall fair headed lad who on leaving the school, intended to work for the Royal Mail underground rail delivery service. Michael Musgrave was short with short curly mousey coloured hair, who gave no clues as to his intentions. Anthony Fitzjohn was of medium height with thick mousey coloured hair, who intended to have an engineering future. In fact I recall being in awe of him, when he made a jet engine component during metal work lessons. I have made no contact with these classmates since leaving school in 1964 and often wonder how their lives panned out.

Although not in my class, I also became friends with two other boys, namely Michael Barnes and Peter Collins. They both travelled into Hackney on the bus, either from Dalston or Islington. They were great characters and I often wonder what became of them as well.

One of the popular pastimes in the late 1950s and early 1960s was to have conker fights. Holes were made through the centre of the conkers which would then have string or laces threaded through the hole and were then secured with a good old fashion knot. Two persons would have the conker fight, which involved having one shot each, at the other's conker. This was achieved by gripping the string with your best hand and swinging your conker at your opponent's conker. At the same time your opponent would stand still with his conker held outstretched in front of him.

The win would be achieved when one player managed to break the other's conker. Some players would soak their conkers in vinegar to harden them. I personally believe this method to be an old wives' tale. It certainly never propelled me to championship status.

Because of the popularity of conker fighting, conkers were very much in demand. My brothers, friends and I, would cycle to Epping Forest in the autumn, where conkers were growing in abundance. Thousands of conkers were collected and placed in large sacks, before being taken back home on the cycle racks

On returning to school we would head straight to the tuck shop, where queues would form to buy the conkers. The acquisition and sale of conkers proved to be very lucrative. Little did we know in those days that World Conker championships were being held at Ashton, near Oundle, in Northamptonshire.

In the school conker fights, I should point out that one point would be given for each victory and conkers would become known as 'Ones', 'Twos' and 'Threes', depending on the total number of wins achieved. The number would increase consecutively as each win was achieved. A very good conker could on occasions become a double figure winner or on rare occasions a treble figure winner. Large groups of pupils would gather round to watch some of the record breaking conker fights.

Groups of pupils would gather during morning and afternoon breaks, to the rear of the gym, where 'fag' breaks would take place. Fourteen was the average age to try smoking at the school, culminating in many individuals smoking for the rest of their lives.

❀ ❀

Nose job

It was during one of the smoke breaks that I realised exhaling through my nose was difficult, and on visiting the doctors it was confirmed that I had narrow nasal airways. An appointment was made for me to see a specialist at a clinic in Hackney. Mum came with me to the clinic on the due date and after introductions the specialist instructed me to sit in a chair. He then placed a white gown around me and tied it in place with a bow to the back of my neck.

He said 'I'll do the right side first Michael and you will suffer a little soreness'. A second man then stood behind the chair and placed his hands firmly either side of my head. The specialist then inserted a tapered shiny metal rasp into my right nostril. As he held the rasp in his left hand, he knocked it up my nose with his right. The pain inflicted was overwhelming and blood poured from my nose. In an instant the specialist connected a flexible tube to the rasp and forced water through the apparatus into my nasal cavity. I was in agony whilst choking up blood and chipped bone from my nose. I can tell you that no one could be more relieved than I when the specialist removed the rasp from my nose.

I was given a cold drink and asked whether I was ready to have the second nostril enlarged. I bet everyone reading about this experience will know how quickly my answer 'No' was given. In hindsight I found the procedure amazing and have breathed well all my life through the enlarged nostril. I'm pleased to report that one enlarged nostril has proved more than adequate to date.

Before leaving the clinic I took a closer look at the rasp, and noted that it had a series of sharp teeth. That observation helped me to understand why I had a mouth full of bone chippings, at the time.

On a brighter note, shortly after the nostril enlargement, Mum announced that she had saved enough money to buy me a brand new bike. This was a first, having a new bike was unheard of. I remember very vividly meeting Mum after school to collect my brand new bike from the shop in Bethnal Green. It was pale blue in colour, with gears and straight handle bars. I was so proud to cycle my new bike home, all be it slowly as Mum walked along side me. The bike had a similar set up, to the modern day Mountain bikes.

It was great to cycle off to far flung places with all the other lads. Two trips spring to mind, the first of course being to Southend, in Essex. That was a great trip, forty miles each way, although we were hit by a thunder storm on the way back. It didn't stop us getting home because we all took a lift on the back of a flat back lorry.

When referring to the lads, I mean my cousins, my brothers and other lads from Aspland Grove. I suppose twelve would be the largest group we would muster for our trips. The second trip failed miserably when we decided to cycle to our cousins in Kent, via The Blackwall tunnel. The Blackwall Tunnel was about a mile long passing from the north bank of the River Thames to the south bank. It was a very busy tunnel, rather bendy and could be quite dangerous. The best method of cycling through the tunnel was to pedal like a maniac and hope that you all reached the other side in one piece.

The misery came when cousin Kenny's chain broke on the south side of the tunnel. The delay resulted in all of us abandoning the trip due to lack of available daylight. Unfortunately, to coin a phrase we never 'conquered' Kent, on our bikes.

The bikes generally provided all of us with an escape from what some people call 'The Smoke' This name is a well-known nickname for London, mainly because of the smog which had been experienced in London for years before we were born. We used the word 'escape' because of the sheer size of London, which stretched some forty miles from one side to the other. Hackney was considered to be very central when considering these parameters and the country side was always considered to be far away, by young adventurers.

Fairly heavy traffic and building after building were the 'norm'. To complete our escape, we took part in a number of different sports and hobbies. I enjoyed boxing at Ridley Road, judo at Upton House and later, some snooker. I must admit that we also played a game with girls referred to as 'Doctors and Nurses'. We were very young at the time and I'll leave the details of that game to your imagination.

I should add that a girl called Anita, who lived in Aspland Grove, regularly played the part of the patient. We didn't have a doctor's surgery to carry out our examination of Anita, but would often visit her home, when her Mum was out shopping. On other occasions I recall that we would hide beneath an open air stage, situated near to Hackney Baths. I remember on one such occasion a brass band started playing music on the stage, as we played doctors beneath it! I should point out that these were harmless games probably played by thousands of inner city kids.

❀ ❀

The First Holiday

I would now like to tell you about a very important event in my childhood years - my first holiday with my parents and family. Mum explained that she had managed to save enough money to treat us to a whole week away at Canvey Island, in Essex. I was fourteen years old at the time and was absolutely thrilled at the thought of a whole week away at the Seaside. Up until this time my only knowledge of holidays came from my cousins, the Hawking family, who spent two weeks every summer in Cornwall.

Mum informed us that we would travel by train to Canvey Island, where she had booked a chalet for us, on a self-catering basis. I can remember helping to carry suit cases, but not helping to pack them. The journey seemed never ending, but eventually we all arrived safely at Thorney Bay Beach Holiday Camp. My first impression was that the chalet was rather small for a family of nine. However Mum soon allocated the bedrooms, and started to organise our holiday home. It wasn't long before Mum had prepared hot food for the whole family.

I remember the days being quite short, with dusk arriving early in the evening. The weather was rather dull, with some rain and strong winds. It was much later in my life that I realised that Mum had only been able to provide such a holiday because it was out of season.

David, Alan and I left the remaining family in the chalet, and went to explore the area. We walked through the site, which consisted of row upon row of chalets and caravans. We then arrived at the sea wall which encircled a bay. The tide was out and the three of us thoroughly enjoyed ourselves, searching for crabs amongst the rocks.

To us three inner city boys, the smell of the sea as we turned those rocks was heavenly. We found crabs, small fish and other assorted crustaceans. Dad had instructed us to be back before dark, but boys being boys, we arrived back late. He was very angry when we returned to the chalet and shouted out very loudly, that we had spoilt the holiday. We were teenagers and didn't understand why he protested so loudly. Of course we all learned later in life about the dangers that caused Dad such concern at the time.

Bunk beds were the order of the day and we all soon snuggled down for our first night's sleep on Canvey Island. In the morning we were all complaining about the cold in the chalet, these places were not very well heated.

Breakfast was followed by a traditional family walk, traditional referring to one chosen by Dad which normally meant quite a lot of pain. As we grew up in Hackney, Dad would choose one of his children to join him on a walk. More often than not the route would be one of several from Hackney to Parliament Hill Fields. I suppose the return journey would entail walking approximately twelve miles. In our opinion, the children that is, the walk was simply too far, for any child to walk. Dad of course didn't agree, and the walks continued until each child had reached fourteen years of age. With the benefit of hindsight these walks were probably the healthiest aspect of our childhood.

Reverting back to Canvey, our family walk with Dad took us along the sea front to the huge petro-chemical works, which had been built behind the sea wall. The site of these huge works was a bit of a shock to the system, they seemed to stretch for miles inland from the coast. The air was filled with the smell of petrol and I felt sorry for the people that lived close by to the works.

Fortunately for all of us Dad decided we should walk in the opposite direction and eventually arrived at the sea side amusement park. At last we could start to spend some of our hard earned money, acquired from our various jobs. The amusements were very limited compared with modern day theme parks, but we thoroughly enjoyed ourselves. The amusements included the 'Wild Mouse', the 'Helter-Skelter', and of course good old fashioned bumper cars.

These were followed by the slot machines which all kids find irresistible. Brothers Raymond and John were still quite young at the time, maybe four and five years of age. Mum and Dad decided it was time to take them back to the chalet, which left David and I a chance to have our first cigarette, of the holiday. My sisters Patricia and June remained with us, but were sworn to secrecy. I seem to remember we all had a hot dog before returning to the chalet for dinner.

As the week progressed the weather improved culminating in Alan and I having several swims in the sea. The sea water was rather cold and we wallowed in black deep sticky mud, which gave off a rather putrid smell. All that to one side, Alan and I had a great time together. Two games spring to mind, the first being sea weed popping, the objective being to squeeze the sea weed until it burst, then squirt the fluid into Alan's face. The second game all kids can relate to, namely, beach stone skimming. The art of this game was to select a nice flat stone and throw it onto the surface of the sea water. The objective being to skim the stone over the surface of the water and in doing so achieve as many bounces of the stone as were possible.

The week at Canvey passed very quickly and we were soon returning to Hackney with sad faces. The family break was great though and I returned to school with new enthusiasm.

On returning to school it was announced that our school was to merge with Wilton Way School. This was worrying news because Wilton Way School had a reputation of being a violent school.

At about the same time of the merger, I commenced my fifth year at the School and as a result of my new found enthusiasm, I was given the role of school prefect. All school prefects were given a badge and I recall wearing mine with pride.

It was at this time that my teacher informed me that I would not be able to sit GCE exams and that RSA exams would be more appropriate. After further discussion with my teacher, it was jointly agreed that I would sit six papers namely Metal Work, Woodwork, Religious Knowledge, Technical Drawing, Arithmetic and Mathematics. If successful with those six papers, I would be adequately educated to apply for engineering apprenticeships, in the London area.

With my goals now set I started to work much harder at school, particularly in metalwork and woodwork. Clearly my future beyond school days would be of a practical nature working with my hands. I was quite chuffed when my woodwork teacher invited me to make my own oak bedside cabinet.

Bertie Glass

My first day at the Wilton Way School had now arrived, and I left home that morning looking forward to the change of scenery. The school was half a mile from home and I recall it being a fine sunny day. As I approached the school I saw a large group of pupils gathered around the school gate. I carried on walking up to the gate and started to make my way through the group of pupils. Suddenly, a large built youth then stepped forward and blocked my path into the school. For no apparent reason he then started raining heavy punches into my face and body. He knocked me to the ground before I had a chance to defend myself.

Amongst the mayhem I could see my brother Alan looking at me with a very worried look on his face. The youth then jumped on top of me whilst I was on the ground. My self defence mechanism then kicked in and I gave the youth a good beating. I later learned that the youth was from Wilton Way School and he had been waiting to batter a prefect. The youth known as Bertie Glass was determined to show his school mates, who was top dog. I was firmly of the view that he chose the wrong prefect for his demonstration.

Alan looked relieved and said he was pleased with my performance. He said he was convinced that Glass had me beat and that I would be badly injured. I told Alan that the old saying 'the first punch always wins' was a fallacy.

I don't want to sound smug about this attack, but I felt that the hooligan culture at Wilton had been shown a good lesson. I merely hoped that the lesson might prevent similar attacks on other prefects. Throughout my childhood I had been taught not to take liberties and not to allow others to take liberties with you.

After the incident I brushed myself down and carried on into the school. I found it to be a very old building but nevertheless quite interesting. I found the woodwork class to be well equipped and soon became involved in the making of my oak bedside cabinet. The teachers were all very pleasant and the pupils at the school, apart from Bertie Glass all seemed friendly.

More good news was on the horizon, in that whilst walking home, I acquired myself a part time job in a small engineering workshop. A note on the door to the premises advertised that the owners needed help on Saturday mornings, in the production of surgical instruments. After a knock on the door and a brief interview, I got the job. The premises consisted of a fifteen feet by fifteen feet ground floor and a similar sized first floor. The owners had lathes, a press, a milling machine, and column drills, together with other smaller machine tools.

Three very nice engineers had formed the company and together made the surgical instruments for a company called Allen Ambury, of Bethnal Green, London. I remember the names Eric and Stan, but cannot recall the third engineer's name. They were all very skilful engineers and had previously worked at Allen Ambury.

My hours of work were set for 8 am to 1 pm and wages would depend on my ability. Well, Saturday arrived and I reported for work at the engineers. I must admit that I was rather apprehensive on arrival but Eric soon put me at ease and showed me the ropes. I was soon making components for two different types of skin grafting instruments. One such instrument was referred to as a barrel type which would be rolled along your leg by means of two small handles. The barrel contained sharp blades which could be adjusted to alter the depth of flesh to be removed from the patient's leg. These instruments were precision engineered in order to remove the skin to thousandths of an inch, in thickness.

The second instrument consisted of a handle with finger grip positions, and a long single cutting blade. This instrument had a supportive column to the rear of the blade that could again be adjusted to vary the cutting depth, when skin grafting.

Once made, the instruments would be chrome plated and polished before being supplied to the customers. I found the work extremely interesting and very satisfying.

During the production of the instruments I became conversant with all of the machine tools in the workshop. This experience would be of great benefit to me in future full time employment.

❀ ❀

Pop music

Because of our age David, Alan and I regularly played pop records on our record player, in our bedroom. It was a great time to be young juveniles with groups like 'The Who', 'The Rolling Stones' and 'The Beatles' being in the charts. My personal favourites were by far 'The Rolling Stones', I thought they were fantastic. Our bedroom had sash type windows which would be fully opened whilst we played our music to the street below. Mick Jagger was my idol and I'm not ashamed to say that I would strut my stuff to his music.

The early 1960s were the greatest time ever for pop music, with many other artists becoming famous at the time. I feel that my generation were the luckiest ever, to have been born in the late 1940s, and enjoying our teenage years in the 'Swinging Sixties' I personally felt that we were experiencing an absolute explosion of pop music.

On one such occasion I was alone in my bedroom playing my music with the sash window open. It was a lovely summer evening and I was standing at the open window looking out into the street. My attention was drawn to the corner shop at the end of Aspland Grove, situated about a hundred yards away. A youth who lived at the shop was standing at a window situated to the rear of the shop. He appeared to be pointing something in my direction. In an instant I heard a bang and a fizzing sound, followed by a heavy blow to my left shoulder. The blow to my shoulder lifted me off my feet and threw me across the room. I landed at the far wall of the room in a heap on the floor. I was in agony and realised that I had been shot with an air rifle.

I managed to stand and made my way to the wall mirror which revealed a ·22 air rifle pellet imbedded in my left collar bone. The wound was bleeding and the impact to my collar bone left me in considerable pain. I ran down stairs to my parents who could hardly believe what had happened. My uncle Harry kindly drove me to the hospital in his car, where a doctor removed the pellet from my collar bone. I had severe bruising to the bone but an X-ray showed that the bone had remained intact.

The doctor wanted us to tell the Police what had happened, explaining that the pellet could easily have caused the loss of an eye or penetration of my brain. I felt that luck was on my side that day and that the boy responsible for the wound should be punished by his parents. Later that evening the boy was dealt with by his parents after admitting that he had shot me with his rifle. He was not completely honest about the matter, explaining that he had been shooting at birds at the time and had shot me accidentally.

The matter was not reported to the police because it was not the way things were conducted in those days. I'm sixty five years of age now and still to this day have the scar on my collar bone to remind me of the event. In retrospect I'm still amazed at the power of such an air weapon. I didn't feel that the youth should be seen by police at the time, mainly due to the fact that I had also fired a pellet gun from my window in the past.

I was soon fully recovered and playing my records in my bedroom again. Great days, with singles like *Little Red Rooster*, *I Wanna Be Your Man* and *Satisfaction*, all of course by 'The Stones'. My cousin Jennifer paid me a great compliment when she said I danced as well as Mick Jagger.

Anyone for cricket

I'll move on now to my next visit to the hospital. I was doing my Saturday job at the engineering workshop and could hear a constant banging on the front door to the premises. Eric was working upstairs and shouted 'Mick, go outside and sort out that bloody noise'. I downed tools and on opening the front door saw a man standing outside who was holding a cricket bat. He was actually playing cricket with a small boy and was using the door as a wicket. It was obvious that their ball had been banging against our front door. I politely asked the man to stop banging the door with the ball, because it was upsetting the engineers. The man became extremely angry and hit me very firmly on the head with the cricket bat. The next thing I knew was Eric was standing above me as I regained consciousness on the pavement outside the premises.

I told Eric what had happened and he looked rather shocked. I had a thumping headache and felt very giddy. Eric took me to the nearby German Hospital where severe bruising and concussion was confirmed. I was given medication and taken home where I slept for what seemed like an eternity. Mum said I had been sleeping for about two days, but the good news was that the sleeping had cleared my headache. The assault was reported to the Police but no one could be traced. However the man's face was deeply etched into my memory banks and I will admit that I was keen to see him again.

Now came the period where I thoroughly enjoyed teasing my younger brother John, who had now reached the age of five or six years of age. His older brother Raymond was much stronger than John and my older brothers and I designed a game called 'The trousers off fight'.

The younger boys would be positioned in the middle of the lounge and made to wrestle. The objective was for each of them to pull down the others trousers, during the wrestle, thereby becoming the winner. Now I must admit that Raymond always won and that the result caused John much embarrassment. I suppose in truth my older brothers and I revelled in the fun despite it being at John's cost every time. I should point out that this was just a game and that underpants were always kept on.

John was a little timid in those days and I now feel it did him no harm and was designed to toughen him up. In fact it clearly did him no harm because he later became a very successful doctor.

Things had settled down and at the age of fifteen I continued enjoying woodwork at school where I finished making my own bedside cabinet. All of the joints were made with hidden dovetails. The cabinet had a single hinged door to the front and a single draw at the top. I French-polished the cabinet and buffed it up to produce a fine sheen to the oak. If I say so myself, the oak cabinet was now a beautiful piece of carpentry and my teacher was very impressed. My woodwork teacher advised that I should put my cabinet high up on top of the class tool cupboard, for safe keeping. It would remain there out of harm's way until the end of term, when I would be allowed to take it home.

One week later I was devastated to learn that an unruly youth in another class had knocked my pride and joy from the top of the tool cupboard, leaving it smashed and beyond repair. Obviously I was very upset about the news of my cabinet's demise. It had taken me many hours of school work to make it. It took a few days to come to terms with what had occurred, but then on a bright note, I reflected on the fact that I had learnt many skills whilst making the cabinet.

Shortly after this I suffered another disappointment when my good friend from school, Peter Bull, let me down over an impending fishing trip. I had been invited to take a week's holiday with him and his family to the Norfolk Broads. I was very excited about the trip because Peter had told me about the large pike we would be catching on the rivers and lakes on the Broads. A few days before we were due to go Peter approached me with a very concerned look on his face. He explained that the trip had been called off by his parents, but he was not able to explain why they had come to that decision. I was gutted at the news, which meant our planned escape to the country was now in tatters.

❀ ❀

Two street gangs

On the sports and hobbies front my judo had progressed quite well and I was about to take my Green Belt grading, which was to be held at West Ham in London. The grading consisted of several bouts of judo, all of which I won, followed by subsequent questions on the subject of judo. I was then delighted to hear that I had attained my grading to that of Green Belt.

My cousin Dennis and I regularly attended Upton House School in Hackney, where our judo club was based. Dennis was very good at judo and had qualified to the grade of Blue Belt. On one particular evening we attended the club and enjoyed a particularly rigorous session of training. As Dennis and I left the premises we were confronted by a street gang of about thirty boys. We were straddling our bikes at the time and about to pedal home. One of the gang told Dennis that judo was for girls, and challenged Dennis to a street fight. In the next instant the youth punched Dennis in the face and knocked him over the top of his bike. Dennis went crashing to the pavement and the youth kicked him about the body several times. This assault left Dennis reeling on the ground in agony.

The youth then turned to me and said "do you want some?' I said 'no mate, you're too good for us'. He then said 'you judo wankers are all the same'. To my relief the bully boys then walked off.

Dennis had a blooded nose and lip. I helped him to his feet and he was quite distraught, saying 'why didn't you help me?' I was a little older than Dennis at the time and quite streetwise, knowing that had I tried to intervene, we would both have been beaten badly or worse. The boy gangs at that time regularly carried blades and knives. It was a dog eat dog situation and you had to bide your time, before getting even with such people. I told Dennis that had the situation become more serious I would have deployed my bike and I wasn't referring to a method of transport.

I'm pleased to say that Dennis later apologised for his rebuke of me and realised that I had saved our skins. The incident left a very bad taste in my throat. However Dennis soon recovered, he was made of better stuff than the street gang. On a bright note I understand that the ring leader was later identified and apparently lost some of his front teeth.

It was now 1964 and that time arrived that we all worried about - it was exam time. I'm pleased to say that I sat my six

Royal Society of Art exams and passed all of them, with flying colours. Subsequently the careers teacher supplied me with details of eight employers who were offering apprenticeships in mechanical engineering. These were all based in the London area and produced an assorted range of products including scientific instruments, farming equipment, and heating and ventilation related items.

The school arranged all the interviews and I attended all eight companies where the interviews were completed. In stark comparison with the present day, I was offered the position of apprentice at seven out of the eight employers, but the one company that I was keen to work for never offered me a position with them. The company was called Hilger and Watts Limited, based in Highbury Lane, Islington, and made scientific instruments, and I had hoped that my work with surgical instruments would have held me in good stead. Nevertheless I felt privileged to be able to select any one of seven apprenticeships, on offer to me.

In due course I decided to accept a job at a company situated in Tottenham, in London, who manufactured a large range of heating and ventilation equipment. This was a large company who had a purpose built apprentice training centre on site, where apprentices spent their first year of training. A pay scale was agreed and I would receive a grand total of £1 19s 6d per week, for my first year at the company.

I spoke to my parents about board and keep, resulting in the lion's share of my wages, namely £1, being given to Mum each week for board and keep. In those early days, I was of the opinion that 19s 6d was a reasonable amount of money for an apprentice to live on.

Tottenham was about four miles from my home which would involve a train journey or a cycle ride via the towpath of the River Lea. I made enquiries about the train fares and found that my 19s 6d would not stretch far enough to buy the tickets. I would be cycling to work for at least the first year - yippee. Well something like that!

Prior to actually leaving school I attended an evening presentation of both prizes and exam diplomas. I had never received a prize at the school and was delighted when called up to collect my RSA Diploma. This was a very proud moment for a boy who had achieved very little at the school until my fifth year. My hand was shaken by the Headmaster for the first time and I was handed a very smart certificate, rolled up in a cardboard tube. It has remained in the tube to this date.

It was shortly after receiving my exam results that my brother Alan shocked the family and got himself arrested aged fourteen. He had been taken to Hackney Police Station with one of his so called friends for theft of cash from the Public Phone Box in Amhurst Road, Hackney. They had apparently forced the facade from the cash box and were caught in the act with pockets full of coins. Mum suffered the humiliation of visiting the Police Station and sitting through the police interview. Alan admitted his wrong doing and apologised to the police. He was very fortunate to receive an official police caution for the offence and returned home in shame.

Dad was not so understanding. He gave him a good thrashing. I spoke to Alan the following day and he said that his mate Terry had encouraged him to do it. He also said that the police had been very pleasant to him throughout the incident. He also said that this was the first and last time that he would be committing a criminal offence.

The reason we were all shocked by his behaviour was because we had always worked for our pocket money and theft was definitely not on the agenda. I'm pleased to say that Alan kept to his promise and resumed to being a respectable person.

❀ ❀

The cut throat razor attack

Alas, my final day at school had arrived in the summer of 1964. A large group of leavers had gathered together and after the final bell sounded, we started to make our way to the back gate. As we reached the gate I became aware of a large group of men who had gathered outside the gate in Frampton Park Road. The men were all dressed casually in denim jeans and work boots. A whisper went around to the effect that these men were there to attack my class mate, namely Malcolm Sammons. Within seconds one the men struck Malcolm in the face with a cut throat razor. I saw the blade of the razor pulled vertically down Malcolm's forehead, through his eyebrow, cheek, lips and chin.

This attack left Malcolm with a very nasty wound to his face and forehead. A huge fight then kicked off between the school leavers and the visiting aggressors. In a purely defensive motion, whatever was at hand was picked up by leavers and used to beat off the attackers. The fighting continued past the school buildings and down Mare Street, before it eventually ended with the school leavers being victorious.

Apparently the assault on Malcolm revolved around his girlfriend's ex-boyfriend, who I assume was responsible for the attack. My heart went out to Malcolm that day, I mean, what a horrendous thing to suffer. I haven't seen Malcolm since that awful day, but I heard through the grapevine that the wound healed well and he made a good recovery. I'm not a religious person, so to speak, but I thank someone for Malcolm's full recovery.

Someone later said that the gang dressed in denim were barrow boys from Bethnal Green Market. I do not believe that to be correct, because I have great respect for people who work in that profession. This is not a pun, but it might be said that there is a bad apple in every barrel.

Before I move on I feel that I should briefly mention my grandparents. They lived on the border of Hackney and Bethnal Green. Granddad worked for the railway on the steam trains and when we visited he would always have a story to tell. He was just a lovely old man and always encouraged us to pick some gooseberries at the far end of his garden. I remember to this day how big and juicy they were to eat. I was fifteen when he became ill and he died soon after. I feel that he always looked on the bright side of life and that some of his optimism rubbed off on me.

My Nan was also a lovely person who lived on to a good old age before dying in my late teens. I have fond memories of parties at my Uncle Harry's where my grandparents would sing along to the old Second World War songs. *Roll out the Barrel*, *It's a long way to Tipperary*, and *Maybe it's because I'm a Londoner*, are three good examples of the songs they would sing. Aunt Rene played the songs on her piano and she was more than accomplished, in that regard. In any street at that time, the piano was the instrument of choice. Although quite young at the time, I always felt a sense of relief in their voices, when the family sung these songs. With the benefit of hindsight I now realise that the relief in their voices related to the end of suffering The Second World War.

Part Two

Work and Marriage

The apprentice

The morning had now arrived in the summer of 1964 when I would start my apprenticeship in engineering. I found the idea of going to work proper, very exciting, and armed with my sandwiches, set off on my bike at 7am. I cycled by road to Clapton Pond and made my way to the banks of the River Lea via Lea Bridge Road. I then cycled along the towpath of the river to Millmead Lane, Tottenham, and continued into Keith Blackman Ltd which was situated at the end of the lane.

At 7.45am I clocked in at the apprentice training centre together with a large number of other new apprentices. We were then welcomed to the company by the personnel manager who introduced us to our trainer Mr Cooper. We were all given blue boiler suits which were to be worn at all times whilst in the training centre.

Mr Cooper told us that he had worked in engineering all his life and had also worked for Keith Blackman for many years. Prior to becoming the apprentice training officer he had worked in the tool room at the company and was therefore a precision engineer. Each of the apprentices was then allocated a work bench and Mr Cooper then showed us around the workshop.

The machinery consisted of lathes, milling machines, column drills, grinders, and a shaping machine. We were shown a display cabinet of tools made by previous apprentices during their training. The tools appeared to be made to a very high standard and were very impressive to look at. Mr Cooper explained that many weeks would be spent learning how to mark out the tool components, from technical drawings. The components would then be made with the use of drills, hack saws and metal files only. We would not be allowed to use the machine tools until we had mastered making the tools by hand.

To facilitate this method of tool making we each had a bench vice, which would be used to clamp metals, whilst working on them. We were all allocated free twist drills, assorted files, hammers, and assorted spanners, to be used at the premises. A large number of additional tools were also available on site, but were to be returned to store when not in use. We were instructed not to visit the main factory, unless given permission to do so, by the management.

After the initial induction we were taken to the employees' canteen, social club and bar. I was pleased to see that they had two full sized snooker tables in the bar area and was keen to learn how to play snooker.

On returning to the training centre we spent time with introductions and becoming acquainted with each other. It was an interesting morning establishing which parts of London the various apprentices actually came from. I recall most of their first names but not many surnames, due to the passage of time.

We were soon making a number of tools, for example centre squares, dividers, G clamps and various punches. I particularly liked the bench work and the shaping of metals using files, seemed to come naturally to me. All the apprentices were given what was referred to as 'Day Release' to attend a technical college. This would take place once a week and would form part of the apprenticeship.

My first college was The City College situated in City Road, Shoreditch, where I studied Mechanical Engineering at City and Guilds level. On the course I studied both theory and practice, which included technical drawing. The course ran for five years in parallel with the apprenticeship. I sat an exam after the first two years referred to as City and Guilds Part One. This was followed two years later by Part Two. During the fifth year I sat an optional paper referred to as The First Class Guilds.

I'm proud to say that I passed all of the papers and that my First Class Guilds was with Distinction. During the five years college work I also attended Hackney Technical College, which proved very convenient, being within easy walking distance from my home.

At the age of sixteen I was smoking cheap cigarettes, which I believe were called Players Number Six. However, I later started rolling my own, using Golden Virginia tobacco and Rizla papers. It was also tradition for lads of my age to visit the local pub. The *Earl of Amhurst* Pub situated at the top of Aspland Grove, became my pub of choice, due mainly to the fact that Brother David recommended it.

It was a typical corner pub, consisting of two bars, one for playing darts and the other being a lounge bar. I of course joined the working men and chose the bar containing the dart board. I occasionally played darts but not enough to become good at it. The pub had a darts team and the players were all quite accomplished. The team was in a pub darts league with matches being held one evening a week, either at home or away. On one such evening the match was at home and the bar was quite packed with people.

One of the opposing team players was rather disappointed with his score and after retrieving his darts from the board, threw all three darts up into the air. More by luck than judgement, no one was injured as the darts fell back to the floor. Dennis Payton grabbed the offender with both hands and told him not to be so stupid, thereby indicating his concerns for the safety of others present. The player told Dennis to Foxtrot Oscar, which culminated in Dennis throwing him through the pub window, out into the street.

The sound of the glass breaking was horrendous and left both the bar and the street, littered in broken glass. The opposing team were unhappy about the way their player had been ejected from the premises. The match had to be abandoned and the opposition went home. On a bright note we were left with a double ration of sandwiches, which were delicious.

On a serious note, the better off members of our team had a whip round and paid the landlord for the broken window. It clearly wasn't the type of damage one could claim for on insurance.

I should mention that Dennis was a member of a very large and respected family who lived in Aspland Grove. The respect related to fighting and not their standing in the Community. In those days fights were not uncommon in the street and were referred to as street fights. Families from other streets would visit your street by appointment, in order to fight.

Whilst growing up I had witnessed some of the fights, but strangely never saw any police in attendance. I believe there was an unwritten rule that dictated that the police were not to be bothered by such matters. Incidentally I drank bottles of light ale at the time which could be purchased for just over a shilling.

Back on the home front, more trouble came to Mum's door when my brother Raymond was arrested for theft. He had been taken to Hackney Police Station together with two other boys for theft of lead, from the roof of a derelict building. Mum had to go to the Police Station to attend Raymond's interview. He admitted the offence and was fortunate enough to receive a police caution.

This was now becoming a problem with two members of our family committing criminal offences. This trend had to stop, because as a family, we had been brought up to be honest. Mum was ashamed to have to visit the Police Station on behalf of her children. Raymond was quite young at the time, but I made it very plain to him that any more criminal adventures would be dealt with by me. In other words he would get a beating.

Raymond said that the Police had been very nice to him, whilst dealing with him for the theft. Furthermore that he had learnt his lesson and would not be getting involved in any more crime. I have little doubt that he was influenced by the two brothers who were his partners in the crime. I'm pleased to say that Raymond kept his promise and remained law abiding for the rest of his life.

At that time money was scarce and I would regularly spend evenings hanging about with friends in the street at the old Hackney Station. For reasons unexplained we would hang around the sheltered bus stop and swing on the bars like monkeys. One such evening I met a girl called Pat, who subsequently became my first girlfriend. Pat was an attractive brunette with collar length hair, in the typical style of the time.

Pat lived near to Hackney Dog Stadium, which was about a mile from my home. As I got to know her more she confided in me that her ex-boyfriend called Johnnie had been sent to Borstal for committing offences of violence. She assured me that their relationship was over and that Johnnie was fully aware of this. All was well until we were having a coffee one evening, in a coffee bar near to Pat's home. We were sat opposite each other with me looking into the premises and Pat looking towards the street.

Pat's facial expression suddenly went from a smile to a concerned look. Within a split second a man standing behind me struck the right side of my head with a handgun. I was very shocked and could see him clearly in the wall mirror situated to my right side. He looked to be very angry and said that he was Pat's boyfriend Johnnie. He said 'has he treated you well Pat?' Pat said 'yes Johnnie. He then said 'It's time for you to go mate' at which point I got up and left Pat with her boyfriend.

This was not the right time for any heroic behaviour and I have not seen Pat since that day. I'm pleased to be able to report that I've not seen Johnnie since that day either. I would add that our relationship was good while it lasted.

I've often wondered whether the gun was a real one or not. The good news of course was that I was street wise enough to leave the coffee bar immediately at the time.

One morning I arrived at work soaked through and believe it or not, it wasn't raining. As usual I was cycling to work and on that particular morning I had suffered a lay in. In order to make up time I was cycling much too fast along the bank of the River Lea. Normally, I would negotiate my way around the large metal chains which secured the river barges. Not this time, you've guessed it, I hit the chain, the bike stopped and I carried on straight into the river.

It reminds me of the saying 'more haste, less speed'. Yes' I clocked in late that morning. Fortunately I was able to take off all of my wet and muddy clothing, which was replaced by my good old apprentice issue boiler suit. Ever since that experience I have always been punctual when going to work.

My fellow apprentices and I were now nearing the end of year one. Examination time had arrived consisting of both practical and theoretical tests. We were given a technical drawing of a hexagon shaped die, which was to be made to fit perfectly into a hexagon shaped hole. Both items were to be made from half inch mild steel plate.

The first step was to blue the metal and mark out the two components. The parts were then roughly cut to shape using twist drills and a hacksaw. The skilful part of accurately shaping the two components with metal files, then followed. I managed to produce a perfect fit between the two components, one being able to slide into the other, with finger pressure only. When held up to the light, no light could be seen to pass through the two components.

Mr Cooper examined my finished product and said he was delighted with it. Not wishing to sound big headed, he also added that it could not have been made better in the tool room. I thoroughly enjoyed the theory exam and passed it with flying colours.

At the end of year one I received 'The Apprentice of the Year' award, which was presented to me by The Managing Director of the Company, Mr Strachan. I was also awarded The Managing Director's prize for best achievements in year one. I was very pleased to receive both the award and the prize, which were both of a monetary nature.

I later purchased a cantilever tool box, a new good quality hacksaw and other assorted tools with the money. In fact I still have the hacksaw to date.

The Good Samaritan

I'll take this opportunity to mention the problems in the 1960s between so called Mods and Rockers. I was certainly not a Rocker and didn't consider myself to be a Mod either. It was a lovely summer evening and I had made an arrangement to meet a mate at Green Lanes, Stoke Newington, a borough of London situated about two miles from home. Among other things I wore one of my favourite bottle green 'V' necked light weight jumpers.

I walked along Sandringham Road and then into Sheckelwell Lane, which formed part of the borough of Dalston. I was as happy as Larry and recall walking past a cafe which emanated with the sounds of pinball machines. I must have reached a point on the road about a hundred yards past the cafe, when I received a heavy blow to the back of my head. I must have been knocked unconscious because the next thing I knew, I awoke lying flat on my back on the pavement.

A young woman was kneeling beside me and she said that I should remain still, because I had sustained a deep wound to the back of my head. I was feeling very dizzy and realised that my green 'V' neck jumper was soaked in blood. I could see a broken bottle neck and broken bottle glass strewn around the pavement. The young women said she was an off duty nurse and had seen a man strike me on the head with the bottle.

She further said that the man had run off up the road and that she had then lost sight of him. I don't to this day know why, but I was convinced that he had come from the cafe. The lady then helped me up onto my feet, whilst holding a handkerchief to my head wound. She was very kind, and although I was a complete stranger, gave me a lift in her car to The German Hospital.

The handkerchief had stemmed the bleeding and after a short wait in casualty I received treatment. The casualty nurse cleaned the wound and administered six stitches. A doctor also examined me and said that I had sustained mild concussion. The doctor advised me to go home and rest for a couple of days, further stating that I should make a full recovery. Unfortunately the young nurse, who had been so kind to me, had left whilst I was receiving treatment. I didn't have the opportunity to thank her for the help and kindness she had shown me.

On leaving the hospital I decided to visit my mate Terry who I was meant to meet earlier that evening. I visited his flat but he had not returned home from Green Lanes. I was actually feeling quite poorly and was pleased to see Terry's neighbour Pauline. She said I looked awful and invited me into her flat for a cup of tea. I took full advantage of the invite and can tell you that I felt much better after a cup of tea.

Terry returned home about an hour later and I explained to him what had happened to me. Based on the nurses description of the man seen assaulting me, Terry said he would visit the cafe and find out who was responsible. I told him to be careful but he said he used the cafe regularly and would tread carefully. I then made my way home and wasn't looking forward to Mum seeing me in such a mess.

As a result of the injury I took a couple of days off work, by way of reporting in sick. Whilst off work I saw Terry and he told me that the man responsible for the assault was a regular at the cafe. He also said that he was not a rocker, but that he was a gipsy. The rockers in the cafe had taken a dislike to me, as I passed that night wearing my bottle green jumper. They had apparently dared the gipsy to hit me with the bottle, as I walked down the street.

I'm sure you can imagine that I was very upset at the time, and wanted rapid retribution. Terry then gave me the bad news, in that the gipsy had gone on his toes. In other words he had made himself scarce.

I'm pleased to be able to report that the wound healed nicely and a week later the stitches were removed. However I was stuck with a bald patch at the back of my head for several weeks. I had resumed work and all seemed to be back to normal.

❀ ❀

The main shop floor

The time had now arrived to go out of the Training Centre and onto the shop floor. I had mixed feelings because I had thoroughly enjoyed my first year in the training centre. Of course on the bright side I would now receive a small pay rise. My wage would rise from £1 19s 6d to £3 10s. How about that, then! In addition to the pay rise I would receive a small piece work payment, yet to be calculated.

I proudly boxed my tools into my cantilever tool box and prepared to leave for the shop floor. It was quite exciting because each of the apprentices would now be attached to an engineer on the shop floor, where we would learn the various engineering processes.

The time had now arrived for the lads to be allocated their locations for shop floor training. We were introduced to our respective foreman on the shop floor, mine being Mr Len Lugar. Len seemed to be a very pleasant man who wore a three quarter length white coat. He was one of three Foreman in charge of the fitting shop, the other two being Mr Alf Laycock and Albert Evans.

I was shown into Len's office where he told me that I would be attached to Tony Drozd for the next nine months. He further stated that Tony, who was Polish, was the hardest working man in the factory and as such I should ready myself for a lot of hard work. Len and I then left the fitting shop and walked to the sheet metal workshop situated on the far side of

77

the factory. I remember the walk very clearly to this day because it was a beautiful hot sunny summer's day.

I was then introduced to Tony Drozd who was said to be forty eight years old. I would describe Tony as a very fit looking man who had a wide face and high cheekbones. We shook hands and I recall that he had a very strong grip. He wore a T-shirt, beige trousers and brown hush puppy type shoes. His work area on the shop floor consisted of about one hundred and fifty square yards of floor space.

Tony had a large work bench which had a bench vice situated to the front of the bench. He also had a typically large wooden drawer on runners beneath the bench. The drawer was used to contain and secure a large array of fitting tools. Tony explained that I would be helping him to build centrifugal fans that were of varying sizes and quantities.

Len then took me to the factory stores where I was given a selection of tools to be used whilst working in the fitting shop. I was quite chuffed because I now had my blue cantilever tool box brimmed full of tools, and they were all mine.

Tony Drozd the hard working Pole

I returned to Tony who explained that our first sandwich break was due. We collected our tea from the tea lady and then sat at his workbench eating sandwiches from our lunch boxes. Within ten minutes a klaxon sounded indicating that work should be resumed. During the break I noticed that Tony had been eating sandwiches which contained both cheese and jam. This seemed rather odd to me, but Tony seemed to be enjoying them.

Whilst chatting to Tony he said that he came to England near to the end of the Second World War. He had been in the Polish Army and had qualified as a heavy vehicle mechanic with the army. He said that he had met his wife Katherine in Scotland and had a family together consisting of a boy and three girls. Prior to working for Keith Blackman he had been a metal polisher in London.

Shortly after our tea break a West Indian guy called Ken drove up on a large forklift truck. I was introduced to Ken who seemed to be a very nice guy. He had a great smile and a cracking set of white teeth when he smiled. Ken regularly delivered all the fan components to Tony's work bay, by means of the forklift truck.

The fans assembled by Tony consisted in the main of an electric motor, three metal arms, a large cast iron frame and an impellor. Tony was paid a piece work rate for each fan assembled and as a result of his hard work received some of the best pay rates on the shop floor. During the assembly a lot of preparatory work was necessary, but I'm not prepared to burden you with the details. The fans were used mainly in factory roofs to improve air quality for the workers.

Tony Drozd,
the hard
working Pole

I generally spent dinner time in the works canteen where a game of snooker might be played with the other apprentices. Playing snooker at lunch time proved to be a very pleasant change from working on the shop floor. It also gave us the opportunity to catch up with each other, on a personal basis.

Tony had moved to Harold Hill in Essex, after marrying Katherine and regularly transported his mates into work in his Bedford van. I was introduced to his mates and they proved to be a very interesting bunch of characters. Compared to me they were all a lot older and had all experienced The Second World War They all seemed to enjoy what I describe as 'every day banter'. They regularly took the 'micky' out of each other, but none of them took offence about what had been said.

The best day of the week was always Friday, can you guess why? Yes you've guessed it, Pay Day. The pay packets were small in those early days but I adopted the view that I was learning the value of money. Added to my basic pay I also received a little extra from my piece work rate, which I was entitled to whilst working with Tony. Of course in addition to pay day, the weekend had nearly arrived, what more could young lads want? I refer of course to being able to go out on Friday and Saturday nights in search of ale, girls and music.

The pop bands

The 1960s of course was a great time for music and a lot of the singers and bands could be seen before they became famous. I refer to people like Rod Stewart and Long John Baldry who both appeared regularly at the *Downbeat Club*, at Manor House, Finsbury Park, London. The atmosphere at the club was just fantastic. Another star in the making that appeared at the *Downbeat Club* was of course none other than Georgie Fame and his band 'The Blue Flames'. I can hear one of their songs now *Monkey go here, monkey go there, monkey go everywhere, do the monkey.* Hopefully someone can remember that one.

Then we had 'The Who', who first appeared in a little club, called Kingdom Hall, at the bottom of Stamford Hill, London. Even at that early stage in their careers, they would smash up their instruments at the end of the gig.

'The Small Faces' also started up at the same time with Rod Stewart being part of the band. They played at Leyton Baths in Leytonstone and became an immediate success.

The fashion at that time was to wear Cuban heel boots which could be purchased new at Carnaby Street, in Soho for a mere £40. Flare bottom trousers and long collared paisley shirts were also all the rage. I would say that if you had all of the above items of clothing at the time, you were thought to be quite well off.

Reverting back to the pop scene another great venue for a night out was *The Cooks Ferry Inn* at Edmonton, London. It consisted of a Disco with a large dance floor, where all the latest records were played. It was a great place with a great atmosphere and I think best summed up by saying that every girl present wanted to leave with a new boyfriend. To every up there is a down and the down in this case, often involved a very long walk home.

I clearly remember on one such occasion thumbing a lift home in the Edmonton area. A small van pulled up with a middle aged male driver at the wheel. He said 'how far mate?' I replied 'Hackney please mate.' I felt much relieved as I sat down in the front passenger seat. It was in the early hours of the morning and there was quite a chill in the air. The driver was very chatty and accelerated up the street at a good pace. We had reached about thirty miles an hour when he placed his left hand on my right thigh and said 'you've got a lovely young leg there mate'.

My first reaction was to say 'stop the car now'. Because he ignored me, I resorted to language I cannot repeat. My second request however resulted in an emergency stop and I was out of that vehicle in double fast time. I'm pleased to tell you that the

81

rather strange man then drove off and was never seen again. I suppose the motto of that story would be to keep on walking and never to thumb a lift.

On another occasion I was walking home from the same part of town when I suddenly found myself walking in a procession of Orthodox Jews. This occurred at Stamford Hill in the small hours of the morning and I was absolutely staggered by the number of Jews involved. For the uninitiated they all had skull caps, long ringlets of hair worn down the sides of their faces, full beards and floor length dark robes. Of course anyone residing in London would have seen one or two Jews of the orthodox type, but I found myself walking with at least a thousand. After a brief conversation I established that they were all making their way to the synagogue at Stamford Hill, for an early morning service.

It was about this time in my life that I knocked about with my old school mate David Everett. David lived on Green Lanes at Stoke Newington, London, a rather cosmopolitan part of town. We occasionally went fishing at the lake in Clissold Park, which was very idyllic. We would catch the typical type of fish species found in park lakes, namely roach, perch, tench and small carp. Sadly life wasn't always so idyllic in a city as big as London.

In the evenings David and I occasionally visited a basement style coffee bar situated close to David's home, in Stoke Newington. It was at the coffee bar that David introduced me to Terry, a friend of his who was a good amateur boxer. He was a very good looking, fit young man, who seemed to have a great personality. I'm very sorry to tell you that he was the next person in my story to be denied the privilege of long life.

Terry had apparently visited the coffee bar where he had become involved in an argument with another man. Terry was only eighteen years of age when the other man pulled out a bowie type flick knife and stabbed Terry to death. David and I were not present at the time, but were both shocked and distraught at this awful news. In hindsight I feel that it was incidents like that made me determined to enjoy every minute of my own life.

Reverting back to the apprenticeship I soon completed my nine month attachment with Tony Drozd and I'm pleased to say that I thoroughly enjoyed working with him. The nature of the work was fairly basic in engineering terms but I developed a very good work ethic under Tony's guidance. I should add that I also enjoyed the occasional pint of beer with Tony and Ken at lunch time on pay day. This would take place at *The Ferryboat Inn* situated near to the Walthamstow reservoirs.

My second attachment was now due and I was taken by Albert Evans to the gas fitting shop. At that location I was introduced to Harold Crow who would teach me all about the building of compressors used in the gas industry. Again some of the early work proved to be tedious and rather mundane but necessary to learn the trade of fitting.

As a fitter you would be given a technical drawing and a large assortment of components from which you would build a product completely made and designed by the Company. In the main it was very interesting and challenging work. Harold proved to be a very good teacher and was soon passing his skills over to me. In addition to the compressor work he also taught me how to do scroll work with wrought iron. I refer to scroll work used in metal fencing, gates and grills around the home and garden.

I had reached the age of seventeen now and started visiting a pub in Tottenham Hale called *The Swan*. On Friday and Saturday nights a group at the pub played soul music. The group were just fantastic performing Wilson Picket and Otis Redding numbers. They had quite a following at the pub including a number of girls who would regularly party with the group at local addresses or Soho clubs. I started spending time at the Soho clubs and had a great time boogying the night away.

We would often stay at clubs in Wardour Street, Soho, until 6am or 7am and were in fact regulars at *The Scene Club*. A second club used regularly was actually called *The Discotech*.

These were great venues where popular 1960s music was played all night long to a packed audience. Everybody in the club would be dancing and the atmosphere was just marvellous.

More often than not I would end up taking a girl home from the club. I would end up literally in any part of London and more often than not I wouldn't have a clue where I was. Sex wasn't really on the agenda due mainly to the fact that everyone involved in that scene, ended up exhausted. I can vaguely recall ending up in Brixton, a place called Southfields and on another occasion Hatfield, Hertfordshire, to name just a few of the locations.

During that same period, the crowd from *The Swan* and I walked from Tottenham to Richmond, where we had the pleasure of watching 'Cream' perform at Eel Pie Island. From memory I believe the group consisted of Eric Clapton, Ginger Baker, John Mayall and one other whose name evades me. It was just a fantastic gig and I would say well worth the fifteen mile walk.

Shortly after seeing 'Cream' I started going out with a girl called Yvonne who lived in a council flat at Highbury. This might make you laugh - her Dad was a dustman, but he did not wear 'gawd blimey trousers'. I hope you recall the song by Lonnie Donigan.

I'd only been going out with Yvonne for a couple of weeks when I was approached by her older brother who invited me out for a drink. He said he had a few interesting mates who would like to meet me. Well, I thought I'll go along, what harm could it bring me, I'm just keeping my girlfriend sweet. The next evening her brother took me to a pub at Finsbury Park and I was introduced to a gang of about thirty blokes. One of them said that they supported the Arsenal football team and would like me to join them at *The Tottenham Royal Dance Hall*, for a meeting with some other fans.

I should point out that I knew very little about football at the time and agreed to go along just to keep the girlfriend's brother happy. I remember it was a Saturday lunchtime when I visited the dance hall and Disco music was being played. Quite a few young people were dancing on the dance floor and the atmosphere seemed great. I was approached by the young male who had spoken to me at the pub. He said 'let's go over the other side of the dance floor and speak to the other fans'.

I made my way to the other side where he then spoke to quite a large group of men. A heated argument then started between him and the group of men. This continued for a few minutes and to my relief things then quietened down. I was rather disturbed at what I had seen and decided it was time to leave. I started to make my way to the exit situated at the front of the club when I realised that both groups of men were all heading in the same direction. As I reached the front doors a large fight broke out all around me. I managed to struggle through the doors and found myself bundled into the street by the opposing sides.

I was quite shocked at what had happened and managed to stand to one side as the fight continued in the street. I knew Tottenham quite well and realised that this massive fight was taking place directly opposite the local police station. To my amazement no police officers arrived to stop the fighting. To my shock horror the men involved in the fighting then drew weapons and started hacking away at each other. This was my cue to leave and as luck would have it a taxi with its 'For Hire' light on stopped and accepted me as a fare.

As the taxi drove off I cannot explain the degree of relief that I felt. I certainly didn't go there with any intention to get involved in a fight or any other form of violence. I decided immediately that my relationship with Yvonne was over and I certainly didn't wish to see her brother again. A few days later I learned that the other group of men involved in the fight were from The Archway Islington and that the two groups were rival street gangs. I wish to make it very plain indeed, unnecessary violence was not my cup of tea. I certainly didn't want to be part of any street gangs. I had been brought up with the understanding that you didn't take liberties with anyone.

I considered fighting to be one thing and the use of weapons entirely another thing. I was genuinely shocked by the events

85

that unfolded around me that day and I hope to this day that no one was injured too seriously.

Several weeks later I visited another pub in the Finsbury Park area together with a mate. Some of the Highbury mob gang were in the pub and on recognising me threatened me with cut-throat razors. We made a swift exit and I'm pleased to be able to say that I lived to tell this story'

❀ ❀

A fight with Dad

It was about that time that I became involved in a fight with my Dad and regret to this day, that particular chapter in my life. It was a Sunday morning and I was in the front room of our house in Aspland Grove, Hackney. Mum was in the room and Dad was shouting at her because she hadn't got any spare cash for his cigarettes. Dad was in a rage at the time and Mum seemed to be frightened.

I reluctantly decided to intervene and said 'that's enough Dad, leave Mum alone'. Dad said 'she always has the last word and it's nothing to do with you"'. I explained that he was frightening my Mum and I wouldn't allow it to continue. Dad said 'I'll take my shirt off then because I don't want your blood on it'. Dad then ran towards me with his fist clenched and directed a punch towards my face. My self-defence judo training came immediately into play and after avoiding the blow to my face, I took hold of Dad throwing him to the floor. He actually came down in a heap on the floor below our front bay window. Unfortunately he was completely winded and was struggling to draw a breath. I helped Dad up and sat him on a front room chair. He seemed to be shocked at my intervention and eventually stood up before retiring to his bedroom.

I felt absolutely awful about what had just occurred and swore to myself that should I ever become a father, I certainly would never assault my own son. Obviously the circumstances dictated what I had to do at the time. However, you never forgive yourself when you assault a parent. Mum appreciated my help at the time but I still feel bad about it, to this day. Sadly my Dad became very reclusive after this occurrence and spent most of his time hiding away in his bedroom.

I didn't understand at the time why Dad became reclusive but now realise that he lost confidence as a direct result of me challenging his authority. Dad would be seen around during the day time but as soon as the evening meal finished he would be off to his room.

Every factory had a bully and Keith Blackman was no exception to this rule. I had completed my attachment with Harold Crow in the gas fitting shop and moved to the general fitting shop where I was allocated my own work bay. This was quite a big step for an apprentice because you would now work independently, without a tutor.

As described earlier, components would arrive at your work bay together with the appropriate drawings. It was now time for me to assess the drawing and build the company products without supervision. During the early days at the fitting shop I had witnessed a man called Bill bullying several apprentices. Bill was a heavily built man who operated a large drilling machine situated to the centre of the fitting shop.

Most of the products assembled by the apprentices had components which needed to be drilled by Bill. Bill had a bad habit of taking hold of people and giving them a bear hug, as they handed items to him for drilling. Then came the day for me to receive my bear hug from Bill. I approached him and placed a large item beside his drilling machine. As I stood up Bill grabbed hold of me and placed me in a bear hug from behind. He had a grip like a vice and I could sense colour draining from my face. I just about managed to blurt out the words 'I can't breathe'. Bill totally ignored me and just carried on with his bullying routine.

Bill had in fact lifted me off the ground and I was now beginning to feel faint. I again tried to speak to Bill, but couldn't draw a single breath of air and was now completely exhausted. I decided in desperation to show Bill's shins the heels of my boots. I delivered a series of firm back kicks to his shins which caused him to release his grip on my upper body. I'm very pleased to report that Bill's shins were now bleeding and he began to whinge about me fighting dirty. As I gained my breath back, I told Bill that I was one apprentice who would not be putting up with his bullying.

Quite a few of my fellow workers came over and congratulated me on my victory. I on the other hand was actually annoyed that Bill had made me retaliate. I was there to learn a trade, not to be embroiled in a fight with fellow workers. The experience left me feeling a little upset. Bill approached me again later that day and apologised for giving me the bear hug. We both shook hands and moved on.

I have fond memories of fresh water fishing trips at Keith Blackman which were organised by a long term engineer by the name of Sam Woods. Venues were arranged throughout the year and we would travel by coach to far flung places such as The River Ouse, at Blunham, in Bedfordshire. We also visited locations in Cambridgeshire and Norfolk. These were great escapes from London and we thoroughly enjoyed our day whether we caught fish or not.

In my later years at the factory I took over the running of the Angling Club and found it both challenging and enjoyable. I recall one elderly engineer called Fred who caught a wonderful bag of bream, which won him the match at Swaffam Prior on the Fens. Then there were Mr and Mrs Nutt who enjoyed the swing tip method of fishing when we visited the River Thames at Marlow, Sonning Meadow, and a place called Leathern Bottle. They also liked to catch bream and would not be in the least insulted if I was to say they actually looked like bream.

We had a points scoring system and would award prizes at the end of each season. The prizes were always fishing related consisting of for example, a fishing reel, a landing net or maybe a keep net. Of course we all enjoyed our sandwiches and other assorted goodies half way through the day. The matches were usually on Sundays and were generally well supported by workers from many different parts of the factory.

I actually found my job very rewarding at the factory and worked on many different types of products. On a couple of occasions I went on the road to install new equipment together with one of the outside fitters. I found that aspect of the work rewarding and recall visiting the County Hall at Bedford to install a large ventilation fan in the basement of the building. This was in the late 1960s and we would travel by train or works van. It was great to work away from the factory occasionally and of course a good meal could be had on expenses.

On another occasion I was thrilled to be able to assist in the installation of a six ton cast iron gas booster at Kensal Rise gas works, in London. I suppose we're all boys at heart, but I saw these installations as big boys' toys. I suppose the thrill for me was the fact that I had been involved in the building of these machines and then had the pleasure of installing them. What more could a young engineer ask for?

Everything seemed to be sailing along nicely in my life and then calamity called. It was a normal weekday evening and I attended my judo class at Upton House School. Well I was one hour into the class when during a practice session I fell badly and broke my little toe. For those of you, who have never broken a toe, let me tell you that it is a very painful experience, culminating in a visit to Hackney Hospital.

At the hospital I was feeling rather sorry for myself, as us men do. I received treatment consisting of strapping the broken toe to another. I was then discharged and allowed home with the aid of a stick. I remember my cousin Dennis accompanied me home and that we arrived home quite late in the evening. Dad was in bed as usual and Mum was nowhere to be seen. This was odd because Mum was always at home and her not being there rang immediate alarm bells.

I went up to my bedroom where I met my older brother David who had clearly spent his evening at the local pub. David was half asleep but managed to explain that my brother Alan, whom he referred to as 'fatso', had hurt his stomach and gone to hospital. He assured me that the injury was minor and furthermore that we should both retire to our beds for a night's sleep.

The following morning it transpired that Alan had been injured very seriously indeed and Mum had spent the whole night at his bedside. The whole family were now in a state of shock, particularly when it was explained that my brother Alan had broken his neck and had been placed in traction.

No one of course was in greater shock than Alan who was fixed by his head to what was described as a Rieker frame. On entering the ward that morning I couldn't believe the sight that met my eyes. Alan's head had been shaved both sides and a surgeon had drilled two holes through the sides of his skull. A large calliper had then been literally screwed into the sides of his head. Alan was laid on his front on the frame, with his face positioned through a hole in the frame.

This position left him staring straight at the floor beneath the frame. In an effort to speak to him, visitors had to crouch down below the Rieker frame. Suffice to say he was not in the mood for a long chat and clearly had difficulty with his speech. A steel cable which was under tension was lead from the callipers to a pulley wheel situated at the headboard. The cable then passed over the pulley wheel and dropped vertically downwards where it was fixed to a tray of weights.

It was awful to see your normally healthy younger brother fixed to that frame in the manner described. The duty doctor explained that the set up with the Rieker frame was entirely necessary and had been designed to stretch the spinal column. He further explained that Alan's vertebrae situated at C5 position in the neck had been fractured and his spinal column may have been pinched or severed.

The doctor further explained that C5 was a particularly high break in the neck and was indicating paralysis from Alan's shoulders to his toes. He also said that Alan would probably remain in traction for a period of three months. I found myself feeling angry at David's remark about 'fatso' that he had made about Alan the night before. I should add that this was typical

90

of David's sense of humour and that he meant no harm by his remark.

Mum was completely worn out but took the time to explain that Alan had broken his neck at his gymnastics classes. Alan was quite a good gymnast and attended the classes at his school, Hackney Free and Parochial. Yes you've guessed it, my old school that I had left three years earlier. We were later told that Alan had been practising a double somersault in the gym, and that the instructor had not been present, to support him on landing.

Alan had lost his footing on landing and had been propelled downwards into the safety mat. His chin hit the mat first and because his body was being propelled forwards, his neck had been broken. It was accepted that the school gym instructor should have been supporting Alan at the side of the equipment. Unfortunately Alan was placed in the recovery position at the time of the accident and with the benefit of hindsight should not have been moved until the paramedics arrived.

Hackney hospital had done all they could for Alan, but were ill equipped to continue his treatment and it was decided that he should be transferred to a spinal unit. Within days he was taken by ambulance to Hackney Marshes where a helicopter landing had been arranged, to fly Alan to Stoke Mandeville Hospital. The Hospital was a well-known spinal injuries unit situated at Aylesbury, Buckinghamshire.

I'm sure that Alan would have been delighted to take such a flight, had it been under different circumstances. Prior to the accident Alan had a superb physique mainly due to his love of sport, which included his love of gymnastics and competitive swimming. Sadly his physic was to dwindle away over the forthcoming months of hospitalisation.

However, with the brilliant support of the medical team at Stoke Mandeville, Alan remained upbeat and optimistic about his future. It was simply a wonderful place for such seriously injured people to be treated. He became a good friend of another spinal injury patient by the name of Turan, who had broken his neck in a swimming pool accident.

Unfortunately progress for both patients was very slow, mainly due to the nature of spinal injuries. The patients in the main remained in traction for three months, which was followed by many months of physiotherapy. It's fair to say that in those days very few of the neck break patients, were able to walk unaided again.

The visiting fell largely to my brother David and me, who were both working at the time. Our four remaining siblings were of course still attending school. Alan spent a total of two years at Stoke Mandeville and Sundays for David and me were generally spent taking the train back and forth to the hospital. Mum would regularly prepare Alan's favourite lunch which - wait for it - were chicken sandwiches. Let me tell you, these sandwiches simply made him smile. At the time David and I were very important couriers. The journey took two hours each way involving walking, buses and a train. David and I generally stayed all day with Alan and returned home late on Sunday evenings. I suppose one could selfishly say that our teenage lives were put on hold for those two years. Boys needed to be boys at that age, but David and I knew that our visits to the hospital were a crucial part of Alan's recovery programme.

Stoke Mandeville at that time consisted of rows of military type wards, interconnected by enclosed corridors. The corridors allowed access for wheelchair patients to make their way around most parts of the hospital. Some of the corridors were quite steeply sloped which resulted in wheelchair races. Some patients, identities unknown, would, for example, race to the canteen. Crashes occurred but no one was ever held to account.

The hospital was equipped with a swimming pool and this facility helped the paraplegics and quadriplegics enormously during their recoveries. They also had a sports field to the rear of the hospital which was used to great effect by many of the patients. The field had been set up many years earlier allowing many patients at the hospital to take part in the sports, which would eventually become the Paralympics.

On one of our visits to the hospital Alan introduced us to a very unfortunate young lady. She was a very attractive lady aged about thirty years and we met her over a tea break in the hospital restaurant. She had also broken her neck resulting in paralysis and was also quadriplegic. I regret to say that despite proper introductions at the time I have forgotten her name. I clearly recall the details of her accident however because the circumstances were quite bizarre.

She had been sitting in a comfy chair in the lounge of her home and had been reading a book at the time. The next thing she recalled was waking up and being completely unable to move. She had apparently fallen asleep whilst reading her book and had broken her neck as her head dropped to the arm of the chair. This lady became one of my heroes, because having been dealt such a devastating blow, she remained very positive about her future whether paralysed or not.

During Alan's first year at the hospital it became fairly clear that he would not be able to walk again. This was obviously a bitter blow for Alan despite much optimism on his part throughout the first year of hospitalisation. He regularly suffered serious headaches because of kidney problems. And also because of the paralysis, he would sweat profusely without warning. These sweats were referred to as cold sweats which resulted in shivering also.

Alan was left with shoulder, neck and head movement only, but despite those limitations he mastered the art of holding things in his hands by locking his wrist and elbow joints. It wasn't long before he mastered the art of holding a pint glass with liquid in it. This feat could not be carried out until he had first pushed his wheel chair to the local pub and yes, you've guessed correctly, the glass would then be filled with lager. In those early days he liked the lager referred to as a red top. This consisted of the normal pint of lager topped with a dash of blackcurrant juice.

Brother Alan in the centre in his wheel chair

After about twelve months in the hospital it was decided that Alan had recovered sufficiently from his injuries to be allowed home for a whole weekend. Fortunately my Uncle Harry had a car and kindly offered to do the trips back and forth to Stoke Mandeville. The trip involved collecting Alan on the Friday and returning him Sunday evening. Uncle Harry was a wonderful uncle and did several of these trips for us over the following twelve months, before Alan was finally discharged, and came home for good

In preparation for his homecoming the local authority carried out a number of home improvements to make life more practical for both Alan and Mum who became effectively his carer. It was great having Alan home but it took a lot of adjustment on both his and our parts. He enjoyed having a bet on the horses and would peruse the newspaper in great detail to find his winners. He could then enjoy watching the race on the television in the afternoon. He also enjoyed a few games of cards for the odd shilling or two.

During the weekends that Alan came home good, old Mum would work her butt off to ensure that Alan was as comfortable as possible. She also had the task of dealing with Alan's bowel evacuation which had to be carried out each morning. I will spare you the finer details but will remind you that we're talking about the 1960s and leave the rest to your imagination. The disposal of the urine was somewhat easier passing into a rubber bottle by means of a catheter.

Mum had the task of dressing and undressing Alan. This required a considerable amount of time until good old Mum perfected the art of dressing a paraplegic. This sounds harsh but Mum was dressing a person who could do very little for himself. Mum, David and I also had to learn how to stand Alan upright to assist his general circulation. This was achieved by standing in front of Alan whilst he was seated in the wheelchair. You would then press your knees against his and take hold of the waistband to the back of his trousers, with both hands. You would then pull Alan towards you and he in turn would rise up from the chair, whilst you held onto him for dear life.

The object of the exercise was to hold him upright for as long as was possible, thereby improving his circulation. Alan generally enjoyed the embrace but not when I was occasionally unshaven. The first time that I stood Alan upright I was quite shocked to find him towering above me. He appeared to have lost an awful lot due to his injury, but on the plus side, the traction procedure made him taller. He would say 'I'm now tall, dark and handsome', and of course I would agree.

Alan was eighteen years of age now and civil proceedings had begun, in an effort to obtain proper compensation from the local authority. He had taken legal advice and had been advised that he would be awarded considerable damages for neglect on the part of the gym instructor. We were very much a working class family and certainly didn't understand the legal system at the time. Alan and members of the family eventually attended the civil court in London where he was advised by council to accept a settlement. It was explained that these cases could be very hit and miss, resulting in some paralysis cases not receiving a penny in compensation. This opinion worried Alan considerably culminating in an out of court settlement of £20,000, compensation. Of course in 1968 this seemed to be a large sum of money, but as timed passed we realised that it wasn't, bearing in mind the degree of paralysis that Alan had suffered.

In the mean time I continued my apprenticeship at Keith Blackman Limited and managed to pass my first part City and Guilds exams. I was now nineteen years of age and had started to work on a piece work basis. For the uninitiated, piece work meant that for each machine that I built at the factory, I would receive an additional payment, on top of my normal wage. Thankfully the days of earning £3 or £4 a week were now over. I now started working very hard indeed and regularly took home in excess of £30 a week.

Mum of course was given a long awaited rise from my much improved wage packet. I was very happy having waited the first three years of my apprenticeship to earn a decent wage. Although the work was very exacting, I thoroughly enjoyed it and actually revelled in it. I feel that I had developed a very determined work ethic from a very early age and this had put me in good stead for the future.

I was given a work bay situated alongside three of the company's top fitters, namely Reg Hasler, Len West and Charlie Hearns. I learnt many fitting skills from those three engineers and feel indebted to them to this day. All three had served their country in the Second World War and all had great respect for their fellow men. I actually feel privileged to have met them and worked with them. I have long since lost touch with them and often wonder whether they lived to a good old age or not. I certainly hope they did and on a bright note hope that at least one of them is now enjoying their nineties.

At about the same time my Polish friend Tony moved his work bay from the sheet metal workshop, to the fitting shop. His new work bay was now a stone's throw from mine and we resumed the pleasure of taking our sandwich breaks together. I guess old habits die hard and Tony was soon bringing an additional sandwich to work each day for me to enjoy. I found Tony to be a very considerate individual who would often enquire about my brother Alan's progress. He would also ask how my Mum was coping, having absorbed the fact that she was Alan's main carer. He was clearly a very kind man, making these remarks about people he'd never even met before.

The time was passing quickly and before we knew it Alan was discharged from Stoke Mandeville Hospital and allowed home for good. His earlier weekend visits had prepared him well for everyday living back at home, and I'm pleased to say that he settled in very quickly.

❀ ❀

An invite for dinner

Not long after Alan returned home, Tony Drozd invited me to his home for Sunday dinner. I was thrilled about the invite having known him for about three years and I was now about to meet his family. The plan was for me to take the train to Liverpool Street Station where I would be met by his daughter Danusia. Tony handed me a photograph of Danusia and said she would meet me about midday.

Well Sunday soon arrived and I travelled three stops from Hackney Downs Station to Liverpool Street Station. On arrival at Liverpool Street I made my way to the platform where trains arrived from Harold Wood Station. Whilst waiting for the train to arrive, I took a long hard look at the photo of Danusia. Liverpool Street was a very busy mainline Station and I didn't want to suffer the disappointment of not finding her.

As expected when the train arrived it was nearly full and I did not see Danusia alight from the train. I checked the terminal area and as the crowds dispersed I saw a beautiful young lady standing near the stations shops.

My beautiful Danusia

I walked up to the young lady and said 'excuse me, are you Danusia?' She replied 'yes, you must be Mick'. I said 'yes, I'm pleased to meet you'. We then decided to go for a coffee whilst waiting for the next train to Harold Hill. I noticed that Danusia had smudged mascara on her cheek and pointed this out to her. She thanked me and removed the mascara with a tissue.

We sat chatting over coffee and I remember thinking how smartly dressed Danusia was. I can recall to this day exactly what clothing Danusia was wearing. She had a smart brown suede jacket on, a yellow crimped blouse, a pleated skirt and red, green and brown medium heeled shoes which had a tassel to the front. Danusia was about 5'7" tall, of slim build, with short brown hair, green eyes and an attractive facial look.

I was in a state of shock because Danusia was simply a stunner, a really beautiful young lady. As I realised how good looking she was I began to regret mentioning the smudged mascara. I didn't need to worry because she had taken my remark as one made in good faith.

Whilst chatting I learned that Danusia worked in an office in the City of London, as a clerical worker. Also that she had been educated at a Convent school which was of course an all-girl school. The train for Harold Wood soon arrived and I recall pulling out of the Station into bright summer sunshine. It was the 4 May 1969, and I can say without any doubt it was to be the most important day in my life.

We were chatting all the way to Harold Wood Station and I recall in some detail the walk from the station to Danusia's home. The weather was glorious as we made our way along a road named Gooshays Drive. This was a wide road with well cut grass verges and handsome mature trees lining it. The occasional shade from the trees was most welcome as we continued to walk for some distance, in hot spring sunshine.

I remember us reaching Harold Hill swimming baths which was situated in a nice looking park. We then crossed a large roundabout and after a short distance reached Montgomery Crescent where Danusia led me to her home situated at number 145. I was no great walker in those days and was feeling the effects of the one mile walk from the station. Danusia's house was situated in a row of neat and tidy terraced houses with small but tidy front gardens.

The house had a happy look about it before and after the street door was opened. I was given a warm welcome by Tony who led me through to the kitchen where he introduced me to his wife Katherine. Whilst talking to Katherine I enjoyed the aroma of a Sunday dinner cooking in the background.

Katherine seemed to be a very pleasant lady whom had produced a beautiful and apparently well-mannered daughter Danusia.

I was also introduced to Danusia's sisters, Bernadetta and Catrina, who both seemed to be very pleasant. If my memory serves me well, Danusia's brother Martyn was upstairs in his bedroom studying. I may be wrong about this but I feel that I met him later in the day, probably when dinner was served.

Introductions were now over for the time being and Tony said 'It's time for a pinta at *The Bear*'. Katherine said 'I won't be going because I'm doing the dinner'. I said 'Come for a beer Kath, Tony told me you were the sociable type'. Following my remark Kath took off her pinny and gave me an embarrassed glance. We all then climbed into Tony's Bedford CA van and he drove us to *The Bear* pub in Harold Hill.

The pub certainly lived up to its name when I saw the resident pet bear in a bear cage to the rear of the pub. It was a beautiful animal and had apparently been at the pub for several years. It was clearly a major attraction for the local children, together with a number of other pets and birds. The pub landlord had created quite a menagerie in the garden at the rear of the pub. It proved to be a very pleasant lunchtime pint with Tony and his family in the pub garden.

We returned to Danusia's home for a splendid Sunday roast consisting of braised steak, roast potatoes, and vegetables. We were joined by Martyn at the dinner table and all became well acquainted by the time dinner was completed. I won a few points back from Kath when I congratulated her on her cooking. I do believe the dinner was then rounded off with good old spotted dick and custard.

Danusia and I then forced ourselves up from the table and went for a wonderful walk through the country lanes of Harold Hill. By the time we returned home we had walked seven miles and both felt that we had become very well acquainted. Later that evening Danusia and I took the bus to Romford Railway Station. It was in the arched brick entrance to the station that

100

Danusia and I had our first kiss. I must admit that I was instantly in love with her and that kiss was simply the best.

I arrived home in the early hours of the morning and recall to this day creeping around in order not to disturb my brother Alan. I went to bed dreaming about my new found girlfriend and I can tell you that I slept like a log.

I resumed work the following morning and thanked Tony for a wonderful day with his daughter Danusia and his family. From that Sunday onwards Danusia and I became very close and took every opportunity to be together. We bonded very well together and Danusia soon became a regular visitor to my home in Hackney. All my family thought Danusia was a wonderful girlfriend. My Dad in particular grew very fond of Danusia and started referring to her as 'D'.

I must admit that Danusia was occasionally overwhelmed by the sheer number of Rines in one house. Dinner time could be a bit of a squeeze at the dining table, particularly when we were all in attendance. Danusia was of a quiet nature, but handled her new situation very well indeed. She got on well with my parents and proved supportive to my brother Alan's situation.

A particularly memorable moment for Danusia and me during our early courtship was seeing the musical *Oliver* at Leicester Square Theatre. It was a great musical and we found that most of the songs have remained in our memories ever since. Oliver Reed played one of the leading roles as Bill Sykes and has remained a favourite actor of mine ever since.

Whilst visiting Danusia at her home I got to know her sister Bernie quite well. She was very slim, a good looker and to this day has always had a good sense of humour. Catrina on the other hand could be very moody, although I must say she was a stunning looker, for such a young girl. Catrina was only twelve years of age and soon turned into a pleasant young lady. Martyn seemed a nice chap but spent most of his time studying, in relation to his job in Insurance.

There came a day when Danusia, Bernie and I decided to spend a day out at London Zoo. One of my apprentice friends Kenny Bateman showed an interest in coming with us and I told him I would check it out with the girls. Bernie asked me what Kenny was like and I told her he was a good laugh. The girls agreed that Kenny could come along and that a blind date between Bernie and Kenny could be fun.

Kenny and I met at Liverpool Street Station and the girls joined us after coming in on the train from Harold Hill. First impressions were not good for Bernie because Kenny had arrived wearing a rather loud large checked jacket. After introductions we took the tube train to the Zoo and had a great day out. I'm an animal lover at heart and thoroughly enjoyed seeing all of the animals at the zoo that day. Unfortunately for Kenny romance was not in the air that day, between him and Bernie. Kenny was a lovely natured person but shall we say didn't have the looks that Bernie had in mind.

A special hug

Danusia and I had been going out together for three months when it was confirmed that she was pregnant. As you can imagine things hadn't quite gone to plan. However, I was very much in love with Danusia and asked her to marry me. Danusia accepted my proposal and we had a very special hug. The hug is still very clear in my memory having taken place at Bruce Grove Railway Station, a Station situated close to my place of work.

After the hug I think both of our lives changed enormously because we were now expectant parents. That evening Danusia and I travelled to her home to tell her parents that she was pregnant. We were full of trepidation and wrongly assumed there would be some fireworks in the Drozd household. Tony answered the door and stood in the hallway with a hammer in his hand. I immediately thought this is the wrong time to give him our news.

However, they say fortune favours the brave so I said 'Tony, Danusia and I need to talk to you and Kath in the kitchen'. We walked through into the kitchen where Tony placed the hammer onto the worktop and I can tell you I was quite relieved to see that. Katherine was in the kitchen where she greeted Danusia and me with her normal pleasant smile.

I asked Kath to sit down on a chair and then said 'Danusia is pregnant'. Kath looked somewhat stunned but Tony smiled and took out his wallet. He said 'You two go to the shop and bring some drink to celebrate'. He then handed me a £10 note at which point Danusia and I made a quick exit via the street door. We were all smiles as we walked down the road and both agreed that the meeting with her parents had gone much better than we had expected.

We went into the local off licence shop and bought some beer for the men and some sherry for the girls. On returning to the house we noted that Kath had been a little upset, but brightened up when we explained that we wanted to get married. The drinks were then poured and Tony proposed a toast to the expected child. He also said 'Tor blooming things', which meant great, in his way of putting things.

From the moment the wedding plans started Kath was fine and quickly overcame her initial shock. In those days it was considered inappropriate not to marry once a child was expected. This wasn't a consideration for Danusia and I because we were in love and keen to marry. I had been brought up in the Church of England religion and Danusia was a Catholic. We decided to marry into the Catholic religion and this involved visiting a Catholic church in Straight Road, Harold Hill, where I took religious instruction, in preparation for the wedding.

We decided to marry at The Most Holy Redeemer Church at Petersfield, Harold Hill, it is a beautiful but modern church. Danusia and I happily informed my parents of our marriage plans. Although a little surprised at the news they both seemed to be pleased. The date for our wedding was set for Saturday 8 November, 1969, and all our guests were duly invited. Danusia and I visited a jeweller's in Mare Street, Hackney, where we selected and ordered our wedding rings.

The reception was then planned and it was agreed by both parents that it would be held at Danusia's home. From memory I believe we invited over sixty family and friends. Danusia had a beautiful wedding dress and we decided to have five bridesmaids. My brother David was chosen to be my best man and proved to be a good choice on the day, as we swallowed the traditional shorts at the *Pompadours* pub. David advised me that the shorts would assist me greatly at the pending church ceremony.

Time seemed to fly whilst making our arrangements and before we knew it the wedding was upon us. I'll never forget the day because although cold and windy, it was a sunny dry day. Shall we say, not the normal weather to be expected in November. I'm pleased to say that all the guests arrived safely and that our wedding went off without a hitch. The ceremony was marvellous and I walked proudly from the church with my beautiful bride on my arm.

We all returned to Tony and Kath's house where we had a great reception and of course a good drink. Although not proud of myself I recall having about ten pints and ten brandy chasers, before leaving for our honeymoon. A good friend of mine then drove Danusia and me to Clacton-on-Sea, in Essex for our honeymoon. We stopped at a hotel on the sea front for three nights full board.

We had a good night's sleep and I recall my pride being hurt the following morning when Danusia purchased a hot water bottle from Woolworths. In fairness to her, proper central heating had not fully arrived in those early days and of course she was now three months pregnant. Danusia and I soon settled down resulting in a very pleasant time together at Clacton-on-Sea. I would say that the weather was dry, bright and rather cold.

Opposite   Danusia and me with five Bridesmaids

My lovely Parents-in-Law, Tony and Katherine Drozd

After our honeymoon we returned back to Danusia's home to an upstairs front bedroom which Tony and Kath had allowed us to use whilst looking for a place of our own. Danusia and I soon set about decorating the bedroom to our own taste in preparation for the arrival of our baby. Having moved into Tony's house I had the new found luxury of being driven to work, yes you've guessed it, Tony was now my chauffeur.

In truth, I was just another passenger in Tony's van travelling back and forth to Keith Blackman Limited. I found the trip very entertaining due mainly to all the different characters that travelled with us. Firstly we had Charlie Green a store man who had a moustache similar to that of the comedian Jimmy Edwards. He also had spectacles similar to those of Eric Morecombe. The lenses were rounded with the appearance of thick glass.

Another friend of Tony was called Butch who was a highly skilled metal spinner. He was quite short and stocky due to the nature of the work that he had done for many years. He had rather a stooped appearance from bending into the spinner all those years. He just loved to puff on his pipe blowing a sweet smelling smoke into the air around him. I can see him now knocking his pipe free of ash and other sticky residues. He would then fill the pipe again from his tobacco pouch, and light up as quick as was possible.

Tony smoked Golden Virginia tobacco in his Rizla papers which were cigarettes better known as roll ups. He would light up and after one or two puffs on his roll up, he would stop smoking. Tony would then continue speaking to the other passengers, whilst the roll up, now stuck to his bottom lip, hung down on his chin. This was a very funny thing to see up close and personal.

Another passenger called Frank worked in electric motor production and testing. He always seemed to think he was a cut above the rest and would usually wear a collar and tie. His world came crashing down when it was discovered that he had designed and built himself a caravan with the firm's materials. Frank made the mistake of failing to obtain permission from the Management.

Tony's van was a Bedford CA type which seated about ten people and had sliding doors situated on the near and offside of the vehicle. He would drive it to Keith Blackman and back five and a half days a week. It was twenty miles each way and the passengers all chipped in to help with the fuel costs. I actually travelled the route with them for one year and can say that I was never bored with the journey, thoroughly enjoying the banter.

Another fond memory of mine whilst living at Montgomery Crescent was the smell of egg and bacon being cooked by Tony in the mornings. The good news was that he prepared one rasher of bacon and one egg together with a slice of bread for good old me. It was a great way to start the day before travelling to good old Tottenham.

Shortly prior to my wedding I finished my five year apprenticeship and was delighted to receive my Diploma for City and Guilds in Mechanical Engineering. Additionally I had a first class City and Guilds Certificate for my final year of engineering studies. The certificates were presented to me rolled up in cardboard tubes and have remained in the tubes ever since. I would like to place on the record the fact that I was extremely proud of my City and Guilds certificates.

On completion of my five year apprenticeship I'm pleased to report that my wages increased considerably and I felt that this reward was long overdue. Danusia and I started to talk about the possibility of finding and renting our own flat in the London area. This would be no easy task because flats in London could often be a pipe dream for young couples, at that time. This was brought about by the generally exorbitant rents for such properties.

Time was moving on fast and before we knew it Danusia was eight months pregnant and finished working in the City, in preparation for childbirth. We had finished decorating the bed room and had purchased all the necessary items for the baby's arrival. This was a very exciting time for Danusia and me, being on the verge of parenthood.

Nicola's breech birth

Our daughter Nicola was born on 8 May at Rush Green Hospital, but not without the complication of being a breech birth. For the uninitiated this meant that Nicola was born feet first, causing concern to all present and additional discomfort to Danusia. However, the doctors did a great job delivering Nicola without further complication. I was present at the birth and will never forget the moment when her tiny feet popped out. She was a little cracker and has remained so ever since.

After about a week at the hospital Danusia and baby were discharged. The three of us soon settled down together at Montgomery Crescent. I should add that Nicola and the parents had very little sleep for the first year of her life. She unfortunately was an incessant screamer and we never managed to establish the reason for her behaviour.

I took driving lessons at about that time and managed to pass the Driving Test after my third attempt. Tony kindly gave me his old Bedford CA van which Danusia and I put to good use for both work and pleasure. We were thrilled to be able to travel independently to places like Southend-on-Sea and Canvey Island, both seaside resorts in Essex.

Good news also came along in the shape of our own flat which was situated at Umfreville Road, Haringey, North London. A friend found the flat for us, which consisted of one bedroom, living room, kitchen and bath room, all situated on the first floor of a terraced house. Danusia and I soon set about painting and decorating the flat, resulting in a cosy little home for mum, dad and baby daughter.

Steven's birth

Time passed very quickly and before we knew it Danusia was expecting our second child. We were again thrilled to bits with the news and preparations were soon underway. Our first son Steven was born at Finsbury Park Hospital, North London, on 21 September 1971. Unfortunately because of some stupid bureaucracy at that time, I was not allowed to attend the birth of my son. In any event we were gifted with another lovely healthy child who was born without any complications. Steven proved to be a wonderful baby boy who slept throughout most nights. This of course was very welcomed news for Danusia and me, as we also slept well through Steven's infancy.

It was about this time that my brother Alan ordered a new Ford Cortina 'L' saloon car, which had been specially fitted out with a view to him learning to drive. The collection of the new car fell to me, and with much excitement I made my way to the main Ford dealer in North London.

At the garage I was presented with keys and led to the vehicle which was in a lovely metallic green colour. On entering the car I familiarised myself with the specially fitted controls and then left the garage to head home to Hackney. I could visualise Alan sat there eagerly awaiting the arrival of his new car. As I made my way along Edmonton High Street a lady jumped out onto the pedestrian crossing. To avoid hitting the lady I braked firmly and stopped just short of the crossing. To my shock and horror, a car then skidded at some speed into the rear of my brother's new car.

I found the jolt of the impact, coupled with the sound of breaking glass quite shocking. I got out of the car and must say felt that I was responsible for the accident. Fortunately the other vehicle, which was of the larger variety, had not sustained any damage. The driver was keen to drive off and left me picking up the pieces. Alan's car had of course been damaged, consisting of rear end dents and scratches. One of the rear light glasses had also been smashed to pieces. I can tell you that the air was blue for a few moments, as I vented my verbal anger.

I wasn't blaming anyone other than myself as I uttered those words, but in doing so, I felt some relief. As you can only imagine, I was mortified at the thought of explaining to Alan that I had crashed his new car. I drove the rest of the journey very gingerly indeed. On arriving home I recall entering the house full of trepidation. Much to my amazement Alan's only concern was for my wellbeing. He actually said 'the car can be repaired, but not the human body'.

Fortunately Fords were very understanding and the car was repaired as good as new in double fast time. Having acquired the car Alan was now champing at the bit for a long awaited ride out. We were soon clocking up the miles, at weekends in

110

the main, this being the time that David and I were available to drive.

Alan thoroughly enjoyed the trips which of course took his mind off being trapped in the house, for best part of the average week. We would normally take a pub lunch whilst on the road and I can tell you that the journey also included loud music from the car stereo. Alan unfortunately had mastered the art of revolving the volume button on the stereo. He had grown his hair long and would sit in the front seat of the car rocking with his head, to the music.

David and I were encouraged too drive fast to add to the excitement of the rock music. In hindsight I of course realise the speeding was somewhat dangerous, but it was easy in all the circumstances to get caught up in the moment. Alan made several attempts at driving his car, but despite all of the alterations that had been made he was unable to achieve his goal. I should point out that Alan was very capable when it came to accelerating the car. On the other side of the coin he was hopeless at steering and braking.

I should add that the decision not to drive came after a huge effort on Alan's part and it certainly wasn't due to a lack of effort on his part. He was of course very disappointed at the realisation that he would probably never be able to drive.

❀ ❀

A difficult Christmas

All was moving along smoothly for Danusia and me until December 1971 when our Steven began to suffer with large swellings to each side of his neck. He was only now ten weeks old and the swellings began to affect his breathing. We took him to the doctor's where he was diagnosed with mumps. However the medication had no effect and the swellings were now frighteningly large. After a further visit to the doctor's he was admitted to Great Ormond Street Hospital in London.

It was now Christmas 1971 and the hospital doctors established that the swellings on Steven's neck were in fact abscesses. I believe it was Boxing Day that he was taken into theatre where both abscesses were lanced. A large quantity of puss was removed and the poor little lad was given a stitch to each wound. I can tell you that Danusia and I were quite shocked when we visited shortly after the surgery and found his dressings and the bedding rather blooded.

At the time we felt that he was far too young for that type of treatment, but in hindsight realised that other parents had children at the hospital with very serious illnesses. Steven was discharged a few days later and I'm very pleased to say made a full recovery. Danusia and I are indebted to Great Ormond Street Hospital for the wonderful way that they dealt with our son Steven. We also wish to thank my sister in law Bernie who baby sat Nicola for us during this difficult time.

In the New Year, Danusia and I started taking a serious look at the property market in various parts of London. We were happy with our little flat but were suffering harassment from a deranged lady who lived in the ground floor flat below us. We were told by estate agents that we would need a deposit of £800 which was a huge target for us at the time. We both saved as hard as we could for a number of months, only to be told that the deposits had in the interim been raised enormously.

I made enquiries at work and established that a transfer might be possible to The Northampton Lift Company, in Northamptonshire. At the time I was quite shocked at the thought of moving so far out of London. I was part of quite a large family whom had all traditionally resided in the London area. It was simply unheard of to move beyond the Borough of London, which you had been born in.

Danusia and I decided that we would buck the trend, if a property could be found at the right price in Northamptonshire, we would go for it. After further visits to the local estate agents we obtained information about dwelling houses that were being built in Northamptonshire, at a small village called Irchester. The properties were being built by builders known as K. J. Lawrence who had an office in Midland Road, Wellingborough, Northamptonshire.

112

We decided to drive up to the area and take a look at the site at Irchester. One thing I remember particularly about the site was that on our arrival it was raining and the site was like a quagmire. Prior to the visit we had established that a certain plot on the land was available to us, where three bedroom terraced houses were to be built. A foreman builder showed us to the plot which was situated in a small close which would be named Saxon Rise.

Danusia and I later visited the builder's office where we were shown all the relevant plans and detailed drawings of the terraced dwellings. The manager said we could purchase a house for £4,800, and would be able to do so after lodging a £50 deposit with him. We decided to go ahead and purchase the house off plan. We handed the manager our deposit and he gave us a receipt indicating that we had thereby completed the purchase of a pending dwelling, to be built on the plot earlier visited that day.

Danusia and I were delighted to be buying a newly built three bed roomed house, at a price which was effectively half the price one would pay in London for an equivalent property. I managed to obtain a mortgage with The Nationwide Building Society and engaged a local solicitor to act on our behalf. All seemed to be running smoothly until we received a letter from K. J. Lawrence stating that our cheque was enclosed and that the dwelling was no longer available to us.

I drove straight to the manager's office at Wellingborough, entered his office and slammed my cheque for £50 on his desk. Very few words were exchanged with the manager who was seated comfortably behind his desk. I did explain to him that the sale of the dwelling would be going ahead as planned and furthermore that I did not wish to hear from him again until completion of the sale.

The building work continued satisfactorily, contracts were exchanged and Danusia and I were soon the proud owners of a wonderful little home in Northamptonshire. I then learned that my transfer as an engineer to The Northampton Lift Company was no longer available, due to no fault of my own. This was

113

obviously a blow to us at the time, but being a qualified engineer I assumed I would find employment in engineering in Northamptonshire.

We decided that Danusia would move to the new house with the children and that I would continue to work at Keith Blackman until a new post arose. Money was rather tight at the time what with solicitor's fees and the mountain of other fees connected with buying a house. My Father in Law, his friend Val and I, decided to use our three vans to move our furniture to Northamptonshire.

Part Three

Northamptonshire here we come

The day arrived and after the three vans were loaded I will never forget the day that we drove in convoy to Northamptonshire. I know this sounds daft but to Danusia and I this was a great adventure, based on the fact that no one else in our family had ventured so far from London before. After what seemed to be an endless journey up the M1 motorway we all arrived safely at our new home. The house had been finished off perfectly and looked simply beautiful.

It was February 1972 and we wasted little time unloading the three vans, it actually helped us to keep warm in the winter weather. Tony and Val left shortly afterwards intent on journeying home before dark. Danusia and I soon had the storage heaters on, which warmed the house up nicely. We soon had the children settled in comfortably and the furnishings organised.

I had arranged a whole week to settle in but received very bad news only a few days after arriving. My father had been hospitalised for the previous two weeks and died peacefully after a long battle against lung cancer. He had also suffered a brain tumour prior to the cancer. His prognosis had not been good prior to our move north, but it came as a nasty a shock nevertheless. This was not the best way to start our new life in Northamptonshire and we soon returned to London to comfort Mum and help a little with arrangements.

It was a particularly sad time for Danusia and I because of course we had hoped that Dad would have had the pleasure of seeing us settle in the new home with his grandchildren. Not long after Dad's funeral Danusia returned to Northamptonshire and I carried on working as planned at Keith Blackman. It was decided that I would live at my Mum's house in Hackney until my new post in Northamptonshire came along. I was now travelling in my own van to Tottenham each day, via Clapton and Stamford Hill. For the uninitiated that meant solid traffic the entire way and leaving home early in the mornings. Danusia and I were not happy at being parted but both accepted the old adage of 'no pain - no gain'.

Danusia obviously found it difficult living with our two children on her own in a completely new area of the country. I would work Monday to Friday and then drive up to spend the weekend together with Danusia and the children. Occasionally overtime would be available on the Saturday morning and we could not afford to decline the offer. On those occasions I would drive up to Northamptonshire on the Saturday afternoon.

I recall on one occasion Danusia broke down under the stress of loneliness and caught a bus back to London with the children. The pressure was certainly on for me to find a job. An opportunity arose at a company called Alumasc which was situated at Burton Latimer, in Northamptonshire. The company were looking for mechanical engineers to work on their production lines in their factory.

I attended for an interview which was successful and was given a tour of the plant. I was impressed with the set up and the type of engineering work required of me. Everything was coming up roses until the details of the proposed wages were explained to me. The wages on offer to me were in fact half what I had been earning at Keith Blackman Limited. I couldn't take up the job opportunity because I would be unable to pay my mortgage.

At the weekends Danusia and I would do the weekly shop in Wellingborough town centre. Nicola and Steven would of course be with us, the former running riot and the latter sleeping in the push chair. Our favourite shop at the time was called Hillards, which was situated to rear of K. J. Lawrence Office. The store was the equivalent of a modern day supermarket which allowed a young family to do economical shopping.

❀ ❀

A change of direction

One such Saturday we had finished the shopping and were walking along Midland Road in Wellingborough, when Danusia said 'I've had enough now'. She then explained that our priority was for me to find a job. We were just passing Wellingborough Police Station and Danusia said 'Get a job in there'. I said 'where?' Danusia said 'in the police station'.

Danusia had spotted a recruiting notice at the side of the main police station door. It depicted a police officer in uniform and words to the effect 'This could be you' and 'please enter for more information'. I was now in a state of shock because I had never ever thought of becoming a police officer. After further consideration and continued prompting from Danusia I entered the building and enquired about joining.

The person at the front counter was extremely helpful and handed me all the necessary information, together with an application form to join the Northampton and County Constabulary. On leaving the police station I again joined Danusia who was patiently waiting on the pavement outside the front door. I told her that I had the application forms and she was simply delighted. I on the other hand was somewhat shell shocked.

117

After driving home Danusia and I read all the information and it soon began to dawn on me that a career in the police could be quite special. I found it a little daunting because the only job experience I'd had was in engineering and police work would entail a lot of paperwork. On the other side of the coin I had experienced considerable life skills after working in a large factory for eight years.

We completed the application forms in very quick time, I refer of course to my secretary and me. Alas, after posting the forms off it was time to drive back to good old London for another week at the factory. The rest of my family were delighted to hear about my intention to join the police force. I was saddened not to be able to tell my Dad about my new potential career!

The lads at Keith Blackman couldn't believe it when I told them I hoped to join the police in Northamptonshire. A couple of weeks later I received a letter inviting me to visit Hornsey Police Station to sit an entrant's exam. I assumed I would be shown to a nice quiet office to sit the written exam. How wrong could one be, as on arrival I was shown into a locker room where police officers changed into their uniforms, in preparation for their next shift.

As luck would have it, two shifts were changing all around me as I sat this very important paper. As the police officers came and went it seemed to me that I was sat in a war zone. They all found it hilarious as the duty sergeant explained that I was sitting the entrants exam for what he called 'the sticks. I should perhaps explain that I was sitting the paper at a Metropolitan Police station, where in those days rural forces were referred to as 'Cabbages North of Watford'.

Despite the pandemonium I managed to complete the paper which consisted of a short essay, ten spellings and some arithmetic. The duty sergeant took a look at the paper and after correcting two spellings said 'that's fine, sorry about the banter from the lads'. This was an experience that I shall never forget, in particular the loud clattering of the locker room doors. Some of you will deduce from this paragraph that my spelling was not and never will be one of my strengths.

It seemed to take ages for my results to come through from Northamptonshire Police and I can tell you I missed Danusia and my lovely children enormously. The letter finally arrived and I was delighted to see that I had been granted an interview which would take place at Police Headquarters. I was fairly confident that I would enjoy the occasion, based on my assumption that it would be similar to those for my engineering jobs.

I remember that it was a lovely spring day that I arrived at Northampton for my interview. I had never been to Wootton Hall before and recall very clearly the long narrow lane which led from the main road to police headquarters. Danusia and I had travelled by bus from Irchester and said our goodbyes at the entrance to the lane. She kindly joined me on the journey to give me moral support. I suppose some would say 'are you a man or a mouse?' Given the chance of a reply, I would say on that occasion 'a mouse'.

As I approached Wootton Hall I remember being impressed with the grandiose look of the building which sat to the rear of a square green. On entering I was shown upstairs to a corridor where I sat together with other applicants. John Fairy stands out clearly in my memory bank as he preceded me for the interview. John and I chatted and I believe he said he was some kind of book keeper. He seemed to be a very quiet and polite individual.

Within minutes of meeting John he was called in for interview and I waited patiently for mine. Well it seemed that no sooner had John gone in, than he was back out again. I was then shown through into the interview room and found myself standing in front of a very large desk with two impressive looking men sat behind it. The one on the left was in full police uniform and the other was smartly dressed in civilian clothes.

A large high backed chair stood to the front of the table and I stood waiting, to be seated. The uniformed officer shouted out the words 'are you sure you want to join the Force?' To be honest, I was stunned for a moment by his remark. I regrouped and said 'yes Sir, I do. He then said 'the last interviewee only wanted information'. He then said 'you'd better have a seat then'. I sat in the chair which stood about ten feet from the front of the desk.

The uniformed officer introduced himself as Deputy Chief Constable, Mr Church. The other officer introduced himself as Detective Superintendent Peter Eads. I noticed that Mr Eads was smoking a pipe which had a very pleasant smelling tobacco.

The room was large and ornate with large windows giving good views to the rear gardens. Mr Church then spoke about my application form in which he had noted that I had been good at snooker. He then said that in his view it might be said that a good snooker player might be the sign of a misspent youth. I explained that I had been good, but not that good. Mr Eads appeared to smile on hearing my reply.

Mr Church noted that my school qualifications were not particularly academic. I agreed and pointed out that I had been more of a practical individual at which point Mr Eads seemed to come to my rescue. He pointed out to Mr Church that I had received a Managing Director's prize and an Apprentice of the Year award. At that moment I can tell you that I was warming to the Detective Officer.

Mr Church then said he had concerns because two of my brothers had been arrested for crimes in the London area. He went on to say that I may have slipped the net and may also have also committed crimes in the London area. I can tell you that I was a little upset at his remarks, but realised that I could use them to my advantage. I pointed out that I had been so impressed with the way that the Metropolitan Police dealt with my brothers, that I later decided to join the police myself.

Mr Church did not look convinced and Mr Eads again had a smile on his face. He then commented that he noted the fact that I had good references from my former employer. I told Mr Eads that I was very proud of my work records at Keith Blackman and very much appreciated the references.

Mr Church then wound up the interview and said I would be informed of the result in due course. Both men then shook my hand and Mr Eads said he had enjoyed the interview. I was of course pleased at his remark and found it slightly reassuring. I later spoke to John Fairy and told him about my dilemma on entering the room. He apologised and said that he had only come along that day to glean information about the force. As we parted company we both had a bit of a stress relieving giggle about it.

As I left the building I recall thinking it's over to them now, I've done my best. I should add that the long walk back down the lane to the main road was somehow more enjoyable. Danusia and I met up again and after a nice lunch in Northampton, caught the bus back to Irchester. I updated her about the interview and added that I had met a very nice man, namely Mr Peter Eads.

Within a week I had conformation that I had been accepted by Northampton and County Constabulary as a new recruit and would commence a two year probationary period on 2 June 1972. This meant that I would undergo two years initial training and could be dismissed from the force, if I failed to meet their expectations at any time during that period.

I was now delighted because I could move in with my wife and children in the knowledge that I had a great career ahead of me. It would not be all plain sailing because I was still to be paid only two thirds of my Keith Blackman salary. For the first year I would receive £84 a month after stoppages. This was clearly going to be a very tightly run ship bearing in mind that my monthly mortgage was £32.

In the interim period I returned to Keith Blackman to complete my notice and bid goodbye to many friends that I had made during my eight years there. Many of the men were reaching retirement age and I knew as I shook their hands that I probably would never see them again. This proved to be the case particularly on hearing that the factory would close down within a couple of years of my leaving.

Unfortunately my father in law Tony had to retire early following a stroke and a heart attack. He subsequently underwent open heart surgery at The London Hospital and I'm pleased to say made a very good recovery.

If my memory serves me well I spent a short period of time at force headquarters where I was kitted out with all the necessary uniform. This entailed visiting the stores at headquarters where you were measured up by a very pleasant and enthusiastic gentleman. You were then allocated with what seemed like a never ending quantity of clothing and ancillary equipment. This included a helmet, a flat cap, two tunics, two pair of trousers, six shirts, two ties, a leather belt, boots, a great coat, a rain coat, a body warmer, a cape, a baton, a whistle, and handcuffs.

All of the above was brand new and when first worn seemed as stiff as a board. On returning home I assume all new recruits did the same as I did and paraded all the new kit in front of the wife.

Whilst at Headquarters I was pleased to meet another new officer, PC Terry Hancock, who was starting on the same date as me and fortunately for me had his own car. Terry lived at Irthlingborough and said he would be happy to help me with transport to and from the police training school. Terry had been a lorry driver and similar to me had recently purchased his own house.

Prior to starting the Initial Training Course, all new recruits were sworn in under oath to honour our Queen and Country, promising to carry out our duty without fear or favour. Furthermore that we would uphold the laws of the land, keep The Queen's Peace and protect life and property. I decided at that early stage of my new career that I would fear no one whilst carrying out my duty. I also decided that I would be as fair as possible when carrying out my duty.

Three other young men had joined the force at the same time namely, Clive Appleton, John Askew and George Stephenson. The training centre, known as Ryton-on-Dunsmore, was situated close to Coventry in Warwickshire. It was approximately fifty miles from Northampton. The Initial Training Course would take thirteen weeks to complete and for our intake started on or about 2 June 1972. We were referred to as Course 483 if my memory serves me well.

The new recruits made their way to the training centre on the Sunday evening, all full of mixed emotions. Clive Appleton for example was full of confidence having been a police cadet for three years prior to joining. Others were not so confident including the likes of former engineers and lorry drivers. We were obviously less academic and the thought of learning a career all over again was quite daunting.

On the plus side, swimming, self-defence and physical training would form part of the course. These subjects I felt would come more naturally to me having grown up with that type of regime. Well the first Sunday arrived and after saying our emotional goodbyes we were on our way to Ryton. On arrival I could see that the training centre stood on what I would describe as an old military base.

It had a large drill square to the front with several single storey elongated buildings to the sides and rear of the square. The entrance gate was manned by security staff that checked the occupants of each arriving vehicle. We had each been allocated a single room in the elongated blocks to the rear of the square. The rooms were rather small but adequately furnished with a single bed, wardrobe, desk and chair. The shower and bathroom were at the far end of the building.

After unpacking we all made our way to the bar for our first pint of beer with the locals, at the police bar on site. However I did meet one of the locals in the guise of Steve Dogget who was propping the bar and looked like part of the furniture. He was a great guy who seemed to know all the ropes and he went on to state that he had been at the centre for four weeks. I've got to say to us new recruits it was like meeting an old sweat.

PC Steve Dogget turned out to be another fine recruit from Northamptonshire and will be referred to later when seen cheating on the cross country run. The following morning soon arrived and it was time to attend my first class in full uniform.

123

There were about twenty four probationer constables in the class and after introductions by the staff each officer stood up and introduced him or herself. We were then instructed to leave the class and attend the drill square. None of us knew why we were standing at the side of the drill square and were a little surprised at the sound of loud military band music. In fact several of us starting laughing, at the sound of this unexpected music. The laughing soon stopped as we saw a grim faced drill sergeant march onto the square.

The drill sergeant was clearly shouting instructions at other officers who were obscured from our view by one of the buildings. All became apparent as uniformed police officers marched onto the drill square in squads. There were three squads in total, all dressed very smartly, consisting of about twenty four officers per squad. They were clearly marching to the beat of the military band music and I can tell you that I was very impressed with what I was witnessing.

They continued marching onto the square carrying out various formations as they did so. It was just incredible that police officers could march onto the square like well-seasoned soldiers. It then dawned on me that I would be marching on the same square probably in the very near future. The squads came to a stop and were made to stand at attention, ready for inspection by the training centre commandant.

The drill sergeant and commandant then inspected each constable. The object of the exercise was to show us that our boots should be highly polished. The uniform also needed to be spotless with trousers well creased. After the inspection the officers formed into squads again and quick marched off the drill square. We then returned to our classroom and started our police education.

The subjects consisted of crime, traffic, and general police duties. We had each been allocated a number of books to be used both in the class and also when doing homework. Learning law consisted of learning definitions off by heart which would then need to be recited to the class, at the drop of a hat. An example would be an offence of theft, the definition of theft being as follows:-

A person is guilty of theft if he or she dishonestly appropriates property belonging to another, with the intention of permanently depriving the other of it.

Having learned the definition of theft you would then be required to learn the meaning of each word forming part of the definition. I could now see why Mr Church who interviewed me at police headquarters had concerns about my non-academic background.

I could see straight away that I personally had a mountain to climb with regard to learning definitions, particularly on hearing that there were several hundred, all to be learned verbatim. Occasionally you would be called to the front of the class to talk about the most recently learnt definition. I found that quite testing having spent eight years working mainly on my own on the engineering shop floor. It's fair to say that the language used was very different to that at the training centre.

The classroom work was fortunately broken up by various forms of physical exercise. The instructors had kindly designed a cross country run for all of the recruits, how kind of them, I thought. It was a stinker, consisting of nine miles through woods at the rear of the training centre. The trainer insisted that all runners had to complete the course without stopping. The earlier mentioned Steve Dogget had different ideas on the subject and had found a small shed where runners could rest up.

The above plan failed miserably because more often than not the trainer ran with us. I could only assume at the time that the trainer had an informant, otherwise known as a grass. We did the run once a week which was exhausting but became easier as the weeks passed. I recall seeing Steve in the shed one day and remember he was sweating profusely. I would describe Steve as heavily built at that time, although others would say he was fat. Steve was very tall and whilst being diplomatic I would say his build was proportionate.

Clearly the most difficult task on the course revolved around the wonderful swimming pool which was indoor and on site. All probation officers on the course would be required to learn how to swim and failure was not an option. In addition to that rule all persons on the course would also need to learn how to life save to Bronze Medallion standard.

Much to my surprise, a lot of my colleagues were unable to swim and to meet their objectives could take additional swimming classes in the evenings. I was quite an accomplished swimmer but found the training very arduous. To obtain the Bronze Medallion you had to tow an effectively unconscious victim, twenty lengths of the pool on your back. To achieve this you needed to be both very fit and a very strong swimmer.

Each individual also had to tread water fully clothed for about ten minutes. Heavy weights would be placed on the bottom of the pool at the deep end. Each individual whilst fully clothed would be required to swim down to the weights and recover them to the side of the pool. Much to my amazement the whole class passed the Bronze Medallion in life saving, and some of us went on to achieve a Gold Medallion.

The classroom work continued at a pace and I fully admit that I struggled with the sheer volume of laws and procedures to be learnt. I recall phoning my brother Alan to inform him that I was finding the course very difficult. He wrote me a letter the following week encouraging me to crack on regardless. It was a gentle reminder for me in that I was able bodied and brother Alan was not. I felt rather upset at the thought that he had gone to the trouble of typing a two page letter with paralysed arms. In those early days he typed by using two small sticks with rubbers on the ends. It was definitely one digit at a time typing.

As a result of his letter I had no further doubts about my abilities and simply got on with the task. I have kept Alan's letter and can say that I treasure it to this day.

It seemed in very quick time that Class 483 were back on the drill square and learning to march to the military band music. I recall very vividly standing to attention on parade when the drill sergeant inspected our squad. He was a brute of a man from the West Midlands Police whose name I'm pleased to have forgotten. He came up behind me and said that I was too stocky. He then struck me across the back with his parade stick and told me to stand upright. I found the blow from his stick to be very painful indeed. For a split second I wanted to punch him on the nose, but quickly realised that he was testing my ability to remain calm when under fire.

I'm pleased to say that he never struck me again and retired later that year. Prior to retiring, I wish to make it clear that he taught our squad to march in formation very well indeed. I feel in hindsight that I had met a wonderful disciplinarian and sadly very few of his type are left today. Suddenly the name of my Drill Sergeant has returned to my memory banks, despite forty years of water passing under the bridge. He was a former Regimental Sergeant Major by the name of Police Sergeant Jim Suthers.

I'm tempted to bore you with more details of the lessons taught at the training centre but frankly can't be bothered. I'm only joking of course, because the teachings will become evident in cases that I subsequently became involved in.

In addition to the swimming, we also enjoyed playing a type of water polo which increased our general fitness. Cricket was also available although I wish to place on the record that I was a hopeless cricketer. I did however enjoy a day out at Eynsham Hall, Oxfordshire, home of another police training centre. We gave them a very good game of cricket but I sadly remained seated in the reserve's chair.

Weekends were thoroughly enjoyed at home with Danusia and the children. I can recall as many others no doubt did, leaving the wife and children on Sunday evenings to return to Ryton. I personally always felt rather sad, which was probably due to my children being so young at that time. Nicola was now two years old and Steven was only nine months. It was quite hard for Danusia because all our relatives were in the London area and we had insufficient time to make new friends locally.

The thirteen weeks soon passed and I'm pleased to say that only one individual on my course failed the course. It was a guy called Barry from Warwickshire who simply refused to have his hair cut, when instructed to do so by the Drill Sergeant. Barry seemed to be a great individual and we were all surprised when he adopted his stance on haircuts. This was another test of the discipline rules that all bar one of us adhered to.

My Passing Out Parade

128

The military band music was played, and with great pride Class 483 did our formation march around the parade square accompanied by other squads. It left all of us with a feeling that will stay with us for the rest of our lives and that was a feeling of accomplishment as a result of good team work. My family told me after the parade that they were very impressed by the standard of the marching. My father-in-law, Tony, had served in the Polish Army and he thoroughly enjoyed the event.

The commandant as was custom made a short speech and wished us all the best in our new careers as we returned to our police forces. We packed our cases and said our goodbyes before escaping from the training centre. It was great to know that we had completed basic training and now had a short break to be enjoyed with our families.

The rest of Class 483 were made ready for our passing out parade early in September 1972. My wife Danusia and children were in attendance, together with my mother and father-in-law. Class 483 marched onto the parade ground with our heads held high. As was tradition we all wore white cotton gloves, immaculate uniforms and highly polished black leather boots. I'm proud to say that we were all now very fit and well trained for our parade.

❀ ❀

My first police station

After our break, the Northamptonshire officers and I spent two weeks at our own headquarters learning local force procedures. We were then told which police stations to report to for on-going duties. I was told to report to Wellingborough Police Station where I would become a member of Sergeant Roberts' shift. I considered myself fortunate because Wellingborough was only three miles from my home at Irchester.

A present from Danusia

The town had a population of about sixty thousand people which included three council estates, many privately owned houses and a couple of large industrial estates. At that time Wellingborough had no shopping centre as such, but numerous terraced shops situated along the town centre streets. It also had a mainline railway station for commuters back and forth to London. The town had a couple of night clubs together with many pubs and working men's clubs.

My tour of duty started on the late shift consisting of 2pm to 10pm and I reported to the shift sergeant accordingly. In those days you paraded together with the other members of the shift, in front of the duty sergeant. Each officer had to present his or her baton, whistle, handcuffs, gloves, radio and torch to the sergeant for inspection purposes. I remember my first shift very clearly indeed because I was the only constable parading for duty. The fact that I was starting duty on my own did not exactly fill one with confidence.

The duty sergeant Trevor Roberts briefed me from the wad of messages received that day. He then handed me a set of car keys and said you will be Panda Areas 1, 2, and 3 providing cover for all of the beats until the others report for duty tomorrow. He briefly explained that some were off sick, some had been on courses and others had taken leave.

I gathered together all of my necessary equipment and made my way out to the rear station car park where I saw my first ever patrol car. It was referred to as a Panda car and consisted of a Morris Minor with a black and white livery, hence the name Panda. In those days I was informed that the Morris Minor was adequate for the job and packed a 1000cc engine under its bonnet.

Prior to starting the engine, I filled in the log book which recorded each officer's mileage and booked on with the station control room, my radio call sign being Whisky Whisky 663. I'm struggling to recall whether anything interesting happened on my first duty but I'm pleased to say that it was miraculously quiet. I think I dealt with a minor road traffic accident and a stolen bike. I remember finishing the shift at 10pm and reflecting that the best part of it had been in my lunchbox.

The following day after parading with the shift I was placed on a one month attachment with the shift traffic car. The car was a typical high powered vehicle driven by PCs Spragg and James, otherwise known as Derrick and 'Sid'. They were both highly regarded and very experienced traffic officers. Other officers on the shift were PCs Lee, Percival, Mundy, Cassidy, and Exall, who were all quite experienced police officers.

I recall the traffic car crew being sent urgently to a serious road traffic accident on the main A45 road at Earls Barton. I only just managed to get into the car before it sped off at incredible speed with klaxons at full blast. 'Sid' drove the car at well over a hundred miles per hour to the scene, which was at the dip in the road beyond a set of traffic lights. Two cars had collided head on causing enormous damage to both vehicles. Drivers and passengers in both vehicles had been injured quite badly resulting in ambulances taking all of them to hospital.

I was placed on traffic control duty which entailed stopping all traffic heading towards Northampton. I found it interesting watching ambulances come and go, followed by break-down trucks which were used to move the victims' cars. The traffic officers then swept up all the broken glass and removed other metal debris from the road. I was then instructed to open the road to traffic and stood waving the backlog through.

The traffic officers had started a road traffic accident booklet, which they then handed to me for completion of all the relevant enquiries. I could see that they had sketched a plan in the booklet, showing all the relevant positions of the cars involved. The details of the injured had also been listed which allowed me to take their written statements at a later date. The object of the exercise was clearly to teach me about actions to be taken at the scene and also how to put the accident file together.

Later back at the station 'Sid' and Derrick explained that I would be dealing with numerous incidents and traffic offenders whilst on attachment with them. They were of the opinion that I would deal with in excess of a hundred offences whilst attached to the traffic car team. This proved to be the case and over the next four weeks I reported many different drivers for various traffic offences. I didn't particularly enjoy that aspect of police work because some of the offences seemed rather minor. In hindsight however I now realise that all traffic offences are placed on the statute books to protect the wider public.

It was a fact of life that probationer constables in those days were expected to submit a large number of minor offence reports. It was looked upon as learning the ropes. At a very early stage in my new career I became more interested in real crime. For the uninformed amongst us, real crime means burglary, robbery, criminal damage, stealing cars, assaults in all their different forms and fraud, to list but a few.

I want to thank Derrick and 'Sid' for the four weeks working with them because they also taught me about being observant. They were constantly checking individuals in the street to see whether they were up to no good, resulting in arrests when necessary. They also taught me about criminal intelligence which related to the sightings of individuals at specific locations and recording such sightings. I also learnt to record details of description and clothing of persons suspected of crime.

I worked a short while with other officers on the shift and learnt that town centre disorder needed to be dealt with firmly but fairly. In those early days, I'm referring to shop windows being smashed by drunken yobs, fighting in the street, and general drunken behaviour, none of which would be tolerated. I remained at Wellingborough for three months and then transferred to Rushden.

Rushden was a smaller town situated close to the Bedfordshire border. It had the main A6 and A45 roads passing through it and as a result attracted quite a lot of passing criminals from linked towns. The linked towns included Bedford, Luton, Kettering and occasionally Corby, in relation to the A6 Road. Not to forget Wellingborough, Northampton, Huntingdon and St Neots which were linked by the A45 Road.

Moving from Wellingborough Police Station to Rushden Police Station was like going back in time. Wellingborough Police Station was relatively modern compared with Rushden which seemed to date from the time of the ark. It was more like a police house than a police station. I don't wish to sound ungrateful because it was a wonderful and warm stone built building, which dated quite a way back in time.

The station's moment of fame came when it was used for the filming of *Hunter's Walk*, a television series about rural policing. Poorly paid probationers such as I, were delighted to hear of the cameras coming, because we could appear in it as extras and earn a few quid. I specifically recall appearing as an extra on three occasions and earning £40 on each occasion. Danusia also played the part of an extra, thoroughly enjoyed it and also earned £40.

Because Rushden was smaller, each shift had fewer officers than Wellingborough, and I soon became acquainted with them. I had another shift sergeant now and as a probationer constable, I didn't find him particularly supportive. He seemed somewhat aloof and didn't seem to be fond of Londoners. Despite this set back the support staff were brilliant and I learnt a lot from the other officers on the shift.

I remember Phoebe Smith the switchboard operator who was always helpful and always cheerful. I also remember the old office PC Bert Ireland who was also a lovely man to work with. PC Christopher Cross was the senior man on the shift, a well-educated man who had come from the banking world. Chris had about three year's service and was always keen to pass on his experience to other shift members.

The Flying Squad

I was manning the station alone one night when I heard someone banging loudly on the door. To my surprise when I opened the door I was confronted by the site of twelve men all dressed in Crombie type coats. One of them introduced himself as a Detective Superintendent and said they were Flying Squad officers from London. He then opened his Crombie and showed me his handgun which was in a holster, situated just above his waist. I was reassured when he also presented his warrant card which confirmed his identity.

He further stated that they were on a job in Rushden and were all armed for that purpose. Being a probationer I asked the obvious question 'what job is it?' He explained that it was high profile and as such he was unable to give me any information about the job. He said that they needed to crack on and that they would be in touch with the results. It transpired that when armed they merely had to report to the local police when in the area.

When they left I could hardly contain myself and phoned Wellingborough control room and passed on the information. We all then waited with baited breath wondering what would happen next. Within one hour our control room received a call from the same Detective Superintendent, who stated that they had arrested Bertie Smalls an infamous criminal from London. He also thanked us for all our help and said he and his team were on their way back to 'The Smoke'.

It later transpired that Bertie had been living off Melloway Road, Rushden, for the previous two years, unbeknown to Northampton and County Constabulary. He had in fact been living next door to a Police Inspector. Suffice to say that the Inspector was rather surprised at the news of such a high profile arrest.

I later learned that the arrest of Bertie formed part of a big operation to arrest and convict numerous London bank robbers. The operation proved highly successful, culminating in over twenty bank robbers going to prison for life. I believe Bertie Smalls also went down and served a lengthy sentence for bank robbery. On reflection I found my brief meeting with the flying squad, very exciting indeed.

Attempted murder

It was soon after that event that I was again alone on night duty at Rushden Police Station. Other officers were also working but were tied up with commitments elsewhere. I received a phone call from a member of the public who stated that there had been a burglary in Southfields, Rushden. It was a male caller who sounded very drunk and struggled to string his words together. I locked the station and made my way to Southfields, informing my control room whilst on route.

On arrival at Southfields which consisted of two rows of prefabricated bungalows, I became aware of someone moaning out loudly, as if in pain. From the 'T' junction of Park Road and Southfields, I could see that one of the Southfields street doors was open. I also saw that light was emanating from the hallway into the street. As I approached the open doorway I realised that the moaning became louder and that it was emanating from that particular property.

I entered the hallway and became immediately shocked at what I saw in the bedroom to my left. An elderly lady was lying on her back on the bed and her nightdress had been pulled up over her head. The lady was in a semiconscious state and the moaning sound turned out to be the lady gasping for breath. I pulled her nightdress down from her head and covered her otherwise naked body. To my shock horror I could now see the most awful injuries to her face.

Her face had been badly battered to the extent that the facial swelling had closed her eyes and airways completely. The lady was bleeding from her facial injuries and a considerable amount of blood had been spattered over her nightdress and bedding. I tried talking to the lady but could tell very quickly that she could neither see nor hear me. I called for an ambulance and back-up on my radio, at the same time explaining what I had found. I tried to turn the lady to one side to assist her breathing, but in truth realised she would need at least a tracheotomy to achieve this.

I stood outside to use my radio because of poor reception and whilst doing so heard someone crashing around in Park Road. I walked the short distance to the Park Road junction and could see the figure of a man standing in the public telephone box. The man saw me and started staggering towards me shouting something about a burglary. The man was completely drunk and had blood sodden clothes on. On closer inspection I could see that his hands were simply caked in congealed blood.

He said that he had phoned in having found the burglary. He further said that the blood came from the lady as he tried to help her. I detained the man and took him back up Southfields at which point back-up arrived. The man was taken into custody by other officers whilst I remained at the scene with paramedics. The paramedics quickly accessed the patient and after initial treatment, placed her on a stretcher and took her to hospital by ambulance.

Plain clothed officers later arrived and took charge of the enquiry. Scenes of Crime Officers also attended and started their examination of the scene. I then returned to the police station where I was instructed to make a detailed statement of what I had seen and done in relation to the incident. Prior to finishing duty that night I enquired as to the progress of the victim and was saddened to hear that she was in a coma.

I must confess that on arriving home that morning I felt very upset to have witnessed the possible demise of this elderly lady. It later transpired that the assailant, who I had detained, had previously lived in the prefabricated bungalow. He had been out that evening drinking large quantities of vodka and thought in his drunken state that he still lived at the bungalow. He went on to force entry to the bungalow via the rear door. According to him the lady became hysterical and this caused him to silence her. Sadly the lady whose identity will not be revealed by me, died eight weeks later having never regained consciousness.

It was a rude awakening for me to be dealing with a victim so badly battered, so early in my service. In very quick time I was learning exactly why young constables took an oath to protect life and property. Protecting life and property formed part of the definition of a police constable. I now knew through a bitter experience exactly why we had learnt such important definitions at the training centre.

With regard to the serious cases experienced in my role as a police officer, I wish to state that I recall all of the names of both victims and offenders. My reason for not naming all of them is purely to ensure that I do not upset or offend anyone with knowledge of the cases. My thoughts on this subject are directed more to victims than the culprits.

Not all of the incidents attended involved violence and a good example of an interesting non-violent crime was when I was sent to Rushden Golf Club. A shed had been broken into and a vehicular lawnmower had been stolen. Despite this being in the early 1970s, the mower was worth several hundred pounds and a vital piece of equipment for the green keeper. The mower apparently had a drop bar to the rear for attaching other pieces of equipment.

Although early in service, I decided to have a good nose around the scene and eventually found fresh score marks on the road surface at the front of the club. I showed them to the green-keeper and he was of the view that the marks could have been made by the drop bar. I had the use of a pedal cycle that morning and decided to follow the marks, which continued on the road surface towards Higham Ferrers.

I soon realised that the offender had been worse for drink, because on reaching Higham Ferrers, I found myself going round in circles. He had entered a park called Castle Fields and had left drop bar marks in the grass. He had then left the park and travelled through Higham and into Rushden. The marks continued to be evident in the tarmac until I reached Newton Road, where they seemed to disappear.

I abandoned the bike and had another nose around on foot. The word 'Bingo' came to mind, when I found the drop bar marks again in Trafford Road Park. Again the offender had made his circular gouges in the grass and clearly left the park via a footpath into Trafford Road. Fortunately for me he had not run out of petrol and made his second big mistake.

Yes, you've guessed it, he drove it through his own side gate and parked it in his rear garden. He had hidden it quite well under a large tarpaulin sheet, and had retired to his bed. I was chuffed and carried out a quick inspection of the mower, which miraculously was no worse for wear. I then took great pleasure in waking the thief from a very deep sleep and arresting him. I found it quite funny when he enquired as to who had 'grassed' him up.

I wish to point out that I found it a very rewarding morning's work, which was very much appreciated by one happy green-keeper. The offender turned out to be a prolific Rushden thief, whose arrest did not go unnoticed by the Detective Sergeant. I was in fact complimented by him when he said he admired my tenacity that morning. The results that day again confirmed that good observation paid dividends in everyday policing.

Days off from work were enjoyed with Danusia and the children. We took regular walks to the small recreation park in Irchester, where an old disused steam engine proved popular with local kids. My two were still a bit young to drive it at that time. Yes, you've guessed it, I had to drive it on my own. We would also walk to Irchester Country Park with our children in the pram. We were all very excited when we saw rabbits running back and forth.

Having bought a new house there was plenty of DIY to be done, as and when the money was available. We slowly erected some fences, a shed base and a garden shed. We built a crazy paved patio, a footpath in the rear garden, and laid two small lawns. We later built a Marshalite stone fireplace, with polished wood tops, which together gave the lounge a little character

I'm afraid as in any job the weekends passed to quickly and before you knew it you were back at work. Irchester was three miles from Rushden Police Station and for the first year I travelled in style. Yes, you've guessed it, I walked there and back for each shift. It was OK in the summer but not so good in the winter months. The main problem was that the route consisted of a number of hills and valleys. At a good pace the walk took three quarters of an hour each way. This unfortunately added an extra one and half hours to each shift.

I suppose some people would consider the inward walk as a warm up and the return, a warm down. I just liked it when I arrived home and found time to put my feet up. On a bright note the walking kept me quite fit and as such I feel that it helped me to cope with the shift system. The shifts consisted of seven continuous duties. Starting on a Friday night we did three late shifts, followed by four early shifts of 6am to 2pm, thus finishing on Thursdays at 2pm.

Those duties would be followed by three rest days on Friday, Saturday, and Sunday. On Monday we would commence seven night duties, starting at 10pm and finishing at 6am. You would then have two rest days and resume duty on Wednesday, at 2pm. You would then do mixtures of late and early turn duties for the next seven days.

Any police officer will tell you that those shift patterns were very tiring indeed. On the other side of the coin, the job provided solid security and a good pension scheme. The team spirit and general camaraderie kept the vast majority of officers going. However my friend Terry Hancock, who I had joined with, found police pay provided insufficient income for him to live on. He unfortunately resigned only a couple of months after completing initial training at Ryton-on-Dunsmore.

John Askew and Clive Appleton were posted to Northampton, where they continued their probationary period of training. George Stephenson was posted to the other side of the county and worked initially in the Daventry area. About once every three months I would again meet these officers at police headquarters, whilst attending probationer training. On a bright note we were always provided with a splendid dinner, at the police headquarters canteen. One of my favourites was the sausage and leek pie, followed by apple crumble and cold cream. Believe me when I say that those girls were the best chefs in the land.

Having digressed a little, I'm now heading back to Rushden to resume normal duties. I quite enjoyed walking the number one beat in those early days. This beat consisted, in the main of the High Street, High Street South, and all of the adjoining roads, situated on either side of these roads. On night duty the main objective was again to protect life and property. It was also important to maintain 'The Queen's Peace'.

Rushden High Street was well known for drunken disorder, particularly at weekends. This was mainly because of the fact that it had eight pubs along its length and quite a large number of eateries where people gathered at pub turn out time. I formed the view at quite an early stage in my service, that I would not tolerate drunken behaviour, whenever possible. I recall one night in particular when I saw an elderly man walking along the High Street, with his small dog on its lead.

I observed approximately forty young men purposely blocking the elderly man's route along the pavement. I could see that the man was becoming distressed by their actions and

140

he actually stepped into the road to avoid them. Several of the young men also stepped into the road and again blocked the older man's route. I was appalled at their behaviour and stepped from the shadows to inform them. My first priority was the elderly man's safety, so I instructed the group of young men to step aside and allow him through.

The group parted as instructed, with the exception of two young men aged about twenty years of age, who seemed determined to defy me. I moved in close to them and they gave way to the man and his dog. To my surprise the two young men challenged me to a fight behind the shops. I then joined them behind the shops, but realised my mistake when the rest of their gang also came behind the shops. I was more than a little concerned until one of the two said 'you hit him first'. The other one then said 'no, you hit him first'.

I knew by their remarks that they were both cowards and realised it was time for me to respond. I basically wanted to call their bluff and in doing so gain their respect at street level. I told both of them to hit me at once and to be done with it. When push came to shove neither of them had a stomach for a fight and both apologised for their behaviour. I resumed walking my beat and can tell you that at street level, I won a lot of respect from the young men who came behind the shops that night. Some might say my actions were foolhardy, but I feel that you sometimes have to play them at their own game.

One of the main jobs on number one beat was to check the front and rear of all the shops, before duty finished at 6am. The reason for the checks was three fold, to deter burglars, to catch burglars, or secure premises after the burglars had left. If the third option applied, you had clearly failed miserably. I recall checking Boots chemist shop at about 1am and found a forced entry via a rear door. Back up arrived and we surrounded the premises, only to establish that the intruder had already left.

It was very frustrating because we had received a warning notice to the effect that a criminal from the West Midlands was carrying out such burglaries at that time. He went by the name of Politano and his MO (Modus Operandi - method of

141

operation) was to use a brace and bit to gain entry. He would drill a series of holes in wooden doors until he created a rectangular shape. He would then knock out the rectangle and simply climb in.

His target in those days was drugs which were secured in reinforced black metal drugs cabinets. In the trade the boxes were referred to as The DDC, short for the Dangerous Drugs Cabinet. The burglar had been successful having forced the DDC and removed the drugs. These chemist shop burglaries were considered as very serious offences, resulting in both CID and the Scenes of Crime Officer being called to the scene. When they arrived I resumed walking my beat.

I later understood that the target for the chemist shop burglaries was arrested and subsequently received a custodial sentence for a large number of burglaries. I also learned that we had narrowly missed the offender on the night of the Boots chemist break in.

About six months into my probation I recall seeing my brother Alan and it was lovely to see him still making a determined recovery from his hospitalisation. He enjoyed playing cards and we would always sit round a table with our brothers Dave and Raymond. We would play for a few bob just to give the games that added interest and of course hopefully be the winner. It was always lovely to see Alan who inspired others by his enthusiasm and determination to enjoy life despite his severe disability. We would normally meet at weekends, although my job made this difficult in that I only had one weekend off a month.

On these rare occasions, Danusia and I would travel down to Hackney, and subsequently to Cheshunt in Hertfordshire, when my family moved to their new home. Fortunately they had been allocated a brand new bungalow which made life more practical for Alan in his wheelchair. It was a sad day for me when I learned that the old house in Hackney had been demolished. Cheshunt proved to be a very pleasant place to live and Mum continued her good work looking after brother Alan. I would say that Mum was very happy in her new home.

Back in Northamptonshire I received a witness warning to attend Northampton Crown Court, to give evidence in the case of the man who had battered the elderly lady, in Rushden. This was the first time that I had ever given evidence in a court of law and I must confess that I felt very nervous about it. Nerves to one side I was determined to go along and help the court to the best of my ability. The suspect had been charged with murder and here was I having never given evidence for as much as a simple theft.

The good news was that all probationer constables had given evidence, in mock trials at the training centre, and therefore had some understanding of court procedure. I was called very early in the case to give my evidence, which revolved around what I had seen and done at the scene. The case was heard at the old Sessions House in Northampton, which on entering I found to be very dark and rather dismal.

The judge, barristers, solicitors and jury were all in place. I was led to the witness box by the court usher, where I took the oath and introduced myself. The prosecution barrister then instructed me to give my evidence, and asked the judge if I could refer to my pocket book. Your pocket book was a book that you used to make notes at the time you dealt with the incident. The judge directed that I should give evidence without the use of my pocket book.

I didn't let the judge's direction disturb me in any way because I knew exactly what I had seen and done that morning. I gave my evidence and was asked to remain in the witness box, to be cross examined by the defending barrister. I felt rather foolish when he asked me what the population of Rushden was. At the time of the trial I didn't know the answer to his question. You had to address all replies to the judge. I therefore informed His Honour that I didn't know the population of Rushden. The judge I recall did not appear to be happy with my reply. I must confess that I felt a bit of a plonker.

During the trial a lot of emphasis was placed on the fact that the elderly lady had been found in a coma at her home. It was said that she may have had a stroke due to her age and then went into a coma. It was medical experts on the defence side putting this theory forward. The defence barrister was saying that a stroke had caused the coma and his client's assault on her had probably not been the cause of the stroke. It was also said that the suspect had not intended to kill her. The judge directed that the murder charge would be changed to one of grievous bodily harm, either 'with intent' which could carry a life sentence in prison, or 'without intent', which carried only five years imprisonment.

The jury then found the accused guilty of wounding without intent. The accused was sentenced to five years imprisonment. I found myself feeling dismayed at the sentence this man had received. Obviously I do not wish to cast aspersions on His Honour, because that might be contempt of the court process, clearly the judge directed the jury in accordance with the law of the land.

I was certainly of the opinion that the offender had got off lightly, for what I found to be an extremely despicable act. As time passed the offender spent three years in prison and had the audacity to return to Rushden on his release. He was not made welcome by the people of the town and I'm pleased to report that he moved away from the area, very quickly indeed.

An unusual death

A few days after the conclusion of that trial I was on early turn duty working with Chris Cross, when we were sent to a council house in Chester Road, Rushden. Neighbours had reported that the elderly male occupant had not been seen for several days. On arrival we were unable to make contact with the occupant, despite knocking the street door several times. We were unable to see anyone via the front window and made our way to the back.

We both peered through the back kitchen window and immediately saw an elderly male on the floor, who appeared to be motionless. We smashed a small pane of glass in the kitchen window and slipped the catch. I climbed into the kitchen and opened the rear kitchen door to let Chris in. The sight that then met our eyes was absolutely awful. An elderly male who we assumed might be the occupant was crouched face down on all fours. We carried out pulse and breathing tests which were both negative in result. The man was dead and rigor mortise had set in.

The scene that confronted us was quite horrendous. The man was only partially clothed and he had been bleeding heavily from his back passage. We initially formed the view that the man could have sustained an assault via his back passage. He in fact had a large hole in his back passage. Suspecting the worst we decided not to move the body and left it as described earlier, propped up on all fours. In effect he was on his knees and elbows with both hands hidden beneath his torso.

Chris and I updated the control room and carried a check of the rest of the house. The downstairs toilet bowl was found to be full of congealed blood. We then noticed a faint smell of gas and found the gas cooker door wide open. Blood was found spattered on the staircase and adjoining walls. We entered the main bedroom and found the double bed sodden in blood. The ceiling and all four walls were also blood spattered. An old fashioned cut throat razor lay on the carpet beside the bed.

Chris and I were somewhat baffled as to exactly what had happened to the elderly gentleman. On closer examination of the gas cooker we found that the oven's 'On/Off' knob had been left in the 'On' position. A check of the gas meter showed it to be of the coin operated type. Perhaps the old fellow had been trying to keep warm, by using the oven with the door open. At some point he may have run out of coins for the slot meter.

Being unsure as to what had happened we requested CID (Criminal Investigation Department) and SOCO (Scenes of Crime Officers) to visit urgently. The specialist officers described were quickly on scene and fully briefed by Chris on

145

arrival. From that moment onwards no one else was allowed into the house, in order to preserve the scene forensically.

Prior to tampering with the body a series of photographs were taken by the SOCO. The scene was then given a SOCO search which entailed a fingerprint search, of the whole premises. A police surgeon also attended and recorded a number of details in relation to the body. Body temperature was checked for example which may or may not have helped with the timing of death. The police surgeon could not see any obvious signs of a suspicious death and felt that the heavy bleeding from the back passage may have been caused by unattended Cancer.

His suspicions grew stronger when we found that a large quantity of tablets had been regurgitated on the carpet, to the other side of the bed. It was decided to turn the body over onto its back, which would allow us to finish our examination of the body. On doing so we found that the elderly gentleman had slashed both of his wrists. Sadly we now had the whole picture as to what had happened.

The gentleman had clearly been suffering a lot of pain, over quite a long period of time. A subsequent Post Mortem confirmed that he had been suffering with cancer of the bowel. His GP had no knowledge of his illness and it was confirmed that he had not been to his doctor for several years. A coroner's report was compiled indicating that the gentleman had probably taken his own life. Our view was that he had taken an overdose which had failed. He then tried to gas himself by placing his head in the oven, but this also failed when the gas apparently ran out. He then appeared to have used his cut-throat razor in the bedroom, after which he made his way down the stairs and collapsed on the floor.

The Inquest I believe concluded that the man had sadly taken his own life.

Although I found this case quite upsetting, many lessons were learned by me that day in relation to what one should do, at a potentially serious crime scene. I need to point out that whilst writing about this incident, I had the utmost respect for the gentleman concerned and also wish to show respect to any surviving relatives. I would add that it is important for me to be factual and as detailed as one can be forty years after an event. I particularly want the reader to understand what is expected of young police officers, as they learn their trade. Having outlined this case to you, I also hope that people will be more mindful, of elderly persons in need of help in your own areas.

On a lighter note now I want to mention PC Tom Lewis, who was one of the older PCs working at Rushden in the good old 1970s. He was a great guy who stood no nonsense on his beat. His attitude to policing came from his previous career in the armed forces. His style of policing to one side for a moment, leads me to a more important aspect of Tom's duties. He spent a lot of time liaising with the farming community, in and around Rushden.

I think it would be fair to say that his liaison work took him more into Bedfordshire, than it did Northamptonshire. As a direct result of Tom's 'liaison work', he became responsible for organising beaters for the local shoots. I admit coming from Hackney in London, I had not a clue what beating meant. Tom explained that young fit probationers were needed on the farms, to walk the fields and woodlands beating up pheasants.

This would be done in a coordinated manner at the direction of the game keepers. An officer on his rest day would receive a payment in cash, at the conclusion of the shoot. On the more generous farms, a bottle or two of beer might be forth coming at lunchtime. In summary, I've got to say that I thought this was a bloody marvellous way to spend one's day off from real work, but was it?

Tom advised the beaters to wrap up warm and to bring plenty of sandwiches with them. I managed to hitch a lift to the venues, which were normally within eight miles from Rushden. The shoots were mostly in the winter months around Christmas time and would be attended by ten to fifteen farmers. I did about ten shoots during my two year probation and must say that I thoroughly enjoyed myself.

It was great for me to learn a little about country life and see the various animals involved in the process. These included rabbit, hares, foxes, wood pigeon, partridge, muntjack deer and obviously the pheasants which had been reared by the gamekeepers for the shoot. The beaters would form a line across the field or the wood and walk through beating the ground or foliage with sticks. This resulted in bringing the pheasants out of cover, whereupon they would be shot by the farmers, who were aligned at the end of the beat.

Believe me when I say that it was very hard work for the beaters, especially when we were beating across sodden ploughed fields. By the time you reached the far side of a ploughed field, your boots had increased in size three fold. The clods of mud hanging from your boots were quite simply enormous. At the end of the shoot the gamekeeper would pair up the birds, which would then be referred to as a brace of pheasant. The biggest shoot that I attended ended up with more than one hundred brace of birds and a good number of rabbits also.

The best bit of course was the day's wages, which varied according to the amount of game shot on the day. In any event a beater would receive a minimum of £9 and a maximum of £14. At the time any probationer would tell you that this extra cash was most welcomed.

I managed to save most of my beating money and after combining it with a small bank loan, I managed to buy a second hand car. A man who worked for the water board helped me to find the vehicle, which was a white Ford Escort estate car. My memory is a little hazy now but I believe I paid about £250 for it. Max the water board man kindly arranged for some filler work and a respray of the vehicle. As a result we became the proud owners of a yellow Ford Escort estate car. Before you ask, yes I did notify The DVLA of the car's new colour.

Hooray! Danusia and I now had a means of escape, to the countryside, the sea or anywhere else that took our fancy. It was really great because I no longer walked six miles a day back and forth to the police station. We could also drive to Cheshunt to visit my family and also drive to Harold Hill to visit Danusia's family. Our shopping trips by bus to Wellingborough were no longer necessary. We could now do the weekly shop with the car, with adequate room in the back for the children, the pram and the shopping.

All probationer constables underwent first aid training, both at the training centre and at headquarters. First aid was taught to police officers, because they were often the first to arrive at the scene of an injury. I was again on early turn shift at Rushden one morning when a call was received stating that a man had been shot with a shotgun. I was instructed to go urgently to the fields, to the rear of The Co-operative abattoir, situated on Bedford Road, Rushden.

I raced to the abattoir in the Panda car and made my way up into the fields on foot. I could see a woman waving frantically in the distance. I crossed two more fields to the woman's location, where I could see a man lying on his back on the ground. He said that there had been an accident with his shotgun and that he had been shot in the leg. The man appeared to be in agony and I could see a hole in his trouser leg, situated just below his knee. The lady explained that she was his wife and that the gun had gone off accidentally, whilst she was holding it.

I quickly summoned an ambulance on my radio and asked the lady to meet the ambulance down at the Bedford Road. I suppose that was unfair at the time, but I needed someone to guide the ambulance crew to the patient. I then decided to raise the man's leg upwards to stem the flow of any bleeding. This proved to be a mistake, because as I raised his Wellington boot, his knee and upper leg remained parallel to the ground.

I carefully lowered his Wellington boot back to the ground, with the realisation that his foot inside the boot might be completely detached from his leg. I spent a few minutes talking to the man with a view to keeping him calm. He in turn told me what had happened and seemed concerned that his wife might be blamed for discharging the gun. He said that he had been carrying the gun which was a double barrelled twelve-bore shotgun and had failed to make it safe, when he handed it to his wife. He further stated that he was climbing over the farm gate when the gun went off.

He said he felt a heavy impact to his lower leg which knocked him to the ground. I then carried out a brief inspection of the gun and after making it safe, I found a second twelve-bore cartridge in the chamber. I then heard voices coming up the field and was relieved to see two paramedics had arrived. After giving them a short briefing, they removed the man's Wellington carefully with the use of scissors. They then apologised to the patient for ruining his boot.

I was pleased to see the patient smile at last, as he appreciated their joke. Again using the scissors the paramedic then cut the trouser leg open which fully revealed the damage to the man's leg. The shot gun cartridge had been discharged at very close range and had impacted the shin bone just below the knee. It had then travelled downwards towards his foot, removing most of his shin bone on route.

Fortunately the patient couldn't see the injury whilst lying on his back. I'm afraid, more or less the whole bone had been shattered into hundreds of pieces. The paramedics realised that a small length of bone remained to the rear of the shin and splinted the leg accordingly. It was that action that, believe it or not, saved the man's leg after many operations.

The man was given an injection to relieve the pain and then placed on a stretcher. He was then taken across fields to the ambulance and then off to hospital. I was satisfied with his wife's account of what had happened and allowed her to accompany her husband to the hospital. I was of course duty bound to inform the CID of all the details and they then took on the case. After extensive enquiries the CID were happy that the shotgun had been discharged accidentally and no further action was taken.

As indicated earlier the injured person underwent many operations and I kept in touch with him. I actually saw him a year after the event and he was still optimistic about the continued process of rebuilding his leg. He was very grateful to the police and paramedics for the support he received that day.

I thanked him and told him in no uncertain terms that he was the hero that day. This was the first shotgun injury that I had seen in my new career, but alas it would not be the last.

I now want to explain how my new career, nearly came to a swift end. My shift Sergeant approached me one morning and told me that the Chief Inspector and the Superintendent were at the station and wished to see me. I went to their office and must admit that I had concerns. Frankly you only went to high ranking officers to be commended or to be admonished. Which would it be, I wondered?

On entering the office I observed that both senior officers had stern looks on their faces. The Superintendent said that I had embarrassed the force on a Saturday afternoon when the High Street had been full of shoppers. He went on to say that complaints had been received from the public about my childish behaviour. I had apparently acted out a high wire trapeze act, along a ten yard stretch of the High Street kerbstone. I was in full uniform at the time with my arms outstretched at my sides. I then apparently made my way along the kerbstone by placing one foot ahead of the other.

The complainants said I had been quite good at the balancing act and at no time fell off the kerbstones. The Superintendent said what on earth were you doing acting like this. I must admit that I now felt relieved, because I knew that I was not the trapeze artist. I told the Superintendent that I had not done what he had described and that he needed to make his enquiries elsewhere. The Chief Inspector then assured the Superintendent that I was the culprit.

I was flabbergasted by his remarks and suddenly realised that my shift of police officers had a second probationer, who also had the name Michael. I reluctantly pointed out that he might be able to assist them with their enquiries. The Superintendent said that my probation was hanging by a thread here, and I needed to start telling the truth.

Most of you will find it hard to believe my response, because I just stood up and said 'stuff your job, I'm going home'. I then marched out of their office, gathered my things together and

151

drove home. Danusia was a little shocked when I told her the story but said she could understand my reaction, in the circumstances.

I sat at home expecting someone to contact me from the station. I received no messages that day and had no visitors from the police station. I retired to bed that night fearing the worst, in other words that my rapid exit from the station, had indicated my intention to resign. I loved my job but realised that my reaction had not gone down well.

I'm delighted to say that my shift Sergeant paid me a visit the next morning and requested that I resume normal duty. He explained that there had been a misunderstanding on the management's part, and that my colleague also called Michael had been the trapeze artist. I was informed that the officer concerned had admitted it and had requested a move to another division, the other side of the county.

I don't know to this day what possessed my colleague to act the way he did, but realise that stranger things happen at sea. In hindsight I realised that my response to the allegation was poor, but was relieved to hear that it was not to be placed on my record. Obviously things like this could mean the difference between completing your probation successfully or not. After a number of years I was told that the Michael concerned in this matter had resigned and built a successful career elsewhere.

I was a little shocked one morning when I was sent to Saint Mary's church in Rushden, to deal with an offence of criminal damage. Saint Mary's church was a beautiful old stone building, with wonderful stained glass windows. The church was situated at the end of High Street on high ground in Church Parade. I made my way on foot via the High Street and as I approached I was shocked to see the degree of damage caused to the stone walls of the church.

The offender had used gloss type paint to daub the stonework with three feet tall lettering. With the huge lettering the offender had spelt out the name 'Rommel'. This of course related to the infamous German tank commander from the Second World War. The offender had also painted several similar sized swastikas. He had used red, black and white paint, the remains of which had been strewn about the footpaths. Further Nazi based references were evident on the walls.

The paint was dry and had obviously been applied during the night. The church warden had already been given an estimate of £300 to remove and repair the damage. Empty paint tins were found at the scene and retained for fingerprinting. It was soon established that a Rushden man by the name of Peter, had used this type of insulting graffiti, in the past. I arranged for SOCO to visit and take photographs of the damage. This of course allowed the church warden and his colleagues to remove the offending paintwork, as soon as possible.

Together with another officer I then went to the suspect's home to arrest him. In those early days you would rehearse your lines on the way. I refer to the reason for arrest and the necessary caution, to be given to comply with the law. Mum was at home and explained that Peter was at work on the Ditchford Lane sewerage works building site. It was raining of course and I was no longer looking forward to the arrest.

We had acquired a Panda car and made our way up to the site, which incidentally was huge. We reported to the site foreman who told us that Peter would be found in the canteen block. The site was very muddy indeed and as we made our way to the canteen, I was reminded of my beating days on ploughed fields. We were both caked in mud before we managed to reach the canteen door.

The canteen was effectively a huge shed and on opening the door we found about a hundred building workers tucking into their lunches. One of them jokingly said 'run everybody it's the old bill'. Peter of course was sat at the far end of the makeshift table and of course we suffered some abuse on route to him. I introduced myself to Peter and invited him to join us outside. I explained that he was under arrest for criminal damage to St Mary's church and cautioned him. In those days the caution was, 'you do not have to say anything unless you wish to do so, but anything you do say will be taken down in writing and may be given in evidence'.

Peter had been arrested several times before and chose to say nothing. We then made our way back to the Panda car, where I observed that a six inch nail had been propped up beneath the front wheel of the car. I removed the nail and carried out a thorough check of the vehicle, which was otherwise in good order. A search of Peter's house was then carried out, resulting in a number of exhibits being found. These consisted of note books belonging to Peter which had similar drawings and wording to that found at the church. These related to Hitler, Rommel, and of course the swastikas. He clearly had an interest in all things Nazi.

Peter was taken to Rushden Police Station where he was booked in for interview. In those days the interview was a long drawn out process where contemporaneously recorded notes had to be made of the interview. This meant that every question put to him by the police had to be written down at the time, as did any answer he cared to make in reply.

He of course denied any knowledge of the offence, but could not recall where had spent that evening. Numerous forms were then filled in and he was released by way of summons. In those early days this meant that when sufficient evidence had been gathered against him, he would be sent a summons to attend the local magistrates' court.

Fingerprints were found on the paint tins and were later identified as those belonging to Peter. The photographs of the offending wording at the church were compared with that found at Peter's home and were found to match one another. Peter was subsequently summoned to Wellingborough Magistrates' Court, under the Criminal Damage Act, where he of course pleaded 'not guilty'.

Peter was eventually found guilty and was sentenced to a period of imprisonment. I'm pleased to be able to report that the paint was eventually removed from the walls of the church. This was apparently painstaking work carried out by an expert in stone renovation. The local press gave the case good coverage, which all hoped would deter others from similar behaviour. For me, the motto of this story would be, why use a six inch nail when a smaller one would have done the trick.

❀ ❀

The Motor Cycle Grand Prix

I was thrilled one day when I was told that I would be one of a large number of police officers, who would be policing the Motor Cycle Grand Prix at Silverstone. I wasn't a motor cycle enthusiast as such, but thought that this would be a great event to attend, and of course police. The day soon arrived and I reported at Wellingborough Police Station for the briefing. I was told that I would be outside the race circuit, controlling traffic at a traffic island on the main A43 road situated to the east of Silverstone. I must admit that I found the news a little disappointing, because it would have been great to see the race.

It was actually far worse than I had expected when I was dropped off on foot at the traffic island. I was told that arrangements had been made for me to visit a private dwelling at the side of the road, where I would be given a cup of tea. In the interim period I was to remain at the traffic island in the middle of the A43 road, directing traffic into the venue. The Sergeant in charge said I would remain there at the traffic island until all traffic had entered the venue.

In the early 1970s, the A43 road was a single carriageway and as such was too small to deal with the volume of expected traffic. To facilitate the volume of traffic, the outgoing lane from Silverstone was closed. This allowed us to use both sides of the A43 carriageway, for incoming traffic travelling from the east side of the village.

At the designated time I took up my position on the traffic island and recall to this day a faint droning sound, which rapidly got louder and louder. Literally hundreds of motor cyclists seemed to appear suddenly from a bend in the A43 road and they were all heading my way. As they reached my traffic

155

island they began to pass me on both sides of the road, three and four abreast. This volume of motor cycles and riders continued passing my location for many hours.

There were simply thousands upon thousands of motor bikes and riders. I could feel my body temperature rising with the heat generated by the bikes. The fumes from the exhaust gases were unbearable and after the first hour my eyes were streaming. I was actually quite shocked at the effect this heavy traffic was having on my body. Fortunately the occupants of the house nearby came good and brought the tea to my traffic island.

I feel indebted to them to this very day. At no time was I given relief by the circuit controller and remained on the island for what seemed like a lifetime. The closest I got the circuit that day was when I heard the racing bikes thundering around it, in the distance. At last I received a message on my personal radio, and thought could this be my relief.

To put it in a nutshell the answer was 'no'. I was merely informed that the race had concluded and my traffic control would again be resumed. I remained on my traffic island where I again controlled thousands of bikes and riders as they rode passed in the opposite direction. I worked approximately fourteen hours that day and recall swearing that I would never attend another Grand Prix. In view of my obvious weaknesses, I also decided that day, that the traffic department would not be my cup of tea.

However, it was quite an experience and I can tell you, I wouldn't have missed it for the world. This is of course why Constables serve a two year probationary period. They need to experience all different aspects of policing and if accepted by their force, will then have a good idea of the way forward, in their careers. By the way, on concluding my duty that day, I had a good eye bath and a very good night's sleep.

I was on early turn duty one day when I was sent with another officer to the Rushden Council Depot, in Newton Road, Rushden. The incoming call indicated that a group of dustman had been drinking and had caused damage to council property. On arrival I saw several dustmen who all appeared to be under the influence of drink. The manager showed me into his office and explained that the men had been drinking at the local pub. He had made them aware of his disappointment at their behaviour.

One of the dustmen had then smashed the office phone and given the manager a lot of verbal abuse. He said that he had tried to reason with his men over their behaviour, but they continued to abuse him. I went back out into the council yard and found myself being abused by a group of six dustmen. One of them called Mick said 'what's this got to do with you fucking pigs?' The manager then confirmed that this man, called Mick, was the man who had smashed the phone. Mick was about 5'10" tall and of a very stocky build. I grabbed hold of the sleeve of his coat and told him he was under arrest on suspicion of criminal damage.

Before I could give him the verbal caution Mick threw a punch towards my head. I managed to avoid the punch and firmly took hold of him with both hands. As I did so the other dustmen surrounded me and began to jostle me. Using very firm words I told them to step back or they would all be arrested for assault on police.

All of them then stepped back, at which point Mick tried to head butt me. The blow from his head glanced to the side of my face and I continued to restrain him with both hands. Mick seemed incredibly strong and continued to resist the arrest. I tried to pull him towards the ground in an effort to secure him.

He remained upright and seemed to lose his temper. He threw several punches to my head and face, most of which were now hurting me. I took hold of his left coat sleeve and moved in to carry out a judo throw, known as a double arm shoulder throw. Without boring you with details, this had the effect of raising him off the ground and up onto my back. From that position he was then thrown to the ground and placed in an arm lock.

I'm pleased to say that my colleague had kept the other dustmen under control whilst I made this arrest. We then

157

handcuffed the prisoner and placed him in the Panda car. All the way to the police station the offender continued to abuse my colleague and I. At the police station he started struggling again as we removed him from the car. He was still as strong as an ox and left me completely breathless as we entered the building. Relief was at hand in the shape of another officer who kindly took charge of the situation, by abruptly placing the prisoner in a chair.

Another late finish was now on the cards as we returned to the council depot to take statements and record the crime. I would like to point out that no extra pay was available in those days, for any overtime worked. Yes, you've guessed it, we did it for the love of the job. Mick was later put before the court for the damage and also for assault on police. He was fined quite heavily and made to pay compensation. To his credit he later apologised to me for his behaviour that day and our paths did not cross again.

Death of a young girl

I think it was in my second year as a young policeman that tragedy would strike another youngster. This time it was on the roads and very sadly brought into play by the same man who had earlier stolen the motorised lawn mower. On this occasion his reckless behaviour had far more serious consequences, for the family of a young girl. He had stolen a car this time and after consuming a lot of alcohol, was seen to be speeding around Rushden.

The girl concerned was about sixteen years of age and was seated in the front seat of the car. Knowing the driver I would suggest that he would have been out to impress his front seat passenger. Seat belts were not being worn when he decided to race at high speed down a road known as Higham Hill. As he neared the bottom of the hill, he braked too heavily and put the car into an uncontrollable skid. This resulted in the car mounting the nearside pavement and colliding head on with the trunk of a well-established tree.

I'm very sorry to say that the girl was launched through the windscreen and died instantly. I could list the driver's injuries, but frankly, couldn't care less. Despite the passing of many years, my heart still goes out to the family of this innocent young victim. The actions of the man responsible that day, clearly denied this young girl the privilege of long life.

I refer to this case in the hope that readers might be more inclined to wear seat belts, in memory of this victim. The driver quite rightly received a lengthy term of imprisonment, for the offence of causing death by dangerous driving. In those early days I began to realise that the emergency services were dealing with far more serious cases than young Bobbies like me had anticipated. I hope that this story will encourage people not to drink and drive.

On a much lighter note I want to tell you a short story about team spirit. I was working one night with a colleague and at about 3am I was driving the Panda car in the vicinity of Rushden Rugby Club. We had moved on a little as a police force and as such I was now driving one of the new Vauxhall Viva cars. These new Pandas drove a little quicker than the old Morris Minor. I happened to be patrolling over the rugby field area and found myself losing control of the car, as I approached a downward slope of grass.

I'm afraid to admit that the slope ran out, but the car kept going. This resulted in the Panda car sliding into a stream, situated close to the main A6 Bedford road. My colleague was clearly unhappy about our predicament and as we went into the stream, he uttered a number of profanities. I'm sure you know what I mean, in other words he used several swear words to describe me. These words left me feeling that he was unimpressed with my driving.

It was actually quite shocking because the nose of our new car now stood at the bottom of the stream. The rest of the car stood vertically in the air, leaving my colleague and I leaning against the dashboard. After considerable effort, both of us managed to climb from the vehicle and were now back on dry land. It was a worrying scene to see the Panda car standing on its nose, in a very precarious position. Despite our best efforts we could not right the vehicle.

After a number of covert messages, other colleagues started to arrive at the rugby field. In fact the whole shift of police officers turned up, to first mock me and then volunteer help. There were now six of us trying to rescue the Panda car from the stream, but we could not budge it. We had no other alternative than to summon the early turn shift to join us at the field. Eventually with the help of eight officers we managed to rescue the car from the stream.

None of the shift Sergeants was made aware of my plight that morning and that's why I referred to it, as good team spirit. A thorough examination of the vehicle showed that no ill effects had been suffered. In hindsight I felt that this was more by good luck, than good judgement. I seem to recall that the cakes were on me, the next time we all met. For me, the motto of this story was to keep the Panda car off grass surfaces whenever humanly possible. The lads took the 'micky' for a few months, but it was all good harmless banter.

A short story about cup final day, but don't get too excited, it doesn't actually refer to any team in particular. I had a new Sergeant at the time and he was nearing the end of his service. We were on full night duty and were all chatting about the weather, having just finished what was known as the 'scoff break'. We'd had a busy night followed by a late scoff break and it was now 4.30am, time to do some paperwork. Actually no, it was time for an automatic burglar alarm to activate, which indicated that a burglary was in progress at the Trade Club, Higham Road, Rushden.

The Trade Club was a working men's type club which contained all the normal target material for burglars. The target material being cash from various gaming machines, cigarette machines and pool tables. Additional targets were cigarettes and of course alcohol. The club was a two storey building with a large flat roof to the rear. Four of us raced to the club in two separate police cars. Fortunately the club was only six hundred yards from the police station and this always gave us a good chance of catching the burglars.

I drove my vehicle straight up onto the pavement at the front of the club. As I alighted from the vehicle an intruder jumped from a first floor window and landed directly in front of me. I dived on top of him and held him firmly on the ground. He was a big lad aged about twenty years but I'm pleased to inform you that he had winded himself on landing. He was handcuffed and left with another officer after being placed in the police car. The two remaining officers had by this time 'surrounded' the premises.

I took the quick opportunity to speak with the prisoner in the police car, who kindly told me that two other burglars were still in the premises. On searching the club we could only find one of the two remaining intruders. He gave no resistance when found hiding in an office, and was also detained with handcuffs. One of the first floor windows had been forced open and that gave access to the rear flat roof. As I looked through the broken window I could see the third intruder lying on the roof in a shaded corner. Adrenaline is a marvellous thing in that it helps you choose the right words, at the right time, to encourage someone to surrender. I seemed to choose those words automatically, and conveyed them to the man on the roof. He remained still for a few seconds he then got up and made his way to the damaged window.

He was the biggest of the three men and as he passed through the opening in the window he was taken to floor for handcuffing. They all had Corby Scots accents and new the ropes very well indeed. Without any fuss they explained that they had two stolen cars at the side of the club. These were found to contain large quantities of stolen cash, cigarettes and alcohol. They openly admitted that they had done two other clubs on the way to Rushden.

These additional clubs were at Higham Ferrers and Burton Latimer, both being situated along the main A6 route from Corby. Had they not been caught at the Trade Club, their

161

intention was to keep one of the vehicles and to travel on with their ill-gotten gain to Wembley. Yes, they were making their way to Wembley Stadium to watch the Cup Final. The three burglars were taken to Wellingborough Police Station and given a room at the inn. We then started the arduous task of writing up the case, which of course meant counting all the stolen cash and recording it accordingly.

I recall that we finished work that morning at about 11am after liaison with the CID and SOCO. I was extremely tired but delighted with the night's work. I was determined to keep appraised of the results of the case and later learned that all three men received quite lengthy prison sentences. They had all committed a number of crimes in the past.

These arrests made a very pleasant change because more often than not, the intruders made good their escape before we arrived. Alarm activations always gave police officers a buzz, because you never knew exactly what to expect when entering the premises. In fact later in my story I will refer to premises where a total of nine intruders took part in the burglary.

Blood samples

I believe it's time for a short traffic story now, one which nearly landed me in a spot of bother. This involved a younger member of a well-known, hardworking business family in Rushden. The youth concerned was about sixteen years of age and was seen by me riding a moped dangerously on the road, in Rushden. It was evening time and a colleague and I followed the lad along several roads, watching him weave from side to side on the moped. The youth was unaware of our presence and eventually struck the kerb and fell off.

Fortunately he was uninjured, but smelt strongly of alcohol. The moped sustained minor damage in the collision. I spoke to the youth about what had happened, but he couldn't string more than two words together. To put it in a nutshell he was quite simply drunk. On request he provided a breath test which was positive and as I recall was in fact twice over the drink drive limit. I arrested the youth and took him to Wellingborough Police Station, where he was detained.

The moped was recovered to the police station and his parents were informed of his arrest. The youth's father attended the police station and was shown into the charge room, where the drink drive procedure continued. The charge Sergeant and I explained the procedure whereupon the youth elected to provide a sample of blood for analysis. The duty doctor then attended and took the sample of blood from the youth's arm.

The blood was then divided into two samples which were sealed and placed on the charge room desk. Under the law, two samples had to be taken, one for the police enquiry and the other for the suspect to analyse if he wished. I was then excused from the charge room to carry out certain checks in relation to the youth. On returning to the charge room the charge Sergeant quietly said 'what happened to the blood samples?' I reminded the Sergeant that they were on the charge room desk, when I left the room. He then took me to one side and explained that the samples had disappeared. He then said he would like me to take the rap because he was due to retire soon. He said this amounted to neglect of duty and that a probationer would be forgiven for such neglect.

This may sound harsh but I said I would not take the rap and that a search for the blood samples was the priority. The Sergeant apologised to me for what had occurred and then put a call out for the duty Inspector. The Inspector came to the charge room and started making enquiries into the theft of the blood samples. The youth and his father were interviewed about the missing samples but chose to make no comment. A thorough search of the charge room and adjoining cell block was made, but the blood samples could not be found. The youth and father were also searched, but again with a negative result.

The youth was then released from custody and told that the facts would be reported. Both father and son had big beaming smiles on their faces as they left the police station. The motto of this story is, some you win some you lose. In those early days there were no security cameras in the charge rooms and the result of the Inspector's enquiry was one of no further action. The Sergeant was advised with regard to charge room security and happily retired, soon after the incident. He had completed thirty years loyal service, when combining military and police service.

Strangely I carried out a total of eleven breath test procedures in my own thirty year career, all of which were negative in result. It would seem that this youth robbed me of my one and only positive result. Forty years have since past and I would like to state that the youth concerned, went on to become a very worthy member of the family business. I grew to know the family quite well as time progressed, but they refused to confide in me, as to what happened that day.

The time for all good things to come to end had arrived, and yes you've guessed it, I was back up to Ryton-on-Dunsmore for a refresher course. Perhaps I should explain that all probationer constables had to attend this course after completing their first eighteen months on their division. This course was nowhere near as painful as the initial course, because we were now looked upon as reasonably experienced Bobbies.

The word refresher explains what the course entailed, namely refreshing our memories on what we had been taught on the initial course. Relatively speaking it was quite enjoyable and gave us the opportunity to discuss our varied experiences out on division. When referring to division I refer to our individual police stations, when relating to our individual counties. There were no exams to be studied for, which left us with more time for 'R and R' in the evenings.

I missed my wife and children whilst on the course, but of course was compensated by spending weekends at home. On completion of the course I was disappointed with my instructor's final report, which said I would never be a leader of men, but a good all round supportive Constable. I agreed in principle with his report but didn't like the word 'never'. I grew up in the belief that one should never say never. In other words who could possibly tell how things will be in the future?

❀ ❀

Double Murder

Compared with the initial course, the refresher simply flew past and before we knew it we were all back on our divisions. I was pleased to see that I would remain posted to Rushden Police Station for the foreseeable future. Added to this good news was the fact that I was about to spend two weeks with the CID. This was a normal attachment for all probationers, to give us an insight into the day to day workings of the CID.

I was told to report to the CID office at 9am on the Monday morning and to dress in plain clothes. The CID office was situated on the first floor of the station and consisted of two offices, one for the detectives and the other for the Detective Sergeant. I went to the Detective Sergeant's office and was informed that there had been a double murder in Rushden, during the night. The DS sat me down and explained that due to the murders my two week attachment would be slightly different to the norm. This was because of the fact that all available staff would be working on the murder enquiry, leaving no one available to show me the ropes.

The DS then said that police officers from all over the county would be coming to Rushden to work on the case. He said he had a very important role for me with regard to the team of officers being assembled. He said you will make the tea and coffee for everyone in the team. You will be head cook and bottle washer. He said you will run errands and chauffeur people back and forth when necessary. He then asked if I was happy with my new role and I said whatever it takes to support the team.

Shortly after speaking with the DS a briefing was held with all available staff present. A mother and daughter had been found dead in their home in Newton Road, Rushden and cause of death appeared to be by means of suffocation. SOCO were at the scene and door to door enquiries were to be carried out. A home office pathologist had also been requested to visit the scene. Enquiries had confirmed that the deceased woman's husband also lived at the address, but his present whereabouts were unknown.

The deceased woman was thought to be in her forties, and the daughter was believed to be about thirteen years of age. An examination of the house confirmed that there were no signs of a forced entry. It was suspected that both victims had been suffocated in their beds with pillows. Both victims had small dots around their eyelids which could be caused by this method of suffocation. These two deaths were obviously shocking crimes to occur in such a small town. To this day my heart goes out to the relatives of these victims, who would clearly have been devastated at the time.

As the day progressed word started to spread that a man had attempted suicide in the Bedfordshire area and had been rushed into hospital. The man's life was saved and it was confirmed that he was the husband of the deceased woman. Police officers attended the hospital and liaised with the doctor in charge of the patient. He was subsequently discharged and arrested on suspicion of both murders. He was then brought back to Wellingborough Police Station, where he was detained for questioning. He subsequently admitted murdering both his wife and his daughter by means of smothering them with pillows, at the family home in Rushden.

I recall that the man had been depressed, but with the passing of time I'm unable to tell you the reason he gave, for committing these horrendous crimes. Although my involvement in the enquiry was limited to tea boy, I didn't mind in the least, because I learnt a lot observing the running of the enquiry. I attended all the briefings where I learnt how the various officers presented the results of their enquiries to the team. The Detective Sergeant said he was very pleased with the way I had conducted myself on such a serious enquiry. He added that

166

most officers would have been unenthusiastic about the role he had given me.

Nearing the end of my two week attachment, Terry, the Detective Sergeant, approached me and said I had earned a trip out. He handed me a set of ignition keys to a plain CID car and instructed me to visit the mortuary at Kettering General Hospital, where I would liaise with the mortician. I was also given a cool box containing ice, for the transportation of certain exhibits that needed to be kept cool. Terry also gave me a laboratory report concealed in a large envelope. He said the mortician would place the exhibits into my cool box and I was then to convey them to the forensic science laboratory at Huntingdon, in Cambridgeshire.

I felt great, because the tea boy was suddenly part of the CID team working on the murders. On arrival at the mortuary I was given a brief tour of the premises by the duty mortician. I was shown pull-out coffins which were situated along the walls and contained bodies which were maintained at very low temperatures. I was also shown the stone tables where bodies would be placed, for post mortem work by the pathologist. The mortician struck me to be thick set, wearing Wellington boots, and a body length waterproof apron.

He explained that the Wellingtons and apron served him well during post mortems, particularly when blood might be splashed around. They were needed more so when the post mortem was concluded and a hose pipe was deployed, to clean the mortuary.

After checking the laboratory report, the mortician removed two bagged exhibits from his fridge and placed them in my cool box. He then signed the report which was done to prove continuity of the exhibits. I thanked him for his assistance and also for time spent showing me around, adding that I found it most interesting.

Ensuring that my cool box was safely aboard I then made my way to the Forensic Science Laboratory at Huntingdon. On entering the building I introduced myself to the receiver of exhibits who stood the other side of a counter. He said something like 'hello, what have you got for me today then?' He then requested the laboratory report and on reading it said 'two sets of intestines I gather'. He then fetched a tray and instructed me to remove the exhibits from the cool box, one at a time. I removed the lid from the cool box and took hold of a large clear plastic bag labelled 'Intestine', which I placed on the tray. I then signed the exhibit label attached to the bag and was rather shocked to be staring straight at the first human intestine I had ever seen. I'm afraid what I saw I will leave to your imagination. Suffice to say that it wasn't the most pleasant object to be looking at.

I was then asked to remove the second bag from the cool box and saw that it contained a considerably smaller intestine. I placed the exhibit on the tray and again signed the exhibit label. The pending laboratory examination of the items would establish whether any stupefying drugs had been administered to the victims, prior to suffocation. Other factors may also be considered when carrying out the forensic examination.

I could of course describe the contents of those bags, but feel that it would be unfair to any relatives or friends to do so. I try to show the utmost respect to all parties when outlining details of these cases. Little did I know at the time, but I would be a regular visitor to this laboratory for many years to come. Having learnt several interesting lessons that day, it was time to drive back to Rushden. I actually concluded my two week attachment to the CID that evening and Terry thanked me for my support. He also asked me if I found crime related police work of particular interest. I told him that I found crime work very interesting indeed and looked forward to another attachment with his department in the future.

The end to my two years as a probationer Constable was rapidly approaching and I recall being routinely met in the early hours of one morning, by the duty Inspector. He chatted generally about the police force and indicated that I would be accepted by the force, as a Constable at the conclusion of my probation. I thanked him for the good news and he said 'that's fine you've earned it'. He said that he had been monitoring my probation and had noted personality clashes with a particular officer. He went on to say that he had approached the officer concerned and had advised him to back off.

I thanked him for his intervention and resumed my night shift in the knowledge that he had been my guardian angel. As we parted he said 'I first became interested in you when you were accused of being a tight rope walker', and he went on to say 'the rest is for you to work out'. As my police career grew I came to respect this particular officer, very much indeed.

Prior to the end of my probation I was given the role of tutor Constable. This meant that a new recruit would spend his first four weeks of policing, working with me at Rushden. My first probationer was an officer called Dave and we started our first shift together on night duty. We were on foot patrol and made our way down the High Street checking property. It was a quiet night and I recall we reached the T junction of Wellingborough Road and St Mary's Avenue. I observed a car parked at the junction on double yellow lines and told Dave to write out a parking ticket.

People were in the bad habit of parking on the yellow lines whilst they went to purchase fish and chips, at Skinners Hill chip shop. There had been a history of complaints about this illegal parking, mostly by residents in the area. Dave took exception to my request and said traffic wardens should deal with such offences. It was at that point that I explained to Dave, that he should apply for the post of traffic warden, as he was about to lose his job as a Police Constable.

We then saw the owner of the offending car return to it, having purchased his fish and chips. I'm very pleased to report that Dave then filled out a parking ticket and handed it to the driver. I feel it important to explain that all traffic regulations are put in place to protect citizens, from injuries whilst using our roads and a Constable is duty bound to protect life. This of course doesn't mean that we should hound the general public with regard to minor traffic offences. Probationers nevertheless need to experience traffic law and this can only be achieved by reporting offenders, whilst officers are early in service.

Engineers and carpenters know that their skills come from basic practices, and the situation is no different for emergency service workers. Dave and I later sat taking our refreshment break during which we discussed our differing views on this subject. He conceded that the basics needed to be learned, but added that he found that side of his duty somewhat difficult. He went on to concede that my decision would be final in any similar circumstances.

One other incident of note happened whilst working nights with Dave. We were given the 'Number One Town Centre beat to walk and we were half way down the High Street, with police helmets raised aloft. It was a Friday night and the pubs had started to turn out. There were the normal tipsy people hanging around the eateries, including a bearded man who was supported by two wooden crutches.

The bearded man was the worse for drink and was being a little abusive. I spoke to him and confirmed that he was recovering from a broken leg. During conversation I asked him to tone down his language. As I turned to walk off I felt a blow to the back of my head, which resulted in my police helmet flying to the pavement. The bearded man had struck my helmet with one of his crutches. I was unhappy about what had happened and again advised the bearded man about his behaviour. I had received no injury and my helmet was found to be undamaged. I decided to let him off due to the fact that he had a broken leg. Some people would consider my actions as somewhat naïve.

After further discussion I decided to resume walking but as I turned I saw the man raise his crutch in the air and swing it again towards my head. I managed to duck down as the crutch swung through the air above my head. I moved in and grabbed him with a view to arresting him. He started to struggle resulting in a joint loss of balance, at which point we both fell heavily to the ground. I looked up towards Dave who was now laughing uncontrollably. It wasn't until I got up that I could see the funny side of what had happened.

170

The bearded man's crutches had smashed into several pieces and were strewn around the pavement. This had clearly happened as we fell to the ground. Dave kindly handed me my helmet and advised me to wear the chin strap. On that note I told the man that he was under arrest for assault on police and for being drunk and disorderly. He was given the caution and handcuffed. He was of course conveyed to Wellingborough Police Station and detained. I'm pleased to tell you that he was no worse for wear, after the tumble. He later pleaded guilty to the charges and was fined quite heavily.

The motto of the story is of course to keep your eyes peeled at all times. Also to avoid Dave like the plague because every time I see him, he reiterates what happened that day. Well I hope you like this story because I do, but only in hindsight.

Soon after tutoring Dave I was told that I had completed my probation successfully and was now looked upon as a fully trained Police Constable. This was great news, especially with the realisation that for the time being there were no more courses to attend. There was also a small pay rise on completion of the first two years in the police force. This of course meant that weather permitting the odd trip to the coast was now on the cards. This had to be put on hold when the engine in the Ford Escort blew up. Good old Dave came to the rescue and helped me in his spare time to remove and rebuild the engine.

The engine block needed a rebore and that was carried out at a wonderful engineers called Harrisons of Thrapston. Within a fortnight Dave and I had put the engine back in the car and we were mobile again. I thought it was extremely kind of Dave to give up his time and energy, when he could have been putting his feet up.

It was now midsummer 1974 when we had more good news, Danusia had fallen pregnant and preparations were soon underway for our third child. We were simply delighted with the news, although would both admit that the pregnancy did not form part of plan A. Nicola had turned four years of age and Steven would soon be three years old. They both seemed very keen to have a new brother or sister. What more help could young parents wish for?

The expectant Parents

Prior to the birth of our next child we continued regularly to visit good old Cheshunt, where of course we saw Mum, Alan, Raymond and John. We also took my brothers Raymond and John on short camping holidays. I recall upsetting Danusia when I allowed the brothers to steer the car across a camp field. My brothers and I thought it was fun at the time, but a repeat was not allowed by Danusia.

On the work front things started to move at a pace when the Detective Sergeant approached me and said that he had a six month slot available for me in the CID. He said I'd like you to go home, discuss it with your wife and then let me know if you want the attachment. I was chuffed to bits and new my answer straight away nevertheless I went home and told Danusia about my new attachment to the CID. Suffice to say Danusia was also delighted with the news and I duly informed the DS. I should explain that these attachments were not often available to Constables so fresh out of their probation.

My
wonderful
Mother
Rose

173

On completion of a six month attachment to the CID, a Constable if lucky could be offered a CID course. The CID courses were residential courses held either at Hendon in London, Birmingham in the West Midlands, or Preston in Lancashire. The courses generally lasted for ten weeks, with weekends spent at home. Failure on these courses was not an option, you had to pass the examinations with flying colours to become a Detective Constable.

Before I knew it I was reporting for duty at Rushden CID office. At that time there were four seasoned detectives and the Detective Sergeant working at the old Rushden Police Station. The office was rather cramped and desk space was at a premium. Nevertheless I managed to find myself a small desk with three drawers. I put a few personal items in the drawers and placed an 'in-tray' on the desk top. I was now ready to start work.

Terry the DS briefed us each morning which basically updated everybody, with regard to current crime and details of criminals thought to be active. The detectives also had an input basically updating everyone with the current state of individual cases. There would also be a discussion on any criminal intelligence gathered which we may or may not need to act upon. In very quick time the phones would be ringing and we would be receiving details of incoming crimes.

Quite often prisoners were being held at Wellingborough Police Station, awaiting a CID officer to deal with them. In the main the uniformed officers dealt with the less serious cases and CID dealt with serious cases, where more time would be needed to carry out the investigations. At the outset I found visiting burglaries very interesting, and by being observant you could learn a lot about potential suspects. By being observant you could pick up patterns of crime relating particularly to your area. This takes nothing away from the SOCO because they visit crimes in a much wider area.

I also found it important to be sympathetic to victims who were often very shocked by the crimes they suffered. There was always pressure to conclude one job and get on with the next. I soon formed the view that it was better to dot all of the 'I's' and cross all of the 'T's', before moving on. During your attachment you were known as the CID aide, which meant that you would aid the CID in whichever way they thought necessary. If a person was in custody for a fairly minor crime, the aid would be sent to the cell block to deal with it. On the other hand if the crime was serious, the aid would assist the detective to deal with it.

In those early days, the interviews were recorded by way of contemporaneous notes. The notes were recorded on sheets of A4 paper which had been specially printed for that purpose. This method could be quite hard work because you had to ask a question, which you would write down in full, followed by any answer given. In the more complicated cases this method of recording could amount to numerous pages. At the conclusion of an interview the suspect was given the opportunity to read the notes. Having read them he would be asked to initial the end of each question and to sign the end of each page. Any handwritten mistakes would also need his initials.

This was a very bad practice and gave the suspect far too long to produce his reply. The interviews were conducted after caution and all suspects had the right to free legal advice. On completion of the interview, numerous forms were filled in by the interviewing officer, who would be referred to as the Officer in the Case (OIC). The suspect would be either charged with the offence or told that the facts of the case would be reported. He or she would then be fingerprinted and photographed before being released.

In more serious cases the suspect would be kept in custody overnight with a view to appearing at the earliest available court. A decision would then be made by the court as to whether an offender should be released on bail or kept in custody. Cases going before the court required far more paperwork than those which didn't. The main role of the CID was evidence gathering and this of course took many different forms. Quite often the case would hinge on forensic evidence which often involved the gathering and proper packaging of the exhibits.

A suspect's clothing and footwear often featured as items to be considered for forensic analysis. These items had to be seized and packaged according to their condition. In other words, wet items needed to be dried prior to packaging, otherwise the evidence would be contaminated before reaching the laboratory. Blood sodden items also needed to be kept in a particular way, sometimes in a fridge and sometimes in a freezer. Where blood came into play personal safety was always an issue and special consideration needed to be given to those items.

Weapons and firearms presented special problems not least of which related to getting shot or sustaining lacerations, whilst handling them. Liquids like petrol, paraffin and spirits, all required special considerations, mainly in relation to suspects' clothing and footwear. Special bags were available for packaging such items, where evidence of these accelerants might be sought.

More often than not the SOCO would recover and bag forensic items at a scene, and police officers would recover and bag clothing from the suspects. A good practice when looking for glass fragments on clothing would be to stand the suspect on large paper sheets whilst removing the clothing. This would of course catch any items falling towards the floor and could be wrapped up for analysis, at the laboratory.

The items that I have listed form just a small part of those that a detective needs to consider when dealing with suspects. I will be expanding on forensic aspects of specific cases in more detail when the stories are told. There were no particularly memorable cases that I can recall during my first three months in the CID. I was dealing with bread and butter cases such as theft, handling stolen goods and criminal damage. These cases were useful and I learnt more about the compilation of crime files, which were submitted for the prosecution of the suspects.

❀ ❀

Our son Ian was born

My wife's pregnancy had progressed well and we were delighted when our son Ian was born in March 1975, at The Isebrook Hospital in Wellingborough. I'm proud to say that I was present at his birth and gave Danusia as much support as one could, during the birth. He of course was a beautiful baby and was soon home with the family at Irchester. He was a great baby and slept well at night, this of course allowed his parents a good night's sleep.

It seemed very soon after Ian's birth that an elderly lady had been found murdered in her home at Longland Road, Northampton. CID were summoned from all over the county and gathered in the Campbell Square Police Station briefing room, situated at The Mounts, Northampton. I was sent also with a DC from Rushden and recall clearly to this day arriving at the briefing room. The room was huge and I recall various officers greeting one another like long lost friends. I should explain that officers will have travelled from opposite sides of the county and would be catching up with colleagues they hadn't seen for many months. The Detective Chief Superintendent, Arthur Crawley, then stood to the front of the assembled officers and called for order.

He then informed us that the victim's house had been burgled and that the victim had been suffocated whilst sitting in her armchair, in the lounge of the house. He added that she had been suffocated from behind by means of a spittle bag being pulled down over her head. Whilst being held by the assailant she had also been beaten around the head. Still being rather inexperienced I found the details rather shocking. The Chief Superintendent said that SOCO were at the scene and that a Home Office pathologist would be carrying out a post mortem in due course.

The officers present were then divided into teams of two and instructed to carry out door to door enquiries in the area of the murder. This was considered vital to confirm who might be in the area at the time of the murder. We would also of course be looking for potential suspects and witnesses. Full details of all occupants were written down on specially prepared forms. Part of this exercise was to confirm independently what each individual told us. On occasions, of course, people were alone at the time and confirmation of what they were doing could not be verified.

Intelligence officers would be sifting through information with a view to finding potential suspects. Informants would be contacted to see whether any useful information could be gleaned from them. They would also be tasked with going about their business in the local area to see what was on the grapevine. Enquiries were raised in relation to property stolen from the premises. Other teams of officers made enquiries in local pubs and clubs. A press appeal was quickly put together and circulated locally.

At the second briefing, the cause of death was confirmed to be asphyxiation. No new information had been forthcoming as a result of enquiries to date. An incident room was set up, in order that all information could be properly detained and investigated. The incident room was manned by several people including police officers and civilian staff. In those early days of course, there were no computers and all information was held on an alphabetical card system. Whilst working on that case I met a lot of officers from other parts of the county, culminating in long term friendships being built. I remember with fondness one Detective Sergeant who was working on the crime squad at the time. The officer, known as Mick, spoke very fast indeed and once fired up, it became difficult to stop him talking. His Detective Inspector summed him up one day when he said, 'he's never short of a thousand words'. I personally thought that was a great way of describing the Crime Squad DS.

I remained at Northampton for quite a few weeks on the enquiry and learnt a lot about the people of the area concerned. I also learned a lot about the consumption of both fish and chips and Chinese takeaway. The teams worked at least twelve hour days and of course proper meals were not available. These meals would be eaten late in the evening in the comfort of the CID car.

Occasionally officers would take liquid refreshment in the Campbell Square bar, at the conclusion of duty. It was nice to sit and talk about the weather after such long days.

At an early stage of the enquiry, a suspect was arrested, but after a few days had to be released on bail. There was insufficient evidence to charge the man concerned, despite the fact that all indications said he was responsible. Enquiries continued at a pace and the same man was again arrested, culminating in a charge of murder. Shortly after he was charged, my colleague and I were stood down and we resumed our normal duties at Rushden. I was not involved in the eventual trial but was informed that the male suspected of the murder, later received a twelve year sentence.

Soon after I resumed duty at Rushden, I was seen by the DS who informed me that there was no CID course available for me. He further explained that he was pleased with my six months attachment to the CID and looked forward to me being given another attachment in the near future. The policy at that time was for all CID aides to return back to uniform on completion of the six month attachment. I was very disappointed not to receive a CID course, but was nevertheless encouraged by the DS's kind words. Without further ado, the plain clothes went back in the cupboard and out came the uniform again.

During 1975 and the early part of 1976 a new police station was being built to the rear of the old Rushden Police Station. It wasn't long before we all moved into the new building and the old one was demolished. It was a sad time because those of us who had worked in the old station realised we were losing a building that had been full of character. In fact the new front car park of the current police station stands on ground where the old station once stood. Now there's a piece of history for you.

It was nice to be working in the local area again and I managed to spend a little more time at home with the children.

Ian was growing into a lovely little boy and all seemed to be plain sailing. Big brother Steven and sister Nicola clearly thought the world of Ian and all three played nicely together. We had of course been down to Cheshunt whenever possible and I was aware that my brother Alan was due for his annual check-up at Stoke Mandeville Hospital.

My brother Alan passes away suddenly

It was now the second week of June 1976 and I knew that Alan had gone to the hospital for a whole week. The week normally consisted of a number of tests to confirm that all was going well. It had, I suppose, become a matter of routine for both Alan and the hospital. In fact Alan had already informed my brother Raymond to ensure that the lagers were in place for his return that weekend. I'm sorry to say that the lagers were in place, but calamity was about to strike.

My neighbour Cathy knocked our door early in the morning to inform me that she had received a phone call from my sister-in-law. We never had a phone at that time and Cathy said we could use hers because the family needed to make urgent contact with us. After speaking to my sister-in-law it was necessary to phone my Mum at Cheshunt. I spoke to Mum and was given the worst news in the world. My brother Alan had passed away at Stoke Mandeville Hospital. I was absolutely stunned by the news and of course Mum was extremely upset whilst talking on the phone. I confirmed that my family at Cheshunt were all supporting each other and particularly our wonderful Mum.

I was the nearest to the hospital and it was decided that I should go to the hospital to deal with this awful situation. I found the journey very upsetting and on arrival was shown immediately into the Chapel of Rest, by the local Chaplain. I remember telling him that Alan and I were very close as brothers. Also that we had run together. In hindsight that

180

sounded daft but this is the sought of things we say, when very shocked and upset. The Chaplain seemed very understanding and made me feel at peace, adding that I could stay with Alan as long as I wished. It seemed very strange indeed to be standing next to Alan who was now laid out in an open coffin. During the two years that he had spent at the hospital I had pushed him in his chair past that Chapel many times.

I moved close to Alan and told him how much I loved him. He looked at peace and had one eye slightly open, as if he was looking at me. I felt the need to touch his forehead which was of course stone cold. I spoke to him reminding him of our boyhood jobs and other things we had done together. As far as I was concerned, for my short visit he was still alive. Apart from my mutterings it was completely silent in that Chapel. Well, I said my goodbyes and quietly but reluctantly left the Chapel.

I was then taken to the administration office and given details of what had happened, leading up to Alan's death. He was apparently in his bed soundly asleep when he suffered a massive heart attack. The doctor said that he had been fine prior to the attack and that it had been a complete shock for the nurses on the ward. The doctor went on to explain that paraplegics occasionally suffered such heart attacks because of their paralysis. He said that the ward staff had spent a considerable time trying to restart Alan's heart, but to no avail. It was 11 June 1976, and my lovely younger brother had died at the age of twenty six years.

As the next of kin I had to make a short statement of identification. I confirmed a number of details to the staff which would be needed for later funeral arrangements. I phoned Mum from the hospital to explain exactly what had happened to Alan and she seemed reassured with my explanations. My force had kindly given me one day's compassionate leave to carry out my visit to the hospital. I returned home to Irchester that evening where Danusia and I consoled each other. With obvious difficulty the situation was explained to our two eldest children.

The following day I resumed duty on the 2pm to 10pm shift, which I must confess I found rather difficult to handle. I

181

had given up smoking two weeks prior to Alan's death and I decided that evening that I would never smoke again in memory of Alan. Thirty six years have since passed and I'm very pleased to be able to say that I have never had a cigarette since that day. I feel that I'm somehow indebted to Alan because I used to smoke sixty cigarettes a day. I'd probably have been dead myself now had I continued to smoke.

When I look back at Alan's rather tragic life, I often admire the way he dealt with the difficulty that went hand in hand with quadriplegia. You may recall me referring to having enjoyed a great life. I now want you to know that having a brother like Alan inspired me to enjoy every minute of my life. I have suffered dark moments like all families and sadly will suffer more as my story continues.

I tutored two more probationers at the new police station, namely Kevin and Alan. I thoroughly enjoyed passing on my experiences to both young men and confirm that they were both quite successful Constables in their careers. Dave who I mentioned earlier went on to a successful time in the CID. Kevin spent many years as a rural police officer and Alan spent many years in the traffic department. It was a couple of years ago that I was shocked to hear of Kevin's death after a period of illness. He was a great character and always made me laugh. He is sadly missed and I often think of his wife and family.

Within four months of returning to uniform duty, another CID attachment became available and I'm pleased to say that I got the attachment. It was effectively another six months aide to the CID with the promise of a CID course, all being well. I continued where I left off and again dealt with a lot of everyday crimes. The duty DS then entrusted me to work on the infamous Yorkshire Ripper case. Yes, you heard me, the Yorkshire Ripper case.

All right, what I did was somewhat limited, but come on, this was high profile stuff. I was now becoming a real detective. I was working on a case where numerous women had been murdered. On a serious note, one of the victims was a young student from a neighbouring town, namely Kettering in

Northamptonshire. Some of you will recall that a tape recorded message was sent to the Ripper team in Yorkshire and the maker of the message purported to be the Ripper. The incident room in Yorkshire had established that the message had been recorded on a Phillips type pocket recorder.

All forces throughout the country had been requested to visit the retail outlets for such recorders to establish where they had been sold and whom to. In that regard I visited a local supplier at Higham Ferrers, and carried out a visual search of all the records, dating back several years. A detailed statement was taken from a member of staff and all the relevant documents were acquired for the attention of the Yorkshire Police team. I felt quite important when I addressed my resulting package of documents to the Detective Chief Superintendent of the West Yorkshire Police, which were of course sent by recorded delivery.

Peter Sutcliffe was eventually arrested and charged with all the murders. The audio tapes turned out to be made by a hoax caller who was later identified and given a very heavy prison sentence. I felt that this individual deserved a long sentence for wasting the time of police, who were working hard to prevent further murders

Unfortunately, violence was never very far away whilst working in Rushden. On this occasion it was late on a Saturday night at the Athletic Club, Newton Road, where a Disco had taken place. An ambulance had been called to a stabbing involving a sixteen year old victim. An offender had been detained by club officials. I visited the scene and found the victim had already been placed in the ambulance. He had sustained several stab wounds to his back, two of which were believed to have punctured his lungs. He was having difficulty breathing and the blood colour indicated to the ambulance crew, that his lungs were probably punctured.

The patient was given some oxygen before being taken off to hospital. A large Bowie type knife had been found on the disco floor, which had a blade measuring six inches in length. I recovered the knife which was blooded and placed it in a knife tube, which was then sealed in a forensic bag. Such knives were better protected, when placed in the tubes, which consisted of a reinforced clear plastic body.

I was then invited into the club officials' office where I was introduced to the offender. I recognised him straight away as one of the local biker boys by the name of Julian. He knew me and nodded his head as if to say 'yes, it was me'. I asked him what had happened and Julian replied that he had stabbed the youth with his Bowie knife. I told him he was being arrested for wounding and cautioned him. He went on to say that he didn't know why he had done it and went on to say probably the booze. I enquired as to what he had been drinking and he replied 'ten pints of snakebite'. This meant pints of cider and a dash of blackcurrant.

He was handcuffed and conveyed to Wellingborough Police Station by my uniformed colleagues. Because of the amount of alcohol consumed, he was bedded down for the night with a view to an official interview the next day. I arranged for SOCO to visit the scene to take photographs. Together with other officers, I then interviewed witnesses and written statements were obtained. None of the witnesses could throw any light on the reasons for the attack which seemed to them to be right out of the blue.

The victim had not been seen to show any provocation prior to the attack. It was a complete mystery and shock to all concerned. Julian had apparently been dancing in the head banging style that evening and had given no indication of what was about to happen. I contacted the hospital at about 2am the following morning and it was confirmed that my victim had suffered two punctured lungs. He was otherwise a very fit young man who was doing well in all the circumstances. I remember thinking 'Thank God for that'. The sister explained that fluid would be drained from the youth's lungs and that his parents were now with him. I arranged to visit the youth the following morning with a view to taking his victim statement.

I knew the victim in this case and it was like visiting an old friend when I visited the hospital the next morning. In those days we referred to this as local knowledge, meaning that you knew most people in your community. It was a great way of policing, to allow local officers to police their local area, whether you are in uniform or plain clothes. Those of us who have watched *The Bill* on the telly are familiar with them referring to 'their manor' meaning their area of local knowledge.

The youth had slept quite well considering his injuries and was responding well to treatment. The lung drains had been removed and his wounds had been sutured. He was well enough to tell me what had happened and I then sat at his bedside writing his witness statement down. He confirmed that there had been no provocation on his part and that he had been on the fringe of the dance floor when he received the blows to his back. He didn't know that he had been stabbed until he became aware of blood running down his back. He then started to feel a stinging pain in his upper back and realised that he had been stabbed. He turned and realised who had attacked him but couldn't understand why. He remembered getting short of breath and then seeing club people grabbing the offender whom he knew to be Julian. The youth fully supported the view that the offender Julian should be prosecuted for the assault.

I later interviewed Julian who fully admitted the knifing and said that he both expected and deserved to go to prison. He was not wrong and later received a custodial sentence at Northampton Crown Court, after pleading guilty to wounding. The trial judge gave him a one year imprisonment based on his previous good behaviour and the fact that he had pleaded guilty to the offence. I thought the sentence was rather lenient in all the circumstances, but had the desired effect in that Julian was never to offend again. He never explained why he stabbed the youth that night and his lack of reason continues to concern me to this day.

❀ ❀

A child murder

I had only been back in the CID office for a couple of months when another awful murder had been committed at Northampton. This was to be the most horrific case that I had assisted with to date. A girl aged nine years had been invited to a party in a nearby street. She had left home on her own that afternoon to walk to the house concerned. She never arrived as planned, and alarm bells began to ring, with the relative families. The girl's parents started to check the route their daughter had taken.

They walked up the road and turned left at the 'T' junction. Their intention was to carry on walking to the next junction and turn left again. They then saw smoke billowing to their left, at the bottom of an embankment. This embankment was situated opposite a pub called *The Romany*. On further inspection of the smoke the parents tragically found their daughters body on a bonfire, at the bottom of the embankment. The little girl had sustained a serious assault and was believed to have died prior to being placed on the fire. It was a poor attempt on the part of the assailant to dispose of the body.

My heart went out to the parents who were obviously devastated by the awful realisation of what had happened. The emergency services attended the scene but nothing could be done for this beautiful little girl. It seemed much too quick for me to be heading back to a major incident room at Campbell Square Police Station. A large team of officers had again been called in to work on the case and I can tell you that the mood was low. Additional details about the cause of death were now available and it was confirmed that the little girl had sustained internal injuries. SOCO and a search team had been deployed at the scene to recover as much evidence as possible.

The priority was to begin the door to door enquiries quickly, to establish whether anyone had been seen in the area at the time. A team was also sent to *The Romany* pub again to search not only for witnesses but also potential suspects. Details were quickly divulged to the press and local media. Historically the general public take particular note of a child murder and the police hoped for a quick response. The door to door teams concluded at about 9pm and they were all debriefed with the fact that no new information had been forthcoming.

I believe it was the following day that a scout master was found badly beaten and dumped in a Northampton cesspit. He was near to death when found, having nearly drowned in the cesspit. He had been beaten about the head with bricks, and thrown into the cesspit by a local man. The scout master named the assailant, stating that he had known him for many years. I believe the assailant had been questioned by the scout master about the case of the little girl and it was that discussion which had prompted the assault. In any event the scout master was lucky to be alive because he had sustained a fractured skull.

Armed with a name, a team of officers visited a three storey block of flats with a view to arresting the suspect. The suspect by the name of Derek was one step ahead of the officers and managed to climb via a window onto the third storey roof. Officers also climbed up onto the roof to confront Derek, but found him standing near the edge of the roof. He threatened to jump if the officers got any closer. Derek was then seen to climb over the edge of the roof and hang down the side of the building, by his fingers.

Officers were unable to respond quickly enough and Derek just plunged to the ground. As you can imagine he was badly injured as he struck the ground having fallen three floors. Derek was now screaming out in pain and was placed in the back of an ambulance. A well-known police surgeon was the first apparently to administer first aid. Derek had sustained numerous fractures to both legs, some might say that this was rough justice, I would say otherwise. He was taken to Northampton General for treatment and was put under police guard. After initial treatment, Derek was arrested on suspicion of murder and attempted murder. He was brought to Campbell Square for interview and subsequently admitted the murder of the little girl. He said he had become angry when she pulled

187

faces at him and in response had thrown her down the embankment.

He said words to the effect that he then went down the slope of the embankment and found the girl dead at the bottom. He had panicked and decided to put her on the fire. He denied any other form of assault on the little girl. He also admitted assaulting the scout master and admitted leaving him for dead. I'm pleased to be able to tell you that the scout master made a slow but full recovery. I'm sorry to say that the court could do no more to Derek, than to give him a life sentence.

Referring to the title of my book, I need to remind everyone that this young innocent girl was deprived of long life and to this day, I would like to see the law changed. I'm sure everyone knows what I'm referring to and I'll leave it at that. I remained on the incident room for several weeks assisting in witness statement taking and then resumed duty at Rushden.

Despite the passing of thirty six years I have chosen not to name the young girl in this case out of respect for her family. Please rest assured that her name will be remembered by me until the day I die. My own daughter was six at the time and I have had the pleasure of watching her grow and blossom, producing four lovely grandsons for my wife and I to cherish. I can only hope that the passing of time has been of some help to the parents in this case.

Fortunately not all cases were so distressing, and on a lighter note I'll mention a family at Irthlingborough. I had visited a local burglary that day where a large quantity of confectionery had been stolen. I received information to the effect that the well-known Irthlingborough family were involved. I made my way to their house together with another officer intending to search for the stolen goods.

I knew the family very well and intended to search with their consent. After giving the street door the traditional knock, we received no reply. I was not amused when I peered through the lounge window and saw several family members rapidly eating confectionery. I banged on the window and to my annoyance the occupants completely ignored me and carried on munching.

At the time it was necessary to seek authority from the duty Inspector, in order to gain entry to the premises.

I phoned in to obtain the authority and was told to keep the occupants under observation, whilst the Inspector was being consulted. One word summed up my feelings but I'm unable to put it down on paper. The family continued to munch away and I could see my evidence disappearing in front of my eyes. I explained to my control room that time was of the essence and they politely reminded me to wait for the appropriate authority. Two hours passed and the authority eventually came through.

I was about to use force on the street door but was denied the pleasure, when the head of the family opened it and said 'hello Mick what can I do for you?' I explained the reason for my visit and carried out a search of the house. My colleague and I found hidden sweet wrappers throughout the house, and also a few uneaten bars of stolen confectionery. Several of the occupant's children were present and were complaining of feeling sick. I wasn't surprised they had eaten numerous *Mars* bars, Turkish Delight, *Twix, Rolos* and *Bounty* bars.

I then answered the head of the family's earlier question, saying that a cough would be good. He said 'all right, it's down to me, let's go and sort it out'. I then arrested him and took him to Wellingborough for a proper interview. At the station he denied the burglary but admitted handling stolen goods. He was adamant that the family thought that the sweets were a gift from him. The rest of the family were of course given the benefit of the doubt, in that no further action was taken against them.

The time had now arrived for my wife and I to meet Royalty. The new Rushden Police Station was to be officially opened by the Duke of Gloucester. All the police officers were to be dressed in their best uniform and CID officers in suits, which normally would only be worn at the Crown Court. Our wives were all to attend in their smartest outfits, together with their smartest hats. A plaque had been prepared and placed in the front foyer, ready to be unveiled by the Duke of Gloucester.

The High Sheriff, local councillors and other dignitaries were also invited to mark the day.

We had a beautiful summer's day for the occasion and all went off smoothly. I thought it was a particularly nice touch for our wives to be involved in the event. After the official speeches we all adjourned to the first floor parade room for refreshments. I didn't have the pleasure of speaking to the Duke personally, but gained the impression that he was a perfect gentleman.

Soon after this lovely event, we had a new and rather nice wine bar open in Rushden High Street. It was named *Sam's Wine Bar* after the owner, and was a very new innovation, for a small 1970s town like Rushden. The bar soon became popular attracting couples looking for a quiet and pleasant night out. A reasonably priced menu had been created to accompany the wine and a small patio had been built to the rear for sun seekers.

Sam himself was a pleasant middle aged gentleman who engaged well with his customers. The CID was of course most welcomed at the wine bar and it formed a small part of the many bars and clubs that we visited as a matter of course. In my early days in the CID it was considered a duty commitment to visit such places, with a view to gaining criminal intelligence and building good relationships with the town's licensees.

I don't know how it came about but the local skinheads started frequenting the wine bar and resulted in some rowdiness. One theory was that they were coming in for late drinks after their favourite bars had either closed, or, on occasions, had ejected them for bad behaviour. This was not a good situation and we hoped that they would be discouraged from using the wine bar.

Then came the night when my worst fears came home to roost. A large group of the skinheads went into the wine bar on a Friday night close to closing time. They were very inebriated and in very quick time started throwing glasses and other missiles around the wine bar. The proprietor, together with other regular customers tried to regain order but was immediately assaulted by the skinheads. Tables and chairs were also thrown around causing both injuries and criminal damage to the wine bar.

Uniformed officers attended first, followed by myself and another CID officer. We found chaos on arrival with our uniformed colleagues in a street battle with a group of approximately twelve skinheads. We were told that several people were awaiting ambulances and that considerable damage had been caused at the wine bar. My colleague and I then saw two skinheads break away from the uniformed officers. We ran into Station Road and confronted the skinheads, resulting in two arrests. One was compliant and the other, namely my prisoner, resisted violently. He started punching and kicking me which culminated in me returning fire.

I eventually managed to manhandle my prisoner to the awaiting police van and after further confrontation managed to place him securely in the rear of the vehicle. It was of course a long time ago but I believe we managed to arrest eight suspects. Interestingly, one of the eight had placed himself in the back of the attending ambulance. It was only when I visited the real victims in the ambulance, that I discovered the last skinhead, who was falsely purporting to be injured. He was then arrested and placed in the police van.

I'm sorry to say that six innocent people had sustained wounds as a direct result of the skinhead attack that night. These were all conveyed to Kettering General Hospital for treatment. The most serious wound was to a young man's forehead which amounted to a laceration requiring six stitches. Fortunately all of the victims made good recoveries and apart from obvious scaring, settled back down to their various futures. One of them actually joined the police several years after this incident and enjoyed many years as a Constable in the Northamptonshire Force. I'm led to believe that he retires this year, 2013.

All of the suspects were interviewed the following day and later charged with affray. They all received short custodial sentences after pleading guilty at Northampton Crown Court. I feel that the judge took into consideration the average age of the offenders which was in fact seventeen years. It took the wine bar a good few months to regain customer confidence, which it wholly deserved. I'm pleased to be able to say that it remained successful for a good few years after this incident. On the other side of the coin several of the skinheads settled down after release from young offenders institutions.

Murder of a young boy

Before I could say 'boo to a goose', another murder enquiry was underway at Northampton. This was another very traumatic case concerning a fourteen year old boy, who had been found dead lying on his back in a cobbled lane near to Northampton football ground. It appeared that he had either been carried there or taken there in a vehicle. This case is undetected to date and because of that fact I will say very little about specifics of the case. Obviously I can give details which I know where given to the media at the time. However I again do not wish to name the youth out of respect for his family and friends.

The incident room was again set up at Campbell Square Police Station and a large team of officers were called in to work on the case. The cause of death was well documented at the time as being asphyxiation. There were numerous lines of enquiry at the time, many of which were generated by calls from the general public. One theory was that the youth concerned may have visited a fairground at Midsummer Meadow, Northampton, at the time and may have been abducted in that area. All enquiries at the fairground unfortunately ended with a negative result.

Another line of enquiry involved the local 'gay' community and with others I spent a lot of time tracing the persons concerned and subsequently interviewing them. I had never worked closely with the 'gay' community before and found it a very interesting experience. The vast majority that I met were successful individuals, living together as couples, who fully supported the enquiry team, whenever possible. At the time I must admit that I was surprised at the size of the 'gay' community, which numbered in the hundreds. That line of enquiry eventually became exhausted, at which point I was paired up with a Wellingborough detective.

A forensic examination of the victims clothing resulted in fibres being found, which were confirmed to come from a particular type of carpet. The carpet was blue in colour and had been supplied to the Ford Motor Company at Dagenham, in Essex for use in one of their cars. It transpired that the carpet had been fitted into 4,800 Ford Cortina Ghia Saloon cars, in the Cosmos Blue car colour range.

These vehicles had then been sold throughout the British Isles. Requests were sent out to all police forces, with a view to tracing all the vehicles for forensic examination. We were firmly of the view that our victim could have been transported in one of the vehicles. All forces agreed to carry out the work on our behalf, with the exception of the Metropolitan Police, who in fairness had a large number of owners in their force area.

As a result my colleague and I formed part of a team of twenty officers who were given accommodation in London, to carry out the enquiries. My colleague and I were sent to a section house at East Ham where we lived for three weeks. It was in the middle of the summer and our particular area of enquiry revolved around the better off parts of Essex. We were visiting Upminster, Hornchurch, Hainault, Chigwell, Rayleigh, Epping, and Woodford and so on. We were made most welcome by all of the people concerned and successfully acquired the relevant forensic from the vehicles. It was also necessary to write out witness statements from all owners and users of the vehicles to confirm their movements at the relevant times. This was obviously a very man-hour intensive operation with all movements being verified independently. In that regard a further witness statement would be needed, all handwritten by our team.

Having concluded our work in Essex we then moved to Wardour Street in Soho, London and were given a further two weeks accommodation, this time at Trenchard House. I should perhaps explain that the section house at East Ham was in fact a series rooms used normally by single police officers employed by the Metropolitan Police and that Trenchard House was used for the same purpose. We were rather concerned to hear that a Metropolitan Police officer had recently been stabbed on a flight of stairs to the front of the building. I'm unable to expand on the incident, because we were never officially briefed on the matter. However, my thoughts are still with the officer and his family.

The noises in the streets around Trenchard House were constant, caused mainly by traffic and a market place. In the early hours one morning I was awoken by a very loud sound of something being dragged along the street, outside our building. I was shocked when I looked out of my bedroom window and saw two officers from our team, whom had obviously been making all the noise. One of them was sitting in a large plastic bread basket with his legs dangling from each side of the basket. The other officer was pulling the basket along the pavement by means of an attached length of rope. They were both off duty in casual dress and had clearly consumed too much amber nectar.

I then saw two uniformed Metropolitan Police officers approaching my colleagues, who were still in possession of their improvised sleigh. I decided it was time for me to get back into bed on the assumption that peace had resumed in the street below. How wrong could one be. The following morning at our daily briefing we were told by a senior officer that our colleagues had been arrested and taken into custody. They had failed to identify themselves which resulted in our senior officer being called out of bed in the early hours of the morning to put the record straight.

Fortunately the basket was returned intact to its owners and profuse apologies were given to all concerned, not least of which were the arresting officers. Our Detective Inspector can only be described as 'Mr Angry' at the briefing that morning.

Although I didn't approve of their behaviour, I can understand that it is occasionally necessary to let off steam. I'm not making excuses for them but some lengthy cases are very stressful and CID traditionally relaxed with a beer or two. We should of course know where to draw the line on murder enquiries.

At the end of the two weeks at Trenchard House, the whole team returned to Northamptonshire, having completed all of the relative vehicle enquiries. All of the exhibits were sent to the Forensic Science Laboratory to be compared with fibres under investigation. Several weeks elapsed before all of the examinations had been completed. When the results arrived at the incident room there was great disappointment, because none of the fibres could be matched to those found on the body of our victim.

I'm afraid to say that CID work generally has many highs and far more lows. This was clearly a low point in the enquiry because the whole team were convinced that a match would be found between a car's interior carpet and our fibres. At that time there were still a large number of outstanding enquiries to be completed and I was allocated a new partner, a police constable called Charlie. This officer worked at Wellingborough and had shown good aptitude in crime related cases. He had been given a three month attachment to the CID.

The Detective Superintendent spoke to me about Charlie and said I was to keep a tight rein on him, because he tended to go off on tangents. I suppose this was the Super's way of saying that Charlie was very keen. Well as soon as we left the incident room, Charlie was chasing across a building site in pursuit of brick thieves. He of course arrested an offender and recovered the stolen bricks. Charlie of course had just gone off on a tangent. Charlie seemed delighted with his arrest until I told him what I thought about it. I explained to him in very plain language that he had just wasted two hours of very valuable murder enquiry time.

Charlie had trouble digesting what I had told him because he was what we call in our profession 'a thief taker'. The following day the Superintendent gave us an enquiry in

195

London, accompanied by the words 'take him to London and keep him focused on this enquiry'. This proved to be quite an interesting day out. The enquiries were written out by hand in those days on what was referred to as an 'Action'. A fourteen year old associate of the victim had run away from home in Northampton and was believed to be in London. His name was John and we were given a photograph of him, to assist us in our search for him.

Enquiries with some of John's mates had indicated that he may go to London to seek work as a rent boy. This meant that he might seek out men who would pay him for sexual favours. As we drove towards London, Charlie said that the missing boy would be working at somewhere like Piccadilly Underground Station. I asked Charlie how he knew where to look for the lad and he said just watch this space. With Charlie's idea in mind we drove to West End Central Police Station situated in Regent Street and gained permission to park in their rear yard.

We were then shown up to the Vice Squad office where we met the squad's Detective Sergeant. He enquired 'how can I help you lads from Northampton?' Charlie showed him the photo of John and said that we had come to London to arrest the lad in the photo. The DS said 'have you got an address?' Charlie said 'no, but he's here earning rent'. The DS said 'what do you mean by here?' Charlie said 'here in London'. The DS said 'son we've got nine million people here'. He then burst out laughing and was joined in laughter by the other detectives in his office.

Charlie asked what they had found to be so funny. The DS said 'you cabbages north of Watford, that's what'. He then said 'if you find him, bring him here and I'll eat my hat'. Charlie said 'right, come on Mick let's go get him'. One of the DCs in the office then joined in the 'micky' taking, saying that Charlie's checked jacket would go down well in vice. The DS said 'bring that boy back and you've got a job here'.

Charlie and I left the police station and made our way to Piccadilly Railway Station which was quite nearby. From memory I believe the station had six exits which were all packed

196

with people because it was the evening rush-hour. The volume of people was simply horrendous and the thought of needle in a haystack crossed my mind. Charlie said 'you do that exit and I'll do one of the others'. In an instant Charlie disappeared into the sea of people making their way through the underground station. I actually stood there thinking I'll never see Charlie again amongst this never ending throng of people.

Within minutes I could hear Charlie's voice shouting 'I've got him Mick'. Charlie then appeared through the crowds pushing a youth towards me, with his arm up his back. To my amazement it was the runaway boy by the name of John. Charlie said 'I've nicked him for soliciting and he tried to do a runner'. Charlie then marched past me and I could see that he was holding his prisoner in a straight arm lock. This arm lock had the effect of pushing the youth's head downward towards the pavement. It took all my strength to keep up with Charlie who was now on a mission to deliver his prisoner to the Vice Squad office.

Charlie marched the lad up the staircase in the tube station out into Regent Street. He then carried on marching his prisoner along the pavement in Regent Street. He then carried on to West End Central Police Station, where John was received by a charge Sergeant. The vice squad DS then came down to see us and congratulated us on our good police work. He also apologised for taking the 'micky'. I personally thought it was great banter and conveyed this to the DS. Charlie was unable to see the funny side of the way we had been treated. Perhaps Charlie wasn't what we call CID material, because you do need a good sense of humour. You need to let things roll off your back.

We suddenly realised that John had expensive new clothing on, which he had acquired since he left home. When questioned he said he had been stopping with a man who lived in a flat at Tower Bridge, London. He said he had had sex with the man who then bought him the nice new clothes. John agreed to take us to the flat together with the DS from the Vice Squad. At the flat, a man was identified for sexual assault on

John and was then arrested by the Vice Squad. He later admitted spending £300 on John for what he referred to as 'rent boy' money. Prior to leaving London with Charlie and me, John made a witness statement against the man who had sexually assaulted him. The man later pleaded guilty and was sent to prison for sexual assault on a juvenile.

John was interviewed back in Northamptonshire in relation to the murder of his friend. It was established that he had no involvement in the case and that he could not assist the enquiry team. He was returned to his family and was thought to be settling back down nicely with them. I got to know his family during the course of the enquiry and found them to be lovely law abiding people.

I remained on the incident room for a total of four months after which I returned to Rushden and my normal CID duties. As far as I'm aware, the murder was never cleared up and the case remains on file to date. I know that a small team of local officers carried on working on the case for many months after I was stood down. I can tell you that it is soul destroying to work on such a case and never see the offender or offenders brought to justice. In my experience it is never through the lack of trying. I have found that officers work very hard indeed with a view to detecting all murders. I live in hope that I shall hear one day that an offender has been found and convicted of this awful crime. This is another example of a lovely young innocent youth being denied the privilege of a long and happy life.

I want to take this opportunity to explain that our sense of humour must be maintained when working on these simply awful murders. It is the humour which prevents the vast majority of police officers from going insane. As time progresses, I have much worse to write about and want everyone to know that I find no pleasure in doing so!. I'm actually trying to give everyone an overview of what it is like on the front line, experiencing some of these awful cases. It is not all bad however, because along the way police officers have the pleasure to meet some wonderful people.

A holiday with the family

It was now time for a holiday to Somerset with my wife and children. Having lost Alan quite recently we decided it would be nice for my Mum and brother Raymond to join us on the holiday. We actually met them at a junction on the M4 and drove down in convoy. We were heading for a beautiful three hundred year old cottage at Porlock near the Lorna Doon valley. This was just what the doctor ordered, peace, tranquillity and your family around you. What more could a young CID aide want whilst away from police work?

It was a long drive down to Somerset, but well worth it because it was simply a beautiful county. On arrival we were all delighted with the cottage and soon had the old log burning oven alight. After a good meal we had a short walk in and around the farm yard. The setting was stunning with heavily wooded hills and valleys. In the morning we were woken early by the sound of sheep bleating in our front garden. On looking out of the bedroom window I counted approximately three hundred sheep in total. I was relieved to see the farmer open a gate and lead the sheep down a lane to a field, where they were left to graze.

Whilst Danusia and the others did various chores I invited Nicola and Steven to take a walk with me. They were not very keen on the idea but in those early days parents still had control over their children. We set off down a lane into one of the valleys and walked through beautiful woodlands, which were in full leaf. We had only gone about a mile when I spotted several fallow deer crossing the path ahead of us. It was at that point that Nicola and Steven seemed to wake up and enjoy the local wildlife. We kept quiet and kept the deer in view for several minutes, before they took cover in the woods again.

On returning to the cottage we enjoyed a wonderful dinner and curled up nice and cosy on a big old three piece suite. That evening was quite warm and prior to retiring to bed, Danusia

199

and I decided to leave the sash style bedroom window open. We were awoken from a deep sleep by two large bats flying around the room. Danusia was absolutely terrified and started screaming as the bats circled above our heads. I must admit that it was quite disturbing, because we had not experienced such a thing before. They actually made quite a clatter as they flew around the room. After several minutes I manage to steer the bats back out of the open window. On Danusia's instructions the sash style windows remained shut for the rest of the holiday.

Mum was in her sixties but still pretty fit, so we decided to walk downhill to the coast the next day. It was a lovely day and it was great to place Ian on our shoulders for the best part of the walk. He was only eighteen months old and like all little boys, he was prone to leg aches. We walked about three miles to a place called Porlock Weir, which consisted of a small rocky inlet by the sea. Better still, it had an old smuggler type pub with good food and real ale to die for.

Before we knew it the holiday drew to a close and we were driving back to good old Northamptonshire. I must say though that it was great to spend those two weeks with my family catching up on family life, as you do. I would recommend that type of holiday to anyone thinking of going to Somerset.

It was now late summer of 1976 and Danusia said that she wanted to move to the Rushden area, which would make daily shopping easier than living in Irchester. We started looking for another house and put our house up for sale. We looked at several properties and eventually agreed on a house in Prospect Avenue, Rushden. It was a three bed semi-detached built in 1936 that was in need of a lot of renovation. The house had a very long garden which for me was the main attraction. It was a lovely old house and we soon thrashed a deal with the owner, who incidentally was a local bus driver. Before we knew it we had a buyer for our house at Irchester and contracts were exchanged.

It was now time to meet an old adversary consisting of father and son who had their own removal company. I need to refer you back to a young lad who crashed his moped and blood samples that went missing. Need I say any more, of course not, they agreed to do our removal and a very good job they did to. I would recommend them to anyone, but I'm not about to name them because that would be unfair. On a serious note it was a pleasure to see such skilful removal men at work. Every single item arrived at the new home without a single scratch.

Part Four

A Detective at last

No sooner had we moved into our new home I was offered a CID course at Hendon in London. The offer couldn't have come at a worst time because of the state of the house we had just bought. I think they call it 'Sod's Law', but I don't want to dwell on it, so let's get on with the main priority - the CID course. I was absolutely chuffed because I had been kicking around as an aide to the CID for too long now and wanted to be a Detective Constable. The course was normally of ten week duration but for reasons now long forgotten, my course would be crammed into nine weeks. I didn't care, we can do this, I decided.

Danusia and I worked hard on the house for the few weeks we had before I went on the course. Frankly the place was in a mess, but we had no other option than to put off the work until my course was completed. The course began in May 1977 and ended late in July. I was very fortunate to be able to travel with another CID aide from Northampton, who attended the same course.

The CID course consisted of nine weeks of learning criminal law. Criminal law in itself is a huge subject to learn. I have always been a practical person and found studying criminal law very difficult indeed. At the conclusion of the course each officer had to pass a detailed written exam and failure was not an option. If you failed the course you would return to your force and go straight back to uniform. You could not become a detective without this qualification.

Three things struck me as being great whilst at Hendon. The first was pairing up with a guy from Liverpool called John Pinnington. He was great company and clearly quite experienced having gone from job to job, to job, on the streets of Liverpool. He had no knowledge of London and I became his natural chaperone, having been born and bred in town. On the downside we parted company at the end of the course and have not kept in touch since that time. I hope he has kept in good health and still look forward to seeing him one day.

The second great experience was the fact that all of the instructors were experts in their particular field of work. For example, a Special Branch DI would have worked for some years at London's major airports and in anti-terrorism. Robbery would be taught by a DI who had worked on the inner city Robbery Squad and will have nicked loads of bank robbers. The DI who taught us about forgery had worked most of his career on the subject and had recovered millions in forged bank notes. The Vice Squad DI had some very juicy stories which I'm completely unable to repeat.

Putting it plainly, these instructors had dealt with super grasses, gangland killers and illegal drug importers. Most of the instructors however, didn't want to be at Hendon Police College, they wanted to be on the outside doing their jobs. Most told the story that they were there because they had upset the Commissioner. We all knew that they were pulling our legs with that story - or were they? Anyway they were great instructors and I will leave the rest to your imagination.

The third thing was that the Queen's Jubilee celebrations had arrived that year and the Queen was going to visit Hendon Metropolitan Police Training Centre. Preparations were soon underway in the rear field with the cutting of the grass and the erection of marquees. We could see all what was happening from our classroom windows, but didn't allow this to distract us from our lessons. When the Queen arrived, we watched several hundred uniformed police officers, parading in squads in front of Her Majesty.

On the conclusion of the Queen's visit, we had tea and specially made Queen's Jubilee mince tarts, which were very nice indeed. That part of the day reminded me of my childhood celebrations to mark the Queen's Coronation.

Meanwhile back on the course, our early evenings were spent on revision. The latter part of the evening would usually consist of liquid refreshments being taken on or off site. The accommodation blocks were situated in three tower blocks on site. The tower blocks consisted of about twelve floors and I was staggered one night when some idiot raced around the top floor on a motorbike. He was obviously a police officer and had brought his bike to the top floor in the lift. I can only assume that he had been drinking because he was certainly putting his career in jeopardy. Unfortunately he was never identified and most probably had a long career in the police force. He certainly put quite a few people in danger that night and I for one would certainly have grassed him up, had I known his identity.

Exam time was rapidly approaching and I can tell you that one officer's nerves were certainly jangling. The good news was that I managed to pass the exam, but not in glowing terms. Out of sixty nine officers who sat the exam I only achieved a sixty first place. However, I obtained a pass and that alone was most likely to get me my detective status back in my county. 'Yippee' sprung to mind as the course drew to a close. All jokes to one side I had learnt a great deal about criminal law and procedure whilst attending a fabulous course.

On the penultimate evening we were treated to a great night out at a north London restaurant, where we all let our hair down and had a great laugh with the instructors. The following day I recall returning to our county with a rather bad hangover. I vaguely recall being seen by my Detective Inspector at Wellingborough, who was unimpressed with my exam results. I had to wait a couple of days before I was told that a post was available for me, as a Detective Constable at Wellingborough. I was delighted to receive the news and keen to start work at my new police station.

Class 'A' of the Initial Junior Course at the Metropolitan Police Training School, Hendon, May 1977

I am standing on the back row, second from the right. John Pinnington is also on the back row, third from the left

My first priority was to enjoy a long weekend off duty with my wife and children. In truth, Danusia and I spent most of our spare time renovating the house. A considerable amount of the wallpaper was just hanging off the walls and needed stripping back to the plaster. The paintwork throughout the house was so bad that we decided to burn it all off back to the woodwork. Assisted by a mate, I also took a dividing wall out between the front room and dining room, turning the space into a through lounge.

My young family in those early days

Time just flew by and before I knew it I was working in the Wellingborough CID office. I was put on a shift with a DS and two other DCs who made up a good little team. I started on late duty and the first job I was given was criminal damage at one of the local cemeteries. During the night someone had entered the cemetery and smashed approximately £2,000 worth

207

of graves and gravestones. I was somewhat shocked by what had happened and liaised with the local council, with a view to relatives being notified. I had photographs taken by SOCO to be used in the unlikely event of an arrest being made. It was obviously a remote location and the chance of anyone being seen was doubtful. I arranged for local press coverage in the hope that someone may have witnessed the damage or may have heard something on the grapevine. No response was ever made and I never managed to establish who had been responsible.

Shortly after the damage, Pete, a detective on my shift said he needed to nick a bloke in a local pub. I said 'great, let's go and get him'. Pete said 'it's not that easy Mick, it's a town centre pub full of ethnic minorities and they like to kick off'. I said 'have we got a good power of arrest Pete?' to which he replied, 'yes. On that note I said 'let's go then', and after putting our coats on, made our way to the pub. On the way, Pete explained that the bloke was wanted for a DHSS deception and that he was likely to resist arrest. I said 'don't worry Pete I'll nick him'.

In those early days of my policing I feared no one and always without fear or favour carried out my duty. We entered the pub which was called *The Coach and Horses,* situated along Oxford Street in Wellingborough. It was packed and we were not made welcomed by the people present. Pete pointed out the suspect who was two things, one being huge and the other being a pool player, with pool cue in hand. He was enjoying a pint of beer whilst playing pool with his mate. I made my way to the bar and introduced myself to the licensee, at the same time explaining what I would be doing next.

I then spoke quietly to the suspect explaining that he was under arrest and that he would be leaving with Pete and I. He didn't seem to respond at all. I sensed trouble and removed my jacket which I then placed on the bar. I returned to the pool table and noticed that Pete had a concerned look on his face. I walked straight up to the giant and said 'can you hear me this time?' He seemed to realise that I now meant business and said he would like to finish his pint before we go. I thought that his request was reasonable and allowed him to finish his beer. He then put down his pool cue and we left the pub like a pair of old mates.

Pete and I took the suspect into custody at Wellingborough Police Station, where he was placed in a cell. Pete said he was impressed with the way I dealt with the suspect. I told Pete that I merely went in and did my job. The suspect soon admitted the offence and after charge was bailed to the local Magistrates' Court. Before leaving he thanked me for allowing him to finish his pint. I in turn thanked him for putting his pool cue away quietly. These particular lads like a bit of banter.

Another case stood out in my memory at Wellingborough which although common now, wasn't in the 1970s. I started at 8am that day and was sent to Wellingborough Railway Station. On arrival it was confirmed that trains had been stopped running during the night on the route between Wellingborough and Nottingham, because of a phone line breakdown. An examination of the nearby line then revealed that 1,400 yards of heavy electric cable had been cut down from the telegraph poles adjacent to the lines. Power cables had also been cut down and stolen from the main line causing considerable disruption on the route. The local engineer was surprised that no one had been electrocuted.

This was the first time that I had dealt with that type of theft and asked the engineer to explain the contents of the cables. He described the cable as being over half an inch in diameter and made mainly from copper, which carried quite a high scrap value. I recorded the crime and then visited all our local scrap dealers with a view to alerting them quickly. I also sent out a telex message to all other scrap merchants in our county and adjoining counties. Because of the unusual nature of the crime we also put details to local radio and press.

Within a few hours someone phoned in anonymously stating that he could hear a constant sawing sound emanating from a back garden of a nearby house. The house concerned was situated on the Hemmingwell Estate in Wellingborough, which in actual fact was only half a mile from the scene of the crime. This of course brought music to my ears and after a very quick briefing we were off. My colleagues and I parked a discreet distance away from the house and as we approached I could actually hear the sawing sound in the distance.

To my amazement, on peering over the rear garden wall, I could see two males hack-sawing the stolen cable into thirty six inch lengths. It made me laugh a little because they had nearly finished cutting up all 1,400 yards of the stolen cable. Having surrounded the house we gained entry and arrested the two local men on suspicion of theft and criminal damage. After caution one of the men said he was just doing a bit of graft. This in turn started the other man laughing because of course graft in their lingo means thieving. Both were then invited to the police station for subsequent interviews.

The SOCO visited to take photographs of the rear garden and make a record of the thieves' production line. We then seized all the cable and all the tools concerned in the offences, which were duly exhibited. Both the lads arrested were well known by Wellingborough police and soon admitted to me their various roles in the offences. I should add that they had little room for manoeuvre because we recovered the actual cutters that they had used to cut the cable, at the scene. We could match the cut marks forensically between cutters and cable. What better possible evidence could we ask for?

During the interviews I wanted to know how they had carried out the offence without being electrocuted. Both men declined to tell me and referred to it as a trade secret. Detailed statements were taken from all concerned at the railway station. I recall the cost of replacing and refurbishing the cable installations was enormous. The two men concerned pleaded guilty and both received prison sentences. The moral of this story must be if you need to cut stuff up, don't do it in the garden.

❀ ❀

A calculated risk

In my early days in CID, it might be said that I took one or two risks. One such example related to a house burglary in Wellingborough at one of the more prestigious households. The method of entry was most unusual in that the burglar had drilled a small hole in the window frame and then passed wire through to slip the window catch. All of the family silver had been stolen and the family were quite devastated at the loss. Very few people used that method of entry at that time and it certainly wasn't a method used in the Wellingborough area.

I decided to circulate full details to surrounding counties requesting that details of burglars using this method be passed to me. My favourite county, Bedfordshire, came back straight away with a potential suspect from Bedford. He was a regular house burglar and had been known to use the Modus Operandi (method of operation) I had described. I immediately requested that he be arrested during the early hours of the next day and that a search be made for the stolen silver.

The word 'Bingo' springs to mind when I was informed the following morning that the suspect was now in custody at Greyfriars Police Station, Bedford. The search had also been fruitful in that a hand drill and drill bits had been found. A small item of silver had also been recovered, which was similar to one stolen. I visited Bedford and conveyed the suspect together with the items recovered back to our police station. He was booked in by the Custody Sergeant and placed in a cell for subsequent interview.

I took the small piece of silver to the owner who identified it as being stolen from his house during the burglary. On examining the drill bits which had of course been bagged properly by my colleagues in Bedfordshire, I could see remnants of wood in the drill flutes. We now had the opportunity to compare the wood remnants with that at the scene. White paint from the window frame might also be matched forensically if need should arise.

211

On interviewing the suspect, he was initially reluctant to talk, but admitted the items found at his home were his sole responsibility. I gathered from his admission that his brother, who also lived with him, had no involvement in the offence. I could tell that he wanted to admit the offence but had concerns about the likely sentence he would receive. I pointed out that the victims of the house burglary dearly wanted their silver back and I wondered how he might be able to help.

He then suddenly said that he might be prepared to admit an offence if he was allowed out of custody for an hour or so. He went on to say that he could recover all the silver - off the record - if allowed out, alone to do so. This request presented me with a bit of a dilemma, because Custody Sergeants didn't approve of such ideas. I decided contrary to all the rules to release the suspect from custody on the arrangement that he would return with the silver within one hour. I made it very clear to him that I would be very upset if he failed to return.

I then led the suspect to the front door of the police station and allowed him the arranged freedom. I recall the exact time to this day, it was mid-day and I expected him back at 1pm. Under normal circumstances he should have been freed by the duty custody officer and duly recorded on the custody record. As indicated earlier I was now taking one of those risks, because the suspect could have vanished off the face of the earth. I actually saw this as a calculated risk having spent time getting to know the suspect.

All was going well until the custody officer asked to see me in his office. I visited his office where he asked me what had happened to my prisoner. I explained that he had gone walkabout for an hour to recover the stolen silver. The Sergeant said 'fine, but who with and why is there no record on his custody sheet?' The Sergeant was most unhappy when I explained that the prisoner had left unaccompanied. I apologised profusely and assured the Sergeant that the prisoner would be back in custody within the hour.

One o'clock arrived but there was no sign of my prisoner. I decided to wait for him at the station door, in fact I clearly recall peering out of the door, looking up and down the street. Just to increase the pressure, the Custody Sergeant joined me at the station door. At 1.15pm I was very relieved to see my man running towards us carrying a large bag of silver. I bundled him through the station door and explained that I was delighted to see him again. The Custody Sergeant said that he needed to speak to me at length later in the day.

I'm pleased to say that my risk paid off and all of the beloved silver was recovered intact. On the other side of the coin I feel that my career had suffered a few dents that day. My man went on to admit the house burglary fully, and was later sent to prison for the offence. Incidentally we had recovered the correct drill and bits.

The Custody Sergeant spent some time explaining the errors of my ways and kept a very close eye on me when he was on duty. This method of recovering stolen goods amounted to a 'one-off' for me and was not to be repeated, despite dealing with many more burglars in my career.

I spent two years working at Wellingborough and thoroughly enjoyed myself. I dealt with a lot of interesting crime and also a lot of criminals. Another DC in the office, also called Pete, actually loved doing the paperwork, so much so that he suggested that I should lock them up and he would do the paperwork. I actually took him up on his idea and together we turned over an awful lot of detected crime. This of course suited the management who simply loved high detected crime figures.

❀ ❀

Alconbury Air Base

At Christmas time, the CID were invited to visit our American friends at Alconbury Air Base, situated near Huntingdon in Cambridgeshire. The DI arranged for a minibus and driver to take us to the base, where we would be shown into the officers' bar. Alcoholic drinks were free of charge at the officers' bar and a wonderful buffet style tea had been prepared for us, on a large round table. The main objective was to relax together with some of the airman and have an enjoyable evening together. Occasionally, CID officers would attend from Cambridgeshire and Bedfordshire also. It was a great way of liaising with old friends, who we had met on joint operations.

The food was always exceptionally good with the occasional surprise thrown in. On one occasion I remember eating these wonderful crunchy meat balls, only to be told later that they were in fact grilled sheep's eyes. I know what you're thinking, but I was just fine actually, I'd already had six 'Southern Comforts with Seven-Up' and couldn't care less. I seem to recall good country music in the background and very good company. I would describe it as the icing on the cake, after a year's very hard work. I should add that the SOCOs came along also and it was a way of thanking them for their hard work.

I must confess that the base generally only invited two CID officers to the tea party, but at that time of year our memories were poor. The numbers who went along would on occasions swell to as many as twelve. I can honestly say that our American friends never once complained about the discrepancies with numbers. I must confess that when home time arrived, the only sober person on the bus was the driver. I've got a very vague recollection that Christmas Carols were occasionally sung on the way back to Northamptonshire.

Just after Christmas 1978, the management decided that I should resume working with the CID at Rushden. I was a little disappointed because I had settled in nicely at Wellingborough. The good news however was that I could now walk to work and might be able to shed a few pounds in weight. You may recall my jacket, you know the one which I liked to take off in pubs, well, it was getting a little tight around my waist.

No sooner had I returned I was on late duty when officers called '10/9' from The Chinese restaurant situated in High Street, Rushden. In those days '10/9' meant they needed urgent back up and all available staff must attend. I drove at great speed to the restaurant and screeched to a stop at the front door. I opened the door and was shocked to see two injured police officers lying on the floor of the restaurant. One was a Sergeant and the other a young Constable called Mark. They had both clearly been knocked about and seemed a bit disorientated.

I then saw a middle aged male lying on his back with a meat cleaver stuck in his forehead. I recognised the man from a family who lived in Newton Road, Rushden. Before I could give any assistance to anyone, I saw the son of the man described running towards me with a chair raised aloft in his hands. He came straight up to me and went to hit me on the head with the chair. I grabbed hold of the chair with my left hand and punched him as hard as I could in the face. He went sprawling to the floor but jumped up and made towards me again. As he rose from the floor I kicked him in the face with my right foot. The kick left him in a semi-conscious state on the floor.

I then established that this was the man who had attacked the other two police officers. It was then that I noticed that this assailant had what I would describe as a badly burnt face. It transpired that he had gone into the kitchen of the restaurant and had knocked a wok of boiling oil over the chef's arm. The chef, Mr Wong, suffered first degree burns as a result of the assault. Acting in self-defence, the chef managed to throw a second wok of boiling oil in the face of the attacker.

Fortunately or otherwise the police officers arrived quickly and they then suffered injuries also. I'm pleased to say that their injuries were more minor consisting of minor cuts and bruises.

The restaurant had sustained considerable damage during the affray, with broken furnishings and a lot of broken glass. The whole thing revolved around wedding celebrations, in that a 'hen night' had concluded at the restaurant. Amazingly the 'stag party' for the same wedding had ended their evening's drinking, by chance at the same restaurant.

As things quietened down, I found that a waiter, also by the name of Mr Wong, had sustained a deep cut to his head. He had been assaulted with the chair when struck by the man with the burnt face. Two ambulances attended and assisted with all of the injured persons. I arrested the young man who had attacked me with the chair, after confirming his facial burns were superficial. He was taken to Wellingborough Police Station and detained overnight.

His father received eleven stitches to his head wound and after being discharged was arrested for affray. The chef went to Kettering General Hospital for initial treatment but then to a burns unit for skin grafts. The waiter also went to hospital where his head wound was stitched, followed by his arrest on suspicion of affray. It was decided that witness statements would be taken with a view to offenders being interviewed the next morning.

I arranged for all the necessary SOCO work to be carried out at the scene and eventually went home to bed at about 5am. Later that day I carried out interviews of all the suspects including the chef at the burns unit. It was decided that all four participants should be charged with affray and that a jury could decide where the truth lie. I never managed to establish who buried the meat cleaver in the head of the middle aged man.

However, I did manage to show that the father and son 'stags' had been the main players in the affray and that the Chinese had merely been trying to run their business in peace.

The father and son from Newton Road, Rushden were found guilty of affray at Northampton Crown Court and the Chinese workers were found not guilty. The son was sent to prison and his father was kept out of prison by the skin of his teeth.

At the conclusion of the trial I was called back into court by the trial Judge. I must admit that I thought he was about to commend me for good police work, but how wrong one could be. He said 'thanks for putting a good case together officer, but, in future do not appear to be enjoying yourself when you tell my jury that it was necessary to kick an offender in the face'. I of course apologised to His Honour and left court with my tail between my legs.

I'm pleased to be able to report that the chef made a good recovery after two operations and was soon back working in the restaurant.

❀ ❀

More money

On a more important note, a report by Sir Edmund Davis was about to be made public, in relation to police pay and conditions. This had been a long time in the making and most police officers were waiting with baited breath to hear the details of the report. Then it was published, and we were all over the moon with regard to the changes that were to be introduced.

Our basic pay was more or less doubled over night and payment for overtime had also been agreed. This news was just amazing because we had been on very poor pay from the day I joined and now we would reap the benefits. Effectively my money worries were over and holidays would now be enjoyed in the certain knowledge that you could afford them. In CID in particular you had been doing double shifts without any financial reward. Let me tell you, that after working a dedicated sixteen hours without any extra pay, your dedication was sorely tested.

❀ ❀

A trip to Hawick

Trips out were always highly sought after when you were in the CID. I had dealt with a case of criminal deception where a man came down from Scotland and acquired £400 worth of shoes with a stolen cheque. That was a considerable amount of money to a small shoe maker in Rushden and I had been determined as ever to nick him. I had sent one of those old fashioned telex messages to Hawick in Scotland in an effort to trace the suspect. About three months later on a Friday evening I had a phone call from Scotland to tell me the suspect had been traced and arrested. I thanked the caller and arranged to collect the prisoner from Hawick the following day.

Generally speaking, we would fly up to Scotland to collect a prisoner but due to unforeseen problems it was decided to go by car. At the time a young lad called Simon Lilley was doing his month's attachment to the CID and was chosen to join me on the trip. On the Saturday morning we collected a nice Ford Cortina from headquarters and were soon on our way. Simon was a little surprised when twenty miles into the trip, the car driven by me, veered into a pub car park. Yes, you've guessed it, it was time for a good lunch before making the long drive north.

Simon soon got into the swing of things when we were presented with a very fine roast dinner. That was followed by apple pie and, of course, custard. Both courses were then washed down with a pint of very weak shandy. I was introducing Simon to the world of CID expenses. Because of the fact that we would be out of the county for more than twelve hours, we were entitled to a very good lunch indeed. In earlier conversation with Simon he had indicated that he might be inclined towards working in the traffic department. On completing our lunch, Simon said that he had enjoyed it so much, that he may now be moving towards working in the CID.

I loved his sense of humour and could tell we were going to have a great trip north. It was actually a lovely day and I recall that we shared the driving, arriving at Hawick at about five in the evening. The Scottish police officers were very accommodating and after introducing us to the prisoner, pointed us towards the local pub, for our tea. I remember Simon and I had a rather nice salad, followed probably by another weak shandy. To complete our R and R, we also had a game of pool, which was very enjoyable.

Simon and I then collected our prisoner together with some evidence of the crime, which amounted to a pair of worn shoes.

Simon placed handcuffs on the fugitive, who was then placed in the back seat of our car. The prisoner seemed very apologetic about the offence of deception and said that he would certainly be pleading guilty at the Sheriff's Court. I explained that we only had Magistrates south of the border and that he could plead guilty to them. Simon and I again shared the driving and arrived back at Wellingborough at about midnight. The prisoner was booked in at the police station after which Simon and I booked off duty.

The following day, I interviewed the suspect under caution and charged him with the offence. The duty Sergeant decided that the offender would remain in custody to appear at Wellingborough Magistrates' Court on Monday morning. As I returned the prisoner to his cell he mentioned in conversation that he normally played pool on Sunday lunchtimes. I must confess that I had warmed to this prisoner and decided that a game of pool might be on the agenda at lunchtime. This of course depended on one's work commitments, and of course, the security of the individual concerned.

Yes, you've guessed it, I was about to take another chance with one of my prisoners. I feel the need to point out that, CID officers had a duty to cultivate informants and this cultivation took many different forms. It was in fact quiet on that Sunday and I decided that with the assistance of a loyal colleague I would take my prisoner to *The Viking* pub at Rushden for a game of pool. The prisoner complied with all my rules that lunchtime and our trip out went off very smoothly indeed. He was of course booked out of the cell block, but for further enquiries relating to the crime.

The prisoner appeared before the Magistrates on the Monday morning and duly pleaded guilty. He was fined for the offence and ordered to pay compensation to the victim. Later that day my control room received a call from a Scotsman who said he was thumbing his way north and wished them to thank me for my courtesy whilst dealing with him. What more gratitude could a detective ask for?

Shoplifting of course was a common occurrence in most towns, but one young offender by the name of John was particularly good at it. He kept an order book where he noted down items needed by other local criminals. He would then steal the items listed when the opportunity presented itself. He was very organised indeed and would write down details like shoe sizes, waist measurement, and neck size. In his eyes he was running a legitimate business because everything was stolen to order and there would be no waste.

He was actually very good at what he did, but I don't want to give the impression that I was impressed by his work. An example of his dexterity was when a lorry stopped in High Street, Rushden, to deliver electrical goods to Curry's. The driver brought several white goods to the back of the lorry, and started taking them one at a time into the store. John suddenly appeared from nowhere wearing a similar full length white coat to that of the delivery man. John had an identical sack barrow with him, which he then used to load his orders and walk off with the goods.

Using that method, he had successfully acquired fridges, freezers and televisions until his arrest. The good news with John was that whenever arrested he would eventually clear his plate. This of course means that he would admit all of the offences that he had committed. He was in fact, quite proud of his achievements, in as much that no violence was ever used during the thefts. I recall dealing with John on many occasions and it's fair to say that he spent time in both Borstal and Young Offenders Institutions. I must say that I personally found him to be a lovable rogue.

I remember on one occasion telling him that enough was enough and that his crime spree in Rushden had to stop. Shortly after my remarks to him I went on holiday for a couple of weeks with my family. I had a lovely time by the way, and returned, as you do, on the Monday morning raring to go. At the CID morning briefing I was sorry to hear that John had been arrested whilst I was on holiday, on suspicion of stealing

£2,000 in cash. He had denied the offence and had been released by way of refused charge.

It transpired that a young man had been seen to enter a local office at the time of the theft. The young man had been smartly dressed and had confidently walked straight past all of the office staff, culminating in a brief case disappearing. The brief case had contained £2,000 in cash. I spoke to the detective who had interviewed John and he informed me that John had vehemently denied any involvement in the offence. He further stated that John was so upset by the accusations made against him, that he had been reduced to tears.

I gave the case some thought and decided that we should carry out another knock on young John's street door. After giving his door the traditional knock, his girlfriend answered, stating that John was still in his bed. My colleague and I entered his house and to put it plainly woke him from his deep sleep. John said 'hello Mick, I thought you were on your holidays', to which I replied that 'I was, but not any longer'. I asked John what he had done with the money. He said that he had spent most of it and that the remainder was in his Building Society account.

I told John that I was upset with him for continuing to commit crime in my town. He said 'hang on a minute, I thought it would be OK while you were on your holiday - you know - not your problem, sort of thing'. He then apologised to my colleague for doing his crying routine and apologies were of course accepted. I re-arrested John for the theft of the cash and took him into custody for a proper interview.

He fully admitted going into the office and stealing the brief case and cash contents. We recovered the remaining money from his Building Society Account. After his court hearing, young John also took a holiday, which he spent at the Young Offenders' Institution. I should point out that he had in fact committed a burglary, because he had entered the office as a trespasser, which is one of the ingredients needed for burglary.

❁ ❁

A word with Prince Charles

I was soon to meet a member of the royal family, namely Prince Charles who was visiting Barnwell Manor, situated near to Oundle. He was visiting other members of the royal family that day, and I had been briefed as part of a large police presence. I was detailed to form part of a guard on the Prince as he made his way along a path from the church back to Barnwell Manor. He actually stopped and spoke to me about my length of service. He also enquired as to which police station I was from and the nature of my work in plain clothes.

I found him very down to earth to speak to, and was delighted that he had taken the time to stop and speak to me. The only thing that surprised me was that the Prince was a little shorter than I had imagined him to be. When you see royalty on the television, you always gain the impression that they are taller, than in the flesh. Soon after the Prince spoke to me, he made his way back into the Manor House and it would be several years before I had the pleasure of a second meeting. I felt extremely honoured to have been a small part of Prince Charles day out at Barnwell.

❀ ❀

'Watch out Mick, there's been some trouble'

Moving on to a less tranquil setting, it's a typical evening on Rushden High Street and I'm doing the rounds at our local pubs. Very few people would understand the need for CID officers to visit pubs and mix with the locals. Of course there are several reasons for such visits and it might be said that thirst was one of them. All jokes aside, we visited to establish which of our local criminals were using which premises. Also, to make ourselves known to the people of the town, whether they are law abiding or not. I suppose you could say that we were meeting them on their own ground and when possible, as equals.

It was important to communicate with the licensee and his or her staff also. Occasionally we would see persons who were currently wanted by police and could arrange for our uniformed colleagues to visit with a view to arrests. In more serious circumstances we of course had the option of making these arrests ourselves. We would occasionally play pool, darts, skittles and cards depending on the type of premises being frequented. This was of course, good old fashioned policing, which my generation referred to as building one's local knowledge. It didn't always work and on occasions things became more complicated than one might have planned.

It was a Saturday night and I was working alone doing the High Street pub rounds. At about 10.30pm I reached *The Railway* pub which in those days, referring to the late 1980s, was a pretty rough pub. As I entered the bar I found it to be absolutely packed and what I would describe as buzzing. All the regular faces were in and of course all seemed to be in high spirits. One guy who always stood at the bar near to the door said 'watch out Mick, there's been some trouble'. Before he could expand on his remark I found myself being grabbed by several of the locals, who then started pushing me towards the front door of the pub. Before I knew it, they had opened the door and pushed me out into the porch way at the front of the pub.

I grabbed the door handle to re-enter but found the door firmly shut behind me. I then heard this awfully loud screaming voice coming towards me from the High Street. As I looked in that direction, I saw a man running towards me with a Samurai sword raised up above his head. The man was gripping the handle of the sword with both hands and screaming loudly. I instinctively backed up against the pub door, basically because there was nowhere else to go. The man ran straight up to me with the Samurai sword still raised aloft. He had a blooded face and was clearly very angry indeed. I recognised him from another occasion and told him to put the sword down. After a short 'Mexican stand-off', he seemed to remember me, and slowly lowered his sword, presenting it to me by the handle.

223

I can tell you that I was very relieved, some would say in more ways than one. He seemed to calm down very quickly, probably in the knowledge that he had come so close to cutting the local detective officer in two. He was bleeding quite heavily from his nose and both lips appeared to be lacerated. He said he had been beaten up by a gang in *The Railway* pub and intended to retaliate. In the heat of the moment I advised him to go home and seek medical attention. He had the cheek to ask for his sword back, which of course wasn't going to happen. I then made it plain for him to understand, either go home or I'll take you to the station. I'm pleased to say he chose the former option and 'buggered off'.

I then arranged for colleagues to secure the sword at the police station and went back into the pub for a quick half of beer. Suffice to say that no one had any knowledge of any incident occurring in the pub prior to my arrival that evening. Remarkably, that included the pub landlord and the guy who said there had been trouble earlier in the pub. The old saying 'some you win, and some you lose' springs to mind. In any event, I know that my presence that evening probably prevented an awful lot of carnage.

I visited the Samurai swordsman the next morning at his home to see whether he wished to name his attackers. He told me that he would not be able to recognise them and did not wish to make a complaint. He apologised for his own behaviour and said that at no time had he intended any harm to police. It transpired that he remembered me from my dealings on the High Street, with the elderly man and his dog. He was one of the two youths who had invited me behind the shops, several years earlier. It transpired that no one else had been involved in the sword incident. Because the young man had complied with my instructions on the night, I decided to caution him for his behaviour.

The Samurai sword was later disposed of under The Police Property Act. To my knowledge the young man concerned appreciated the fact that I had cautioned him and didn't resort to arming himself with a weapon again. In hindsight I believe that in all the circumstances that night, I was very lucky not to have been seriously injured.

❀ ❀

Footprint in the snow

This next case formed one part of what became my two pet hates in police work. This was a case of robbery, my other pet hate being house burglary. Robbery on the one hand involved using violence on the victim or the threat of violence. House burglary will always be devastating because the victims have often worked hard and long for the property which is stolen. Added to that, the goods stolen are often of sentimental value and never recovered. An Englishman's home is his castle and that's how it should remain.

I've digressed a little from the actual robbery. It was about 7pm on a winter's evening at Queensway, Higham Ferrers, when a local insurance man was out on his rounds. He was carrying his briefcase which contained quite a large sum of cash. It had been snowing, and about two inches of snow lay on the pavement. Suddenly two men grabbed the insurance agent from behind and knocked him to the ground. Whilst doing so, one of the men grabbed the brief case and they both made off to a waiting vehicle parked nearby. As the car sped off the victim noted the make and part of the registration number.

The victim had sustained minor cuts and bruising to his hands and arms. He had been left quite shocked by the suddenness of the attack. Assisted by local residents, the brief car details were written down on a piece of paper. He managed to remember also limited descriptions of his attackers, and also that of the driver. On receipt of the complaint I was on scene very quickly and could see that one of the offenders had left a very good shoe impression in the snow. SOCO were quickly called out and managed to take both photographs and a plaster cast of the footprint.

Door to door enquiries proved fruitless, but with the assistance of a colleague, urgent work started in relation to the vehicle and the suspects. The vehicle was a small dark blue hatchback that we managed to trace assisted by the part registration number. It had been sold at a garage on the A1 road in Cambridgeshire to a man from St Neots. We linked in with our CID colleagues at Huntingdon and after searching through a mountain of cards came up with three potential suspects.

All three fitted the limited descriptions given by our victim. Observations were carried out at their addresses culminating in the suspect car being found in a lock up garage. Assisted by officers from Huntingdon CID we visited two addresses at St Neots and arrested all three suspects. At one of the addresses we also recovered a pair of shoes which matched the shoe pattern found in the snow. The vehicle was recovered to Wellingborough Police Station.

Two of the suspects were a little anti police and made their feelings known. We of course were fearless and would not be put off by their demeanour. On interview at Wellingborough Police Station one of the men admitted driving the car on the night of the robbery. However he maintained that he didn't realise that a robbery was going down that evening until it happened. He went on to admit that he carried on driving the car after the robbery, all the way back to St Neots. He chose not to name the other persons in the car. Having met the other two I wasn't in the least surprised that he didn't wish to shop them.

Our enquiries at the A1 garage indicated that one of two brothers had purchased the car. That person turned out to be one of the two brothers we had in custody. After a subsequent identification procedure, the remaining two suspects were identified as the offenders on the night concerned. All three were charged and remanded in custody. This meant they were likely to remain in custody until the date of their trial at Northampton Crown Court.

226

Several months later I attended Northampton Crown Court where after a fairly lengthy trial all three men were convicted of the robbery. The two brothers who carried out the actual attack received three years imprisonment and the driver received two years imprisonment. I should add that the discarded brief case was recovered near to the scene, but none of the cash was ever found. Old habits die hard and whenever the snow falls now, I think of that evening and that wonderful shoeprint in the snow.

All jokes to one side, I'm convinced that the jury's decision in this case was swung largely by the finding of the footprint in the snow. Nevertheless I appreciate that the car and the identification procedures were the main thrust of the case.

Another case of interest related to a burglary at Steel's chemist shop situated at Market Square, Higham Ferrers. I attended the scene when it was discovered by staff reporting for work one morning. Entry had been gained via a window to the rear and the DD (dangerous drugs) cabinet had been forced open. All of the dangerous drugs had been stolen, together with a number of cosmetic items. The cosmetics puzzled me because the 'druggies' normally went for the drugs only.

The normal scenes of crime work were carried out by the SOCO. No fingerprint marks were found and no foot marks of note could be found. Door to door enquiries failed to turn up any witnesses. The SOCO found good jemmy marks in the wooden window frame and kindly took good casts of the marks. Photos were also taken of the marks relative to their position at the rear of the premises. Partial vehicle tyre impressions were also found on the ground to the side of the premises.

I prepared a telex message informing colleagues throughout the county of the details of the burglary and also requested a press release in local papers. My favourite word comes into play again 'Bingo', the local milkman had been stopped by three people early that morning and they had purchased refreshments from him. He had read the item in the paper and had formed the view that the three individuals had looked like 'druggies'. He went on to say that he was only half a mile from the chemist shop when they pulled up in a noisy old car.

It was about 4.30am when they approached him and he said that there were two long haired scruffy men who looked like brothers, and a girl who was the spitting image of Suzy Quattro. Incidentally he was a fan of Suzy - what better witness could one ask for? I wrote down a detailed witness statement from the milkman and couldn't thank him enough.

On returning to the station I prepared a second telex message which I circulated to all surrounding police forces, with particular interest to drug squads. I gave full details of the case including detailed descriptions of the suspects. I of course placed particular emphasis on the Suzy Quattro look-a-like, because I was now also a fan. Within one hour of sending out the message I had a phone call from a Bedfordshire drug squad officer, who I had previously met at the Alconbury celebrations.

He said he was delighted to be able to identify Suzy for me as a local Luton 'druggie', who lived in a flat in Luton with her boyfriend. He went on to say that the boyfriend had a brother who often stopped at the same flat. He said that the Luton 'druggies' used what were referred to as 'pool' vehicles, which meant that the vehicle was shared by all the 'druggies' and basically could be found anywhere. It was agreed that the drugs squad officer would acquire a search warrant for the flat from a local Magistrate and that we would execute it together the following morning.

Being now full of deep joy, I retired to bed that evening setting my alarm clock for 4am. I was tempted to play myself to sleep with a Suzy Quattro number, but being married, thought better of it. Together with a colleague I arrived at Luton Police Station at 6am the following morning for a short briefing with drug squad officers. Together we executed the search warrant at the local flat and as luck would have it, all three suspects were tucked up in bed. All three were very drowsy and very compliant when arrested on suspicion of the chemist shop burglary. I'm pleased to say that a good search of the flat resulted in the recovery of most of the dangerous drugs that had been stolen from the chemist's shop. Most of the tablets were still contained in bottles which had *Steel's the Chemist* labels on them.

This was the euphoric moment that detectives strive for. I can't really explain the buzz that you get when all your hard work is rewarded with prisoners and the evidence. I'm actually getting a buzz right now as write up this story. The answer to the question on the tips of your tongue is a resounding 'yes', the young female offender looked just like the rock chic Suzy Quattro.

All three prisoners were interviewed and admitted that they had been the burglars. They also admitted that they had taken a refreshment break, compliments of the milkman. They were all brought back to Wellingborough where they were later charged and remanded in custody. All three were found to be reliant on the drugs and entered drug programmes whilst on remand. They all later pleaded guilty to the offence of Burglary and received custodial sentences of eighteen months. I'm pleased to say that our paths were not to cross again. These individuals are what I described earlier as travelling criminals, and it is these particular criminals which are normally the hardest to capture. I hope you found my Suzy Quattro story of interest and ask you to think again before buying your milk in the supermarket.

A true hero

A couple of years ago, I read with some dismay about emergency services who attended a potential drowning and under the new Health and Safety rules were unable to get into the water. The case hit the national news and I believe involved a fatality. This reminded me of a colleague of mine by the name of Mark, who had only been a Constable for a short period of time, when he would be tested by someone in the water. I seem to recall that it was a very cold November night when he received information that a lady had jumped into the fast flowing and freezing River Nene, at Nene Road, Higham

Ferrers. Visibility was extremely poor because of freezing fog, and the water temperature was near to zero. Add to these factors that the river was also in flood, and you begin to picture the scene. Fortunately for the lady concerned, there were no Health and Safety rules in place, to interfere with Mark's lifesaving principles. He realised that the lady would be carried some distance downstream, from the bridge where she had entered the river. He decided in an instant to approach the river a couple of bridges downstream. On arriving at his chosen bridge he decided to remain quiet, in the hope that he would here the lady struggling in the water.

Amazingly he then heard her screams and saw her being carried at speed along the centre of the river. Mark quickly removed his outer uniform and dived straight into the freezing water, to swim out to the lady concerned. He managed to grab hold of the lady, who was in fact of quite large build. He positioned her in the life saving mode and then towed her, a considerable distance to a bend in the river. It was at that bend that he managed to grab the river bank and hold the lady's head above the water. As you can well imagine he was now frozen and completely exhausted, but miraculously had saved a life.

Help was soon at hand from other police officers and the good old general public. The officer and the lady were hauled from the river and were both given first aid, before going to hospital by ambulance. The lady had been suffering with depression and had attempted to commit suicide. She subsequently made a full recovery, which in the freezing circumstances was probably assisted by her large stature. Mark on the other hand contracted pneumonia and sustained damage to his lungs.

Here was a fine example of a police officer going over and beyond his duty to save life. His actions that night were just remarkable and there can be no doubt at all that he saved the lady's life. Mark was very proud of that achievement and went on in typical Mark fashion to make a good recovery. However I heard that in the longer term his damaged lungs continued to present him with occasional breathing problems. I for one feel that this was a real shame, because prior to the incident he had been a picture of good health.

I was delighted to learn that Mark later received The Queen's Commendation for Brave Conduct for his actions that day. He was in fact one of the two police officers who had earlier been knocked to the floor in the Chinese restaurant incident. He certainly had a habit of being at the right place and at the wrong time. Good old Mark. I saw very little of Mark during my career, but recall that he moved to the other side of the county, where he continued his successful police work on the rural area.

Guns would occasionally rear their ugly heads whilst working as police officers. It was a lovely sunny summer's day as I recall, when a young police woman called up on the air for assistance. An incident had occurred at Hillary Road, Rushden, involving a firearm and the officer needed help quickly. I was close by at the time and arrived at the address within minutes.

The street door lay open and I found a very distraught middle aged lady in the lounge of the house. She was crying and said that her son was in the loft. She had heard gunshot coming from the loft and said a police women had gone into the loft to investigate.

I climbed the loft ladder and on entering the loft I was relieved to see that the police woman was safe. A young man who I immediately recognised was thrashing around violently on the loft floor. I could see that he had been shot in the left upper side of his chest and realised that he was thrashing around in shock. I could see a double barrelled twelve bore shotgun lying next to him. It was fairly obvious that the shotgun had been used to cause the wound.

I grabbed hold of the young man and steadied him, in an attempt to prevent further blood loss from his wound. As I did so, he stopped thrashing about, and I realised that he had in fact died in front of our eyes. I attempted mouth to mouth and cardiac massage, but couldn't revive him. My colleague climbed back down the loft ladder to speak to the middle aged lady, who was in fact the young man's mother.

I spoke to my control room who confirmed that an ambulance was on route to me. I then made the shotgun safe and moved it away from the loft hatch. A length of string had been tied to the trigger of the gun. The other end of the string had been tied to the loft ladder safety rail. The young man had apparently committed suicide by means of pointing the barrel of the gun directly at his chest. He had then discharged the gun by applying pressure to the string with his foot.

The ambulance crew arrived and confirmed life extinct. This was a very sad case because the young man had become depressed after being made redundant from his job in the printing industry. He had been trying to find alternative employment, but had been unsuccessful. I had met him on a number of occasions on Rushden Town Centre and always found him to be both pleasant and polite. His Mother was obviously very shocked and saddened by her son's demise. This young man was clearly very disturbed at the time, to be able to carry out such an act, in the knowledge that his mother was in the house at the time.

I organised a visit to the scene by the duty Detective Sergeant and also the SOCO. All the appropriate evidence was gathered together to be laid before the coroner in due course. I should add that the police woman and I later consoled each other with regard to the traumatic nature of the incident. These types of meetings are generally referred to as a debriefing. It took a little while for both of us to come to terms with the fact that this young man died in our presence. In hindsight I feel that the police woman, who was very young in service at the time, acted very bravely when entering the loft, knowing that a gun had been fired. On the other hand, some might say that this was merely another day at the office.

A post mortem later showed that the shot from the shotgun had in fact missed all of the victim's vital organs and that he had died from shock.

❀ ❀

The family at Irthlingborough

They were now at it again, and they were driving the rural officer insane with their constant petty crimes. This time they had stolen two geese from an allotment, leaving their owners very upset, because one of the pair had been sitting on eggs. The eggs of course had also gone missing from the pen. The rural officer was very pleased when I offered to help him lock up the offenders.

The rural officer enquired as to what police vehicle we should take with us. I said we should take the van and lock the whole family up. The rural officer thought I was joking but I told him 'in for a penny in for a pound'. On arrival at the house, the knock on the street door was answered by the father, who said 'how can I help you Mick?' I explained that I wanted the geese that he had stolen. He explained that I was too late because they had disposed of them.

The father went on to say that his son had actually stolen them together with the eggs. His son was in the house, so I arrested him for the theft. I then asked the rural officer to escort the prisoner to the police van. I then asked who had slaughtered the birds, to which the father replied 'I did'. I then arrested the father for assisting in the realisation of stolen goods. I then asked the rural officer to place the father in the police van. It was at that point that the gentleman's wife stepped forward and said that I should lock her up also, because she had cooked the geese. I then told her that she was under arrest on suspicion of assisting in the disposal of the stolen goods. The rural officer was now ahead of the game and said that he would place her in the police van.

To my amazement the eldest daughter then stepped forward and said 'what about me? I knew they were stolen and I ate some for my dinner'. I then arrested her for disposing of stolen goods. All four were of course cautioned on arrest, all indicating that they understood the procedure. I then did the honours and placed the last of the prisoners in the van, which incidentally was now full.

On the way to the police station the father namely Derek said 'why have you nicked all of us Mick, is it because you're fed up with us taking the piss?' I said 'to put it in a nutshell, yes I am fed up with you and your family taking the piss'. All the prisoners were interviewed and reported by way of summons. The matter was dealt with satisfactorily by the local Magistrates and the victim was very pleased with the police action that had been taken.

After that case, the problem family seemed to settle down and their petty offending stopped. Whenever I saw members of the family out and about they would always remind me of the day that they cooked their goose. Ha, Ha.

Some people might be of the view that these arrests were a bit over the top. I would of course disagree, and point out that there are several ways of skinning a cat. Like any other profession you are given a bag of tools and on occasions it is necessary to use them all. Quite often, rural policing involved making a point, and to make that point, you would use the powers made available to you. Failure to use those powers would often culminate in greater problems down the line. My general policy was to nip it in the bud before it blossomed.

Fat Charlie

In the late 1970s, I started to find time to go fishing with the Northamptonshire Police Angling Club. The club was run by a couple of police officers from Northampton, and consisted of trips out to fresh water venues both in and outside the county. It was great fun and the membership consisted of a great bunch of lads, several being civilian staff and friends. If a member had children who were keen on fishing, they could come along and fish also. We usually managed to muster between eight and ten anglers per trip and regularly hired a van for comfortable transportation.

I'm sorry to admit that I never managed to catch many fish on the trips, despite all my training as a young boy. My eldest son Steven, started coming with us on the odd trip and thoroughly enjoyed himself. He was about nine years of age then and developed into a good little angler. One of the anglers was rather stout to say the least and became known as 'Fat Charlie'. After a great day out in the fresh air, what else could anglers want? Yes you've guessed it, fish and chips.

I'm firmly of the view that the trip organisers had their priorities right, in as much that the fish shop location came first and the fishing venue second. These decisions came after many years of experience on the part of the organisers. I have a fond memory of my son Steven after one such trip out. We had enjoyed the fishing that day and had also enjoyed our fish and chips with the lads in the hire van. Steven and I were now driving home in our own car, when he suddenly burst out in uncontrollable laughter. Once he had recovered I enquired as to what had tickled his fancy.

Steven then explained that he had learnt that day why we called Charlie 'Fat Charlie'. Steven went on to say that 'Fat Charlie' was in front of him, in the chip shop queue and had ordered two pieces of fish and a double portion of chips. Steven said he was then shocked when 'Fat Charlie' ate the whole lot in record time. He said it wasn't just the way he woofed it down, but the fact that his face was covered in chip fat when he finished.

❀ ❀

The body in the lake

Before I knew it, reports of another murder were coming from Northampton and all available CID officers were ordered to visit Campbell Square Police Station. A local college lecturer had been found stabbed to death in his car which had been driven into Abington Park Lake, at Abington, Northampton. An incident room was set up and a briefing would take place when all the officers had arrived.

At the briefing we were told that the victim had connections with the 'gay' community in Northampton and enquiries were already well underway in that regard. The vehicle had been found half submerged in the lake with the deceased owner in it. The victim had sustained a deep stab wound to his chest and a cut throat. It was thought that he had died very quickly after the attack. Early indications were that the offender or offenders had then driven the vehicle into the lake with the intention of sinking it below the water line.

With safety in mind, the vehicle and the body were removed from the lake. Thorough examinations of both were then carried out by the relative experts. A colleague and I were then given door to door enquiries in the area of the park. The enquiry with the 'gay' community coupled with good intelligence work soon produced two potential suspects. They were both young males who were known to be part of what was loosely described as the 'rent boy scene' in Northampton.

For the uninitiated 'rent boys' were involved in sexual activity with men and would receive a payment for their illegal services. Quite often, the meetings between men and boys would take place at public toilets, which would be referred to as 'cottages'. I should point out that not all boys forming part of the 'rent boy scene' were necessarily active or for that matter experienced in any form of sex.

The two suspects were soon under arrest and being interviewed about this awful murder. It turned out that one of them was called John, who was the same young man that I had brought back from Piccadilly underground station several years before, in relation to the murder of the fourteen year old boy at Northampton. The interviews of the two suspects were very productive and specific details emerged about the events leading to the death of the college lecturer. The victim had transported the two young men to an industrial estate in Northampton, where he intended to enjoy sex with them.

236

Sexual activity took place in the car involving all three individuals. With John and the other youth in the back seat and the lecturer in the front, the time had arrived for payment to be made. The lecturer didn't have enough money on him to pay the going rate. This angered the two young men in the back of the car who then jointly decided to punish him. One of the two young men then pulled out a long bladed knife, which he then used to stab the victim deeply in the chest. With the realisation that the victim was still breathing, they finished him off by cutting his throat wide open. They then took any valuables on offer and drove the car to Abington Park, in Northampton. The car was then driven along a path to the lakeside where they then pushed it into the lake.

These were clearly two very vicious young thugs who had no respect for life. Their joint actions showed the necessary intent needed for a successful murder charge, and they were duly charged with murder. They apparently showed no remorse for their victim. I'm afraid to say that this was another example of a man denied the privilege of long life. Both of the offenders later received life sentences for murder at the Crown Court.

However, the story didn't end there, because I was reading telex messages several years later, and read that John had taken his own life at Blundeston Prison. It would be wrong of me to comment further having met John's parents some years earlier. I wish to show them the utmost respect because I found them to be lovely, law abiding people, who obviously loved their son, despite what had happened. Again I have chosen not to name either offenders or victims out of a real respect for their relatives, who will have lived with this nightmare for many years.

One of what I called my 'sanity breaks' was now due, and I'd gone off fishing for the day to Thrapston Lakes, which were old gravel quarries near to Thrapston. As I drove home along a road called The Hedges, which was situated close to my home, I saw one of my neighbours flagging me to stop. She looked shocked and said 'come quickly, your son's been injured'. I parked up and followed her into her house where I found my son Steven laid out on her settee. He was only nine years old and had sustained serious burns to his buttocks and thigh.

He was in a lot of pain, and I reassured him best I could, that all would be 'OK'. The lady had undone his jeans at the waist in an attempt to ease the pain. She had then removed the jeans because she could see smoke billowing from his calf area. The burnt out remains of an incendiary device fell to the floor as she removed the jeans. I could see that Steven had sustained a large and deep burn to his calf, with a very large piece of skin hanging down from the burnt area. My neighbour said that she had called for an ambulance and that they were on their way.

Before the ambulance crew arrived, I asked Steven what had happened. He said he was cycling down The Hedges when a local boy was seen to throw something at him. The item thrown had lodged itself in the waistband of Steven's trousers.

Steven said that he could feel instant heat to his buttocks and then to the back of his thigh. He said whatever the object was, it was making its way downwards inside his trousers. To prevent his jeans getting caught in the cycle's chain, Steven had tucked his jean bottoms into his socks. The object, which seemed to Steven to be on fire, carried on downwards .It lodged itself on the back of his calf. It was effectively trapped in the leg of his jeans.

As you can imagine, I was rather shocked to find my son so badly injured and suffering a lot of pain. The ambulance arrived and the crew put sterile bandages on Steven's burns. They also gave him something to relieve the pain. He was then taken to Kettering General Hospital where he was given initial treatment for the burns. The doctor who examined Steven said he had first degree burns and transferred him to Stoke Mandeville Hospital, in Buckinghamshire.

Steven needed urgent surgery, and had a two hour operation which involved skin grafts to his calf. The skin for the grafts was taken from the back of his thighs. My whole family were shocked to see the state that Steven was in. However he was in the best place in the whole world for the treatment and remained at the hospital for a total of five weeks.

In the interim, the assault was dealt with by a police officer from Wellingborough, resulting in a local youth being charged with grievous bodily harm. The incendiary device was recovered and sent to the Forensic Science Laboratory for a proper analysis. It turned out to be a flare from a flare gun, which when ignited reached extremely high temperatures. The youth responsible pleaded guilty at court, accepting that he had been very reckless when throwing the ignited device at Stephen. He was lucky not to be sent to prison, but subsequently apologised profusely to Steven and his family.

After a long period of physiotherapy, Steve was on the mend and before we knew it, back out on his bike. The incident had clearly scarred him for life, but he just got on with it. Whilst at the hospital, Steven also met patients from other parts of the world, including a little boy from Iraq who was paralysed by an unknown virus. There was also a five year old American girl whose hand had been crushed in a train door. The three children become good friends and as such helped one another through their varying ordeals.

Back at the police station it was my turn to work with a young CID aide called Gary. Whilst we were talking, I happened to mention street craft to him, which produced one of those puzzled looks on his face. I asked Gary why he had given me a puzzled look. He said he hadn't got a clue what street craft was and perhaps I could show him. Some would say that Mick had just put his foot in it, but I said we can do this right now.

For the uninformed, street craft is all about observing what is going on around you in any given situation. In other words who is doing what, when, where, how and why. I went on to explain these observations to Gary, before we left the station for a walk down the High Street. On route to the High Street, I asked Gary to walk down one side of the road, whilst I would walk down the other. I explained to him that we would both be looking for anything out of the ordinary and would notify each other, in the event of a sighting of interest.

It was now about 4pm, and all the normal High Street players were milling about. As I walked down my side of the High Street, I observed a man beckoning to another man, on the other side of the street. I read these situations in a body language way, in other words, I ask the question, 'are these two men acting suspiciously?' I decided that they were suspicious and instructed Gary to follow the suspect on his side of the road. I in turn followed mine and all four of us continued walking to the far end of the High Street.

Gary and I obviously kept well back from the suspects and also kept our communications to a minimum. At the far end of the High Street, Gary's suspect walked into High Street South, at which point we lost sight of each other. This was becaue my suspect turned left into Newton Road and continued walking to a car park in Rectory Road. Unbeknown to me, Gary then followed his suspect into a car accessory shop where he stole a car battery. He had placed the battery inside his coat prior to leaving the shop. Obviously no payment had been made for the goods. Gary responded very well indeed, when he decided to continue following his suspect.

A few minutes had elapsed, and my suspect had made his way to the rear of a blue Ford Escort Saloon car, which was parked in the car park. I kept well out of the way and was pleased to see Gary's suspect now walking down Rectory Road, towards the car park. Of course he now had what I would describe as a laboured walk and I was left wondering why. 'Bingo' - the two men met at the back of the car and 'the Street crafters' were moving in. Gary mouthed the words 'car battery', at which point the two suspects opened the boot of the car.

Gary and I grabbed hold of the two men as they placed the car battery in the boot. As we arrested them both on suspicion of theft, we were thrilled to see that the boot was completely full of stolen goods. The two men had travelled from Corby, the well-known steel town, and had been shoplifting all day in Kettering, Wellingborough and Rushden. I arranged for my

240

uniformed colleagues to take the prisoners to the station, leaving Gary and me to recover the vehicle and contents.

We later listed the stolen goods, which consisted of toasters, kettles, food mixers, a microwave oven and a large array of car accessories, together valued at £900. This was quite a good haul of stolen goods for the late 1970s. Both men co-operated fully on interview and fully admitted the offences revealed. They were known to the police at Corby for other previous shoplifting offences. Both men received suspended prison sentences for our offences.

It was a great result for me, because I had shown Gary the perfect example of 'street craft'. Gary and I were quite chuffed with the way the afternoon had panned out. Of course with every up there is a down, we should have finished at 5pm, but didn't book off until 11pm. The good news was that I had a very understanding wife and Gary was a single man. Did you notice me using my 'Bingo' word again, I bet you did.

A shooting

Back to more serious matters. We'd had a busy late shift, and were enjoying one or two beers in *The Railway* pub. I was with my new DS and another DC when the barman called me to the phone. It was my control room saying there had been a shooting at Highfield Road, Rushden and CID needed to go straight to the scene. I'd already worked ten hours and I was not a happy bunny on receipt of this news. The three of us went straight to the address where we found the ambulance already on site. A local man in his early twenties had been shot at his home in both legs.

I recognised the victim as a lad named John, who I had dealt with previously for criminal damage. He was very much part of the local drink and drugs scene. He was lying on his front on a settee in the lounge of his house and was clearly in a lot of pain. As the ambulance crew attended to him I could see that both calves had been shot at close range. His trousers had been removed and both leg calves were more or less missing from his legs.

Frankly it was a horrendous sight to see with the calves missing and no other apparent damage to his legs. I briefly spoke to John who said it had been an accident, but that was quickly disputed by other people present. John was given first aid by the ambulance crew and then rushed to Kettering General Hospital, for emergency surgery. My colleagues and I then established the facts from a witness at the scene. John had been arguing with two other well-known Rushden men, which revolved around an unpaid debt.

One of the men then produced a sawn off shot gun, which was used to threaten John. John had been drinking and in his typical way sneered at them, saying 'you haven't got the bottle to shoot me'. The second of the two men, by the name of David, then instructed the other to shoot John. He in turn told David to do his own dirty work and handed David the gun. David moved to the rear of John and discharged the shotgun into John's lower legs, causing the damage earlier described.

Both assailants were soon arrested on suspicion of wounding, and the shotgun was recovered. One of them seemed genuinely upset about the injuries sustained by John, this being the one who had declined to fire the weapon. He fully admitted his part in the incident and fully expected a lengthy prison sentence for his part in it. David on the other hand was basically a hard man and didn't bat an eyelid about what he had done to John.

He more or less said that John shouldn't have pushed his luck. He also admitted to the illegal ownership of the sawn off shotgun, being a person disqualified by previous convictions, for having such a weapon.

All the normal scenes of crime work were carried out by the SOCO, including photographs and fingerprint work. Detailed witness statements were taken from the victim and other relative witnesses. The shotgun was properly exhibited and forwarded to the Birmingham Forensic Science Laboratory for analysis. Lead shot from the wounds was also sent to the laboratory for comparison with shotgun cartridges recovered from David's house.

On conclusion of all the preparatory work, a Crown Court file was prepared and submitted for the attention of the Crown Prosecution Services. The case came before Northampton Crown Court where both men pleaded guilty to the offences. David being the main perpetrator received five years imprisonment and the lesser offender received one year imprisonment. After release from prison the lesser offender reverted to being a law abiding individual. This type of offence wasn't really his cup of tea and in hindsight I feel that he was lead somewhat by David.

John had a couple of operations including plastic surgery and was soon back on the streets, aided by crutches. The surgeons did a good job on him and managed to save both legs, despite the serious nature of his injuries. Having dealt with this case, I would say that it was a very unusual incident, to have happened in a town like Rushden.

Rushden Golf Club was a regular target for burglary, mainly because of its isolated nature. One such burglary stands out very clearly in my memory banks. It occurred in the small hours, when two intruders forced entry to the rear of the premises. They then forced all of the cash containing items, which consisted of the one arm bandits, a payphone and the pool table. They then moved onto a floor safe which was set in concrete. They struggled for a couple of hours but then realised that they needed more manpower.

Within half an hour, they had summoned four more burglars who joined them at the scene. Together they dug a huge hole in the concrete but still failed to lever the safe from its fixings. Three more men were contacted making a total of nine burglars at one crime scene. With good team work they eventually managed to remove the floor safe and took it away with them.

They all then returned to Huntingdon, where they used a disc cutter to open the safe. The teamwork had not paid off on this occasion, because the safe was in fact empty. I would just love to have been a fly on the wall when that safe was finally opened. I bet that the air was very blue indeed.

Huntingdon was just over our border in Cambridgeshire and detectives based there soon had information about this gang of burglars. All nine suspects were arrested and quite a large quantity of the stolen cash was recovered. A couple of jemmy bars were also recovered which were found to match the marks made at the scene.

A colleague and I went across to Huntingdon Police Station where we assisted with the interviews. I know this may sound a bit far-fetched, but all nine suspects admitted their part in the burglary. One of them even took us to the safe which had been opened during the night. Bad news always followed good, and on this occasion it consisted of a mountain of paperwork. Several of the offenders were already on court bail which meant that remand files needed preparing before we could finish duty. My colleague and I eventually arrived home at 3am after completing an eighteen hour day. The detectives at Huntingdon had also worked long hours to put this case together. The least we could do was to send them a letter of thanks via their Detective Inspector.

The detectives at Huntingdon had trained the locals well in my opinion, because they all pleaded guilty when appearing at our Magistrates' Court. I'm pleased to report that prison sentences were on offer that day, mainly due to the degree of damage that had been caused at the golf club. I should add that courts in my experience take a dim view of criminals that travel across borders to commit crime. I for one would second that opinion, because the aspect of travel, shows how determined criminals are to succeed in their mission.

Another burglary of interest, was one when the intruder used the company's hand operated fork lift machine to convey a large metal safe from the premises. He successfully steered the forklift along three streets in the early hours of the morning, arriving at his house just before day light. Other occupants at the house then helped him to manhandle the very heavy safe into the breakfast room. They placed a tablecloth over the safe and positioned four chairs around it, giving the impression of four chairs and a breakfast table.

I received a telephone call from an informant who suggested I should visit the house and recover the safe. I visited immediately with a colleague and gave the street door my traditional knock. The female occupant stuck her head out of the first floor bedroom window and said 'what the fucking hell do you want?' After further conversation, the kind lady came down and opened the street door. Her next remark tickled me somewhat, when she said she had been up half the night and needed to get some sleep.

My colleague and I were eventually invited in and made our way into the breakfast room. Two of the earlier mentioned chairs were in use, being occupied by a local burglar and his friend. They invited us to sit at the table for a cup of tea. We accepted and sat down in the remaining two chairs. I must confess that as I sat down there was very little legroom beneath the table. It took all my will power not to burst out laughing, especially when my colleague looked me in the eye.

It could be said that we were stringing it out, but it had been ingrained in us over the years, never to refuse a cup of tea. The lady of the house made the tea which was up to standard. Whilst having tea together, we all chatted about the weather and reminisced about previous encounters. I then decided to talk about the lack of legroom under the table, which prompted the burglar to cough up. He said that he had screwed the factory and that the safe was down to him. I then lifted the tablecloth and admired the safe, which of course had been forced open.

I knew the offender, who went by the name of John. He said the others had nothing to do with it and that he wanted to sort it out on his own. I arrested him for the burglary and used the remaining occupants as witnesses. It was later confirmed that the safe had contained just over £100. The safe had been damaged beyond repair and was valued at £600. John was interviewed under caution and gave a full and frank admission. He was later sent to prison for the offence and had a number of further offences taken into consideration. I must admit that my colleague and I had a real good laugh over that particular case.

Princess Diana

I would now like to mention one of those beautiful moments in my police career, which involved royalty visiting Wellingborough, to open the new Victoria Cultural Centre. Prince Charles and Princess Diana carried out the opening, which proved to be very popular indeed, resulting in very large crowds. I attended the briefing at Wellingborough Police Station and was allocated the task of crowd observation. The duty involved monitoring the crowd both prior to the arrival of the royal couple and during the opening of the Cultural Centre.

It was a beautiful day, and all of the crowds were on best behaviour. I saw little of the royal couple at the centre itself, but then mingled with the crowd on one of the nearby pavements. The Prince and Princess then came out into the street and did a walkabout, to the delight of the people of Wellingborough. I considered myself very lucky when the Princess stopped walking and spoke to local people, standing next to me. The Princess struck me to be absolutely beautiful, very polite and very elegant. I stood within three feet of the Princess and couldn't help but notice what beautiful eyes she had. The Princess spent over a minute talking to the people at that location and then walked further down the street.

In very quick time the event drew to a close and the royal couple left Wellingborough for their next engagement. I was left with a very fond memory of the Princess that day, and consider myself privileged to have attended the event. I sometimes wished that all my memories could consist of such wonderful days at work, but alas, reality was soon to strike again.

This time a murder had occurred in Wellingborough on the Hemmingwell Estate. A young man of Afro-Caribbean descent had been attacked in the street and battered about the head with a blunt instrument. He had died as a result of the attack and had been found lying dead in the street. An incident room was set up at Wellingborough Police Station and enquiries were soon underway resulting in arrests of the offenders.

I only played a small part in this enquiry, relating to the *post mortem* examination, which was carried out by the Home Office pathologist, at Kettering mortuary. I was instructed to be present at the *post mortem* and assisted with the bagging and labelling of the exhibits. During the procedure, the pathologist removed the upper part of the victim's skull to assist him, in confirming the exact cause of death. I was present when he counted fifteen bruises on the inside of the skull cap and formed the view that the victim had been struck on the head fifteen times, with something similar to a baseball bat.

I was a little shocked by the degree of bruising and found it hard to believe that anyone could deliver so many vicious blows to another human being. I completed my task in relation to the exhibits, ensuring that they were all appropriately stored. I should also point out for the uninitiated that all exhibit labels needed to be signed by any witness referring to them. The signatures were necessary to prove the continuity of each exhibit in a court of law.

I always found the mortuary a difficult place to work in, and whilst there on occasions, additional corpses would arrive. On this particular day, a deceased child was brought in by a hospital orderly and I found myself asking what had happened to this poor little child. The orderly told me that the little boy aged just eleven, had just died on a ward of cystic fibrosis. I was rather upset to hear that this child had been eleven years of age, because in stature he appeared to be no more than five years of age!

I left the mortuary that day in the knowledge that two families had seen their loved ones, denied the privilege of long life, albeit in very different circumstances. My spirits were lifted

247

more recently when I learned that children suffering with cystic fibrosis have a much longer life expectancy because of advances made in this field of medicine. To this day my thoughts are with both families, in relation to their tragic losses.

A close call

I want to tell you a story now about the night that I got it very wrong indeed and nearly ended up being killed. I was working the late shift in Rushden, and just happened to be in *The Railway* pub, when my control room phoned me. I was told to go to Tennyson Road, Rushden, where a man was in the process of assaulting his wife with a large knife. I jumped into the CID car and drove at great speed to Tennyson Road, where I parked up a couple of doors from the address.

As I got out of the car, a neighbour beckoned to me and told me that she had phoned in about the assault. She said 'he's got her in his kitchen and you can see him from my kitchen'. She said he's completely drunk and it's Bruce Pope the slaughter man. On looking at the houses, I could see that her house had the same layout as Bruce Pope's. I ran into the lady's house and established that a long hallway lead straight through to her kitchen. I quickly glanced across to the Pope's kitchen and could see Bruce Pope holding his wife, with the knife held under her chin.

Time appeared to be running out for the woman, so I ran from the neighbour's house, out into the street and then across the road, where I aligned myself with the Pope's street door. I threw off my coat and ran as fast as I could, in body checking mode, towards the front door. As my shoulder came in contact with it, the door flew open and I went through the opening at great speed. I continued running straight into the kitchen where I collided with the man and the woman

Bruce Pope, whom I had known in the past, grabbed hold of me and forced me onto his kitchen cooker. I had now ended up

248

in an impossible position on the cooker. My back was positioned on top of the gas rings and my legs were hanging down over the front edge of the cooker. My head movement was now restricted by the back upright section of the cooker. Bruce Pope was holding a large boning knife at my throat, the blade of which measured about ten inches long.

I could feel my heart pumping like never before, and because of the position I was in, I was struggling to breathe. I noticed that Mrs Pope had left the kitchen, and I assumed she was safe. Bruce screamed out that he was going to cut my fucking throat. I was somewhat shocked by his words, in the knowledge that he had been a top slaughterman for many years. I decided to humour him and told him that I'd had four pints of beer and that if he cut my throat, it would all be wasted.

My words in fact angered him all the more, with him screaming that it was drink that had brought him to the point of killing me. Being in such a compromising position I decided to try some different words and decided to plead for my life. I told him that I had three lovely children, who all needed their father. He again screamed out loudly saying the courts had denied him access to his children. I formed the opinion that there would be no compromise for me with Bruce Pope. The only option was for me to take the fight to him, but I could not even move, I was completely off balance on the cooker.

Bruce Pope, in his state of rage, had increased his grip on me and pressed the point of the blade to my throat. I tried to move but his body weight pressed down firmly onto my upper body, leaving me completely trapped. I decided that given any opportunity at all, I needed to secure his knife arm. Pope suddenly pulled the knife away from my throat and tried to plunge it into my stomach. I quickly grabbed his wrist with my right hand and held on tightly. As I did so, I saw the blade of the knife stop within inches of my stomach. He was screaming like a madman because this had stopped him in his tracks.

I can tell you that I was holding on for life's sake and very relieved to see several uniformed police officers dragging Bruce Pope off me. No one was more relieved than I to see him leaving the room in handcuffs. I managed to roll off the side of the cooker and spent a few seconds gathering myself together. Mrs Pope then re-appeared and said that apart from the shock of it all, she was fine. I walked towards the kitchen door where a colleague called Stuart was standing. I said 'hello' to Stuart and he said that he thought he was about to see two stone of ugly fat roll across the kitchen floor. I told him that I didn't understand, to which he replied 'I thought he was going to cut your fucking head off'.

I thanked Stuart for his kind thoughts and then burst out laughing. To my mind, this is what policing was all about. One minute you're in considerable danger and the next you're laughing your head off. To this date I think Stuart's sense of humour was just great.

I remember going home the next morning and waking my wife to tell her what had happened. I also remember her rebuking me for waking her, and telling me to tell her the story later that day. There's no truth in the saying that a problem shared is a problem halved. I suppose you need to share it first with someone.

My Detective Inspector spoke to me when I resumed duty and patted me on the back, stating that he wanted to give me a commendation. He went on to say that he couldn't recommend the commendation because a colleague had compromised the situation. The DI was not in a position to expand on his reasons.

Bruce Pope was dealt with at the Magistrates' Court and I was appalled when he was fined £150 for the assault on his wife and the assault on me. This punishment sent a very poor message out onto the streets with regard to knife crime. I know that Bruce Pope came from a very good family, and I want to place on the record that this story should not detract in any way from the good family name.

❀ ❀

A triple murder

Time waits for no man, and my police career was now moving into the 1980s. I have good reason to remember one month in particular. I had arrived at Rushden Police Station for a late shift in November 1981. As I entered the building I bumped into another detective called John, who was always up for a laugh. I remember saying 'hi John, much going on today?' He replied 'you won't believe it Mick, but we've had a triple murder'. I didn't believe it, and carried on into the building to commence my late duty.

The station seemed unusually quiet and it wasn't until I rang Wellingborough control room that I found out why. Three travellers had been murdered in Ditchford Lane, Rushden, and an incident room had been set up, in a disused factory nearby. All Rushden CID, with the exception of me, had been called in to work on the case. I was the only DC left and had been allocated the role of taking on the everyday workload at Rushden. This was going to be an interesting task because we covered a large area of the county. I was nevertheless invited to attend the incident room briefing, where I would be given details of the murders.

I attended the briefing at 6pm that evening where I learned that two male travellers and one female traveller had been shot dead in their respective caravans. I had known the two male victims for many years, who lived in two separate caravans on Ditchford Lane. The female's name eludes me at this time, but she was a local Rushden girl who was living with one of the male victims. The two caravans stood alone on the lane and no other travellers lived there. It was a very isolated spot and a truly shocking and worrying incident.

One victim was quite elderly and the other two much younger. None of them had any known enemies to my knowledge. The travellers had two dogs which had also been shot dead. A huge team of officers was being brought into the area to investigate these very brutal murders. Officers were also drafted in from Bedfordshire and Cambridgeshire to assist us.

251

A thorough scenes of crime examination was undertaken in simply appalling weather. A large search team also attended to conduct a fingertip search of the scene and surrounding area.

On completion of the scene work, the caravans and other relative vehicles were all brought into the underground car park at the incident room. Several bullets were recovered at the *post mortem* and bullet cases were recovered at the scene. The task to find the offenders was always going to be very difficult indeed. Travellers rarely ever informed on each other, in fact I'm tempted to say 'never'. Added to that, historically Northamptonshire had a long tradition of travellers both living in, and visiting, the county. We had four travellers' sites all within four miles of the scene and many others dotted around the county.

I'm sorry to say that despite an enormous effort on the part of all concerned, these murders were never detected. For the first four months of the enquiry I remained at Rusden and never had a day off duty during that period of time. In the early 1980s, the CID office had a staff of two DS's and five DC's. Six of these officers remained on the incident room for four months, at which time I worked alone, on what we call 'Sub-Divisional' duty. I either picked up, or assisted, my uniformed colleagues with all other serious crime committed during that period. Without a shadow of a doubt that was the hardest working four months of my whole career. I must admit that I developed a number of very dodgy shortcuts to achieve all of my goals. Before you ask, let me tell you that with the passing of time I'm unable to recall details of these shortcuts.

Paul

It was also during the early 1980s that I started dealing with a young man called Paul. He wanted to be a hairdresser but failed to get all of the qualifications that he needed for a successful career. He worked for a short time at a hairdresser's in Rushden before being dismissed. It was then that he started going off the rails and started committing burglaries. His first burglary was at the hairdresser's in Rushden where he had been employed. The proprietor arrived at the shop one morning and discovered the break in.

Someone had stolen a large quantity of hair dressing equipment, consisting of hair dryers, brushes, scissors, combs, and various shampoo-type products. Initially there were no suspects, but then it became apparent that an expensive car had been stolen from Rushden, which had then been abandoned at Coventry, in the West Midlands police area. Further burglaries had been occurring on route to the West Midlands, the premises concerned all being hairdressers' shops. I made enquiries into the stolen vehicle and managed to link it to Paul. Coincidently all of the hairdressers' shops broken into had lost similar hair related products to those stolen from Rushden.

As a result of further enquiries, Paul was arrested near Coventry and most of the stolen goods were found in his possession. He was brought back to Wellingborough Police Station where I dealt with him for all of the offences. He was very amenable on interview and fully admitted all of the offences that he had committed. He explained that he really wanted to be a professional hair dresser, and had committed the offences when upset over losing his job.

Paul never made an issue of it at the time, but I know that the break-up of his parents' marriage had upset him enormously, when he was younger. He pleaded guilty when he appeared in court and was sent to a YOI, a Young Offenders Institution, where he served a short sentence. Soon after his release he started committing crime again, but had changed his Modus Operandi. He had moved up the criminal ladder and was now committing very clever deceptions.

He would now put on a smart suit, shirt and tie, to go about his criminal deceptions. Carrying a smart executive case and umbrella, he would visit expensive car show rooms and falsely purport to be a solicitor or a barrister. He would convince the showroom salesman of his high status and would then be allowed to take very expensive cars out for test drives. He was so convincing that he would remain unaccompanied whilst taking the test drive. The cars consisting of Jaguar, Daimler and high value sports cars, would then disappear - along with Paul.

Paul was now a little older and when eventually caught for these offences he received prison sentences. On release from prison, he would continue to escalate his position in society falsely, becoming a Lord, a Count and, on one occasion, a High Sheriff. Highly expensive vehicles continued to go missing having been obtained by Paul's deceptions. He was eventually brought to book and served a further prison sentence. Prior to receiving the sentence Paul assured me that he intended to settle down when next released from prison.

Paul was eventually released from his latest incarceration, and things seemed to quieten down. I had my fingers crossed and hoped that his family would now see the new Paul. How wrong could we all be. Well, let me tell you, very wrong indeed.

I was shocked one day to see a message from colleagues at Kettering Police Station, stating that Paul had been arrested after falsely purporting to be a hospital consultant. He had in fact donned a white coat and examined patients with his stethoscope. One of his so called patients was pregnant and the other had cancer.

Enquiries into these offences revealed that he had used his bogus medical skills at Northampton General Hospital also. Paul was interviewed and again fully admitted these very unusual crimes, stating that he had always wanted to work in the medical profession. He later appeared at Northampton Crown Court where he pleaded guilty to his latest deceptions. His so called medical career was then put on hold when he received a substantial prison sentence.

Eventually Paul was released on completion of his sentence and had apparently received medical treatment. Perhaps he would now settle down to a normal existence. A couple of years passed and I then picked up a story about Paul on the national news. He had unfortunately resumed his unlawful medical career in a different part of the country. On this occasion he

254

had gone into a London hospital, again purporting to be a consultant and on this occasion he had carried out a medical procedure on a patient. I believe the procedure involved drawing fluid from the patient's lung.

He apparently carried out a second procedure on another patient which involved the birth of a child. Paul later received a very long prison sentence for those crimes and I have not heard of him since that time. I would like to say that Paul was a very plausible person, who clearly went off the rails, and eventually put people's lives in danger.

Occasionally, police work involved being in the right place, at the right time. The best example of this was when a Detective Sergeant and I travelled to Peterborough one day, on a routine enquiry. I was driving an unmarked police car along the A605 road near the village of Warmington. As we approached a petrol station which was situated on our nearside of the road, I saw two men in a car, parked in a country lane situated, opposite to the petrol station. I paid no further attention to these men and we carried on to Peterborough. The DS and I visited Thorpe Wood Police Station where we completed our earlier mentioned enquiry. We then made our way all the way back to Rushden which concluded our return journey of about sixty miles.

All good CID men would now assume that lunchtime had arrived. How wrong could we be, when the report of a robbery was coming in at the earlier mentioned petrol station. The DS and I took up the shout and drove straight back out to Warmington. On arrival we found that the proprietor had been working the till, when he was attacked by two male robbers. He had been wrestled to the floor by one man, whilst the other snatched cash from the open till. The offenders had then driven off in a car that had been parked in the lane opposite the premises.

I was simply chuffed at that moment, because I realised I had seen both men in the car earlier that morning. Despite only having a fleeting glance at them both sitting in their car, I could give brief descriptions of them. The proprietor was found to be a little shocked, but a man of stiff upper lip, who quickly resumed work in his petrol station. He was happy to make a statement in which he gave good descriptions of the two suspects. He had suffered some scratches and minor bruising but was otherwise all right.

The proprietor and I both confirmed that the two men had been using a dark blue saloon car, similar to a Ford Cortina saloon. The first of the two men seen by me had shoulder length mousey coloured hair and a gaunt face. The second had shorter brown hair and a more rounded face. Both men were of a similar age being in their early twenties. Their car had sped off in the Peterborough direction after the robbery. The proprietor and I were both of the view that the driver had been the suspect with the long hair.

On returning to the station I put out a detailed appeal to Northamptonshire Police and surrounding counties, which I'm pleased to say, generated an immediate response from Cambridgeshire Constabulary. In fact it was from another mate of mine, who also frequented the Alconbury Christmas celebrations. You've probably noticed by now that I love to plug inter-force cooperation.

As luck would have it, an off duty detective had seen the two suspects returning to their home town of March, in Cambridgeshire, at the material time. The officer knew both men quite well and had recognised both them and their car. Armed with the new information I requested that Cambridgeshire officers carry out the arrests and also requested that the car be seized.

Before you could say 'boo to a goose', both men were under arrest and ready for collection at Cambridge Police Station. I took great pleasure in collecting them from Cambridgeshire and returning them to Wellingborough Police Station. Some Bank of England notes were also recovered together with the suspect vehicle. I told the two men that I was delighted to see them both again. On hearing my remark they both had confused looks on their faces. To ease their confusion I explained that I had seen them both at the scene on the morning of the robbery.

As I made that remark, both men looked dumbstruck and seemed to colour up a little. To cut a long story short, they both knew that they were nicked. Both declined to take legal advice and both said they were ready to be interviewed. During the interview I told them that the proprietor would be happy to identify them on identification parade. I also told them that we would carry out a 'ninhydrin test' on the recovered bank notes and probably find the owners' fingerprints on them.

They both admitted the offence and conceded that they were not the best robbers in the world. Neither could believe their misfortune with a police officer simply driving by, when they were casing the place. They admitted that they had purposely driven to Northamptonshire in the knowledge that they were unknown to police in that county. I decided not to mention them being seen returning to March by an off duty detective. I felt that this would be rubbing salt in their wounds.

Both appeared at Northampton Crown Court where they pleaded guilty and received three years each imprisonment. I recall their names to this date, but see no point in naming them at this late juncture. I hope that they moved on to living a normal lawful existence. I often wondered what the odds would be, to see would-be offenders parked up like that again. I'm not a gambling man but assume those odds would be quite high.

Murder of a little girl

During the 1980s, I was sent to Corby to assist in a search for a six year old girl, who was missing from home. She had waved goodbye to her parents early that morning and had been left to make her way to school on foot. She was alone at the time and had been given some cash to purchase something at the local shop, for her school lunch. She never arrived at school that morning and alarm bells were soon ringing. In view of her very young age a large team of police officers and other volunteers was assembled to search for her.

At an early stage of the search, it was decided to carry out door to door enquiries, based mainly on the fact that the little girl's route to school consisted of a mere four streets. The main emphasis on door to door enquiries of this type would be to search all of the houses, visited by the enquiry officers. Two days elapsed and there was no trace of the little girl, despite all of the relevant houses being searched. The question still remained, had she been taken in a vehicle or had she been taken into someone's house?

It was decided that all of the relevant houses would be visited a second time and further searches would be made. It begged the question, had we missed something? Well in truth we had, because a very sad discovery was about to be made. To this day I'm very saddened and sorry to say that her body was found in the loft of one of the houses. This was obviously a great shock for the family of the child and also for the enquiry team.

The sole occupant of the house, a man in his twenties was arrested on suspicion of the little girl's murder. He was handcuffed and taken into custody at Corby Police Station. A full forensic examination of the scene was then carried out. Her head had been wrapped in cling film and her body had then been placed in a large black bin liner. The initial search of the house had not revealed her body.

A *post mortem* confirmed that she had died of asphyxiation and had in fact been raped. The suspect was interviewed and initially denied any knowledge of her presence in his house. The forensic examination of the scene confirmed that the rape had taken place in his bedroom. The cling film placed around her head had caused the asphyxiation. In simple layman's terms she had suffocated, as a result of the placement of the cling film.

An incident room was immediately set up at Corby Police Station and I was partnered with Graham Timpson, sometimes called 'Reg' for some reason, but more often known as 'Timmo'. This pairing worked well for me, because 'Timmo' was a local

258

Detective Constable who had worked at Corby for many years. He had both knowledge of the town and the local people. On completion of the forensic examination of the house, 'Timmo' and I were given the role of cataloguing all exhibits contained in the property. This was a very important role because every item in the house could be significant in any subsequent murder trial.

'Timmo' and I had only spent a few hours in the house when we made a significant discovery. We found three bags of Cheese and Onion crisps in a large earthenware container, which stood on the kitchen worktop. These were exhibited, bagged and labelled, before being sent for fingerprint work. On completion of the fingerprint examination, identifiable fingerprints were found for both the victim and the suspect. Enquiries were then made to establish the origin of the bags of crisps.

I'm pleased to be able to say on behalf of the enquiry team, that the crisps had been purchased by the victim, at the local corner shop, on the morning of her disappearance. The shop proprietor recalled her making the purchase for her school lunch that day. The prior delivery to the shop was also proven, when comparing batch numbers with the supplying wholesaler.

A large number of letters and other documents found at the house helped in compiling a list of known girlfriends and other associates of the suspect. One of the associates proved later to be crucial in identifying the offender in this case. 'Timmo' and I spent a total of three weeks at the murder scene, gathering all of the exhibits together. From memory I believe we ended up with in excess of six hundred exhibits from the house, all of which were moved into proper storage at Corby Police Station. All items were photographed prior to removal and consecutively listed.

I must say that when we finally turned the key in the street door, we were both ready for a breath of fresh air. 'Timmo' and I then started working on outstanding actions, many of which related to the suspects former partners and girlfriends. It was important to establish why this suspect had chosen such a young girl for his sexual needs. We soon established that he had

259

many girlfriends, but no lasting relationships with them. All of the young women that we spoke to were happy to make detailed written witness statements, about their relationships with the suspect. A common factor surfaced, revealing that he was a premature ejaculator and could not sexually satisfy his partners. Some of the women admitted that they would actually mock him in relation to his lack of prowess in the bedroom.

Although these were highly personal matters, in this case they were giving the enquiry team, a Modus Operandi, a reason for the murder. Clearly this man had been ridiculed by his adult partners and decided to snatch the child for sex without rejection. We felt that this view was reinforced by the fact that he had wrapped the child's head in cling film. After a mountain of work, sufficient evidence was gathered together and the suspect was charged with the murder of the little girl. He was put before the Magistrates' Court and after a short remand application, was remanded in custody.

Routine murder enquiries continued, several of which revolved around his previous friends and associates. 'Timmo' and I had occasion to speak to one of the suspect's best friends, a young man who spent time smoking cannabis with him. He made a witness statement describing the history of their friendship and seemed quite relaxed about it. However, 'Timmo' and I then started to press him a little in relation to the murder of little girl. The young man's body language seemed to change and he appeared to be slightly uncomfortable.

I asked him what had upset him and he assured us that he was fine. I told him that he had become uncomfortable when we had mentioned the victim. He again stated that he was fine and said that we were misreading the situation. He then said that he needed to leave the police station, because he had an appointment elsewhere. 'Timmo' then told the youth that we were unhappy with him, and wanted to know what he was holding back. The friend then said that there was something on his mind and that he would like to go home and think about it. I then showed him out via the station door and told him to visit us at the station the next day.

260

'Timmo' and I then had a chat about the youth, and were both of the view that he was holding back information about the murder. Neither of us could put forward a theory as to what the information would be. The following morning we both attended the incident room briefing, and then caught up on some paperwork. We were both delighted to receive a call from the police station front desk, stating that our witness wanted to speak to us. On a light note, 'Timmo' and I raced down the stairs, to be the first to speak to the witness. Of course we then composed ourselves before stepping through the reception door!

The youth said he wanted to speak to us both behind closed doors. We then took him into a small reception office where he apologised and then handed us two hand written letters. The letters were both addressed to him and had been stamped for clearance by the Prison Authorities. The youth then said that the letters were from the suspect. Before opening the letters I put on a pair of forensic gloves. I then read the letters in which the suspect explained to his mate, exactly what he had done to the little girl.

'Timmo' and I were completely stunned by the contents of both letters. They were both complete and utter admissions to rape and murder of the little girl. He had gone into incredible detail and had clearly entrusted his best mate with the letters, in the false belief that he would keep them hidden. 'Timmo' and I, now had a better understanding, as to why this young man found himself in such a dilemma the previous day. We could both see that it took enormous courage for this youth to come forward with those letters. Although we had nothing to celebrate, these letters would become the icing on the cake, for the whole enquiry team.

It was a great feeling to be able to present such compelling evidence at the morning briefing, the following day. It wasn't all good news though, because somehow the letters had not been censored at the prison. Normally all letters are checked by prison staff before being allowed through the prison gate. Something had clearly gone wrong back down the line, but on this occasion we were delighted with the outcome. The accused later admitted that he had been the author of the letters and also admitted committing the offences. He later appeared at the Crown Court and was given life in prison.

I learned only recently of Graham 'Reg' Timpson's untimely death, resulting from a massive heart attack. I see this paragraph as a good opportunity to say a few words in his memory. He was a truly great detective officer to work with, and had a wonderful sense of humour. I know from personal experience that he carried out dedicated police work on behalf of the young victim in this case. 'Timmo' clearly had great affection for young children. When you spend three weeks of your life with someone like 'Reg' Timpson, at the scene of such an awful crime, you truly get to know the man.

I want to take this moment of opportunity to remember also the child and her family, who were lost to each other that day. I have been very frank about what happened in this case, but only because I want people to realise, what police officers also have to come to terms with. I like to think that my side of the story comes from what we refer to, as being at the front line of policing. We see an awful lot of grief and I'm afraid that a lot of that grief rubs off on us. In truth it was probably the murder of this little girl, that prompted me to name my book *Think of those denied the privilege*.

More by luck than judgement I was about to have an enjoyable break from everyday CID work. The break came in the form of a refresher CID course which I attended in 1983, at Bishopsgarth, Wakefield, West Yorkshire. This was a three week course designed to update CID officers with recent legislation and new practices. It was a very relaxed course with informal lectures and no examinations. All of the officers attending had been detectives out on the ground for some years. The officers came from numerous counties and also Northern Ireland.

262

My CID Refresher Course in Wakefield. I am standing, sixth from the right

Each officer would stand up to introduce themselves, and talk for a few minutes about the area that they policed. I found both Northern Ireland officers to be of particular interest, both having received gunshot wounds during their service in Northern Ireland. One of them who was nearing retirement age, became distraught, when explaining that a colleague had in fact been killed in the same shooting. Both had more than adequate scars to remind them of their trauma.

West Yorkshire Police were of course in the middle of a murder enquiry at that time, namely the Ripper Enquiry. This was the case where many women were being murdered in the Bradford area, consisting mainly of prostitutes. Some of the officers on the course had been working on the case and gave us a talk about the difficulties they were experiencing. They had received huge amounts of information and were still using the card index method of storing it. Computers of course were still in their infancy at that time.

Most evenings were spent having a pint or two at local bars in Wakefield. Two of particular note were the *Pussy Cat* club and *The New York Bar*. I remember that all of the bar staff at the *New York* were dressed in leotards, which I thought to be very strange indeed. Others would call me old fashioned, but I don't really care. All of those wearing the leotards were of course men.

One of the lads on the course took us to Dewsbury, to sample the local curry. I remember walking down what seemed like a back street and arriving at a terraced curry house. The dining area consisted of a number of wooden tables covered with plastic table cloths. There was a piece of blackboard on the wall, which had chalked writing on it, which read, chicken or beef curry.

I chose the chicken curry which was very basic, but delicious to eat, accompanied by naan bread. It was the cheapest curry I have ever purchased but remember it well, despite the passing of thirty years. The other remaining highlight of the course consisted of a visit to Wakefield's Maximum Security Prison, the details of which I'm not prepared to bore you with. To summarise the course, I would say that the lads, the instructors and the accommodation were all good. Alas the three weeks had passed and it was time to return to the grind stone. I'm only joking because it was great to be back with my family.

It was about this time that I decided to apply for a post on the Regional Crime Squad. I took a little time preparing a nicely worded application report for the attention of the Detective Inspector. Within two days of submitting my application I was summoned to the DI's office. I thought great, the job must be mine, otherwise the application normally took two to three weeks. As I entered the office I was surprised to see the Detective Superintendent Ron Beards, sitting with the DI.

The DI said that he and the Detective Superintendent had given my application careful consideration. However, they had decided that I was to remain at Rushden as a Sub-Divisional detective for the foreseeable future. Furthermore, that my next three years in CID would be at Rushden as part of my career planning. The DI then tore up my application and threw it in the waste paper bin. Both had big grins on their faces and agreed that I was needed at Rushden. In those days there was no such thing as a grievance procedure, you just did as you were told.

In truth, they probably already had someone lined up for the Crime Squad role. I was quite happy with their decision and in a funny kind of way felt that they didn't want to lose me. After that day, I decided that I would not apply for any other posts, without consulting the management first. I should perhaps explain that I was now in my mid-thirties and felt that a Crime Squad role suited people of my age. In effect I wouldn't want the role three years later. On that note, there was plenty of good work to be done in the Rushden area.

❀ ❀

Disco mayhem

It was about this time that I had a call from one of my informants, who told me that trouble was brewing, and that a large gang from Wellingborough would be coming to Rushden for a punch up. He went on to say that they were coming on two buses and that the punch up would take place on the evening he was ringing me. Their intension was to visit the *Carriage House* disco in Market Square, Higham Ferrers. They had planned the trip by bus so that the police had no knowledge of their personal vehicle movements. The informant went on to say that there would be over sixty men coming, all intent on giving Rushden a good beating.

It was a Friday evening, and I was the only plain clothes officer on duty at Rushden that night. I visited the police station and fully briefed the duty uniformed Police Sergeant. He instructed me to visit the *Carriage House*, have a beer or two at the bar and to monitor the situation. I told the Sergeant that this seemed to be inadequate action, in relation to the good information, that I had received. The Sergeant repeated his instructions, stating he would provide back up if and when needed.

I visited the disco and notified the licensee about my information. The disco was already well underway so the licensee decided to let it continue, again with a view to monitoring the situation. He had one bouncer working that evening and said that he would remain on the disco floor, to deal with any trouble makers. Within minutes of our discussion I noticed Wellingborough faces passing me at the bar, in groups of two's and three's. These individuals started making their way to the disco floor, which was situated right at the back of the premises.

I told the licensee of my concerns and advised him to join his bouncer on the disco floor. I then phoned the duty Sergeant and updated him as to the number of Wellingborough men entering the premises. He said that I should continue to update him and that he would now consider back up. I returned to the bar and observed a constant stream of new faces, passing the bar and making their way to the disco area. Many of those faces were familiar to me, in that most had been in trouble at Wellingborough before. I was now very concerned for the safety of people on the disco dance floor and again called for support.

I decided to go to the entrance door, where I would be in the best position to prevent any offenders from leaving. I couldn't see the disco area from the front entrance, but suddenly heard all hell break loose. People were screaming and shouting very loudly. I could hear glass breaking and furniture being thrown around. The entrance door was about four feet wide and wedged wide open, obviously to allow people in. I placed myself in the middle of the opening and faced full square towards the disco floor.

With limited resources, I made up my mind that no one would be leaving until I said so. I had received no word of back up and could now see the Wellingborough gang moving in large numbers towards me. They all looked very determined to leave, until I shouted out the words 'no one's leaving'. On that remark, they all stopped dead in their tracks and I heard all of their metal dropping to the floor. They had been carrying an abundance of blades, knives and others weapons.

I had placed my arms out wide either side of me and stood my ground in a 'herding' mode. A lad named Peter, who was at the front said I should get out of the way or they would trample me. I told him that if they challenged my authority, he would be the first to be arrested. The gang started pushing from the rear and with me standing firm, they were all locked in what I would describe, as a bottle neck. I was suddenly aware of PC Alderman standing behind me and peering over my shoulder. He said 'we've got back up out here Mick, we've brought a van load of Bobbies'.

This was like music to my ears and filled me with renewed confidence. Mick then whispered in my ear, that he was only joking, adding that he and one other officer had arrived to give me support. He went on to whisper that other officers were in fact on route. At that point Peter started to push me backwards, followed by the rest of the gang from Wellingborough. I grabbed hold of him and told him he was nicked, at which point the whole gang burst through the door into the street. I hung onto my prisoner who was now throwing punches to my head and face, as we fell to the pavement. I was aware of police officers arresting others in the gang and could see a considerable battle taking place on the pavement.

I was forced to return some of Peters punches, otherwise he was going to cause me serious injury. After a considerable struggle I managed to handcuff him and lead him to the nearby police van. The rear door was open and I tried to manhandle Peter into the van. He stopped resisting and said that he would go quietly. I then made the mistake of allowing him to use the steps situated at the rear of the van. He somehow managed to turn around and head butted me straight in the face. From that point onwards I placed Peter in the van, without any further resistance. I remained in the back of the van with him, with a view to accompanying him to the police station.

I remember sitting talking to Peter when the van doors opened and another violent prisoner was thrown in with us. I wasn't having much luck that night especially when I realised that Peter had loosened my top front teeth, with his head butt. I was actually feeling a little rough when the second prisoner started picking a fight with me. His arresting officer had failed to handcuff him and left me in my second boxing match of the night. He started punching me in the face and head, forcing me to defend myself, by returning blow for blow.

Peter started to kick off again and before I knew it they were both on the attack. When we arrived at Wellingborough I recall the driver complaining because the van had rocked from side to side, all the way. These were two young fit men who took a lot of restraining and I certainly didn't want a rematch.

At the police station it was confirmed that seven of the gang had been arrested. I was quite pleased with that number considering the lack of support from the outset. They were all charged with affray and all later pleaded guilty. A number of injuries had been caused to Rushden disco participants, but fortunately nothing too serious. Affray could easily be proven because we only had to show that people were put in fear, during these assaults. All of the men received appropriate punishments at the Magistrates' Court. All of the weapons were of course gathered together and later destroyed under the Police Property Act.

I later thanked PC Alderman for his good humour at the time of the incident. I particularly liked his line about a van load of Bobbies. I also contacted two detective officers who on hearing my plight, travelled all the way from Northampton to assist me that night. They travelled twenty miles in total and in my opinion showed great initiative, in doing so. Out of interest the offenders confirmed that they had travelled on two buses that evening and had entered the disco in dribs and drabs, to avoid detection. I'm pleased to report that my front teeth recovered and have remained stable to date.

Also during the 1980s we started working what was referred to as the 'night car'. Let me be the first to tell you that the 'night car' role was a job and a half. A detective from Wellingborough area would pair up with a detective from Corby or Kettering area. The official hours worked were 10pm until 6am, during which time the two detectives would deal with all serious crime, committed in our half of the county. We used a plain car and worked seven nights on the trot.

This was a very tiring role, mainly because of the vastness of the area that we covered. You could finish a job one side of the area, only to be sent minutes later to the other side of the area. We would often drive a lot of miles during the tour of duty. However, I felt that the system worked, albeit that you rarely finished duty on time. We dealt with the whole spectrum of serious crime including rape, wounding, robbery, burglary and deceptions. Possession of offensive weapons and firearms was also often on the agenda. Frankly there was never a dull moment and rarely enough time to eat the good old fish and chips.

Referring back to 'street craft', I was working with Dave Hankins from Corby one night when we were sent to a burglary at Raunds Town Football Club. Entry had been gained via a small toilet window to the rear of the premises and all of the gaming machines had been forced and cash contents stolen. Dave said 'what you going to do now then Mick, this one's on your area?' I said 'well I'm going to Rushden to lock up the offender'. Dave said 'oh yes, this I've got to see'.

We then drove the five miles to Rushden and went to a house in Co-op Row. We parked the car up a good distance from the house and approached quietly on foot. We had planned to cover front and back doors, but as we approached the property we heard a clatter to the rear of it. We didn't actually see anyone go, but found the back door wide open. The occupant was present and explained that her son had just done a runner. With the consent of the occupant we then carried out a search of the house, recovering stolen cash and breaking implements. We also took possession of his car parked nearby, which had a nice warm engine.

A search of the area proved futile, and we left to write up our report. Dave asked how on earth did I know who had done the burglary. I explained that the method adopted fitted the suspect to a 'tee'. I went on to refer to the following observations : the suspect liked breaking into isolated clubs; he liked small window entries; and also committed the offence in the early hours of the morning. Add to this the love of ready cash, and you've got your man. He also worked fast to beat alarm systems.

Dave said he was very impressed, but I think he was taking the 'micky'. When we reported for duty the next night we learned that our suspect had surrendered to police and admitted the burglary. A great result, even if I say so myself.

❀ ❀

Late night shoppers

On the last night of that tour, Dave and I dealt with another burglary at a Co-operative shop at Brigstock, when a large quantity of cigarettes and drink was stolen. We visited about 3am that morning and carried out all the initial work on the case. We wrote up the crime report and completed all the other paperwork relating to the night's work, when just before 6am, we received information about potential offenders. Dave and I were on our last legs and to be honest ready to go home.

The word 'conscientious' springs to mind, and on that note we made our way to an address used by the suspects. No back up was available because our uniformed colleagues were changing shifts. The information indicated that two offenders might be at the address in Kettering. We decided in our wisdom that we could adequately deal with two suspects. On arriving at the address the street door was opened by a giant of a man who was well oiled and not happy to make our acquaintance. Dave and I could hear a lot of bottles rattling as we followed the big guy into the house.

Having entered, we were confronted by a total of six men, who were all well-oiled and of Scottish decent. They were all milling around the lounge which was full of bottles of assorted beers and spirits. Cigarettes were also in abundance, strewn around the room, consisting of more brands than you would acquire from the local shop. The big fellow staggered towards me carrying a large glass bottle of cider. He said he was thinking about hitting me with the bottle, because he didn't like the police.

When you deal with drunken Scotsman, you need to choose the right words quickly to gain order. In a raised voice I told him to sit down or I would take the bottle from him and stick it up his backside. I went on to say that the bottle would be pushed so hard that it would probably come out of his big mouth. To my complete amazement this giant of a man went and sat down on the settee. I then told them that they were all

271

under arrest for burglary and would be conveyed to the police station by my uniformed colleagues.

I was of course making this up as I went along, because I didn't actually know whether or not my uniformed colleagues had arrived. But as if by magic, we heard the door knocker and found our uniformed colleagues lined up outside. Dave and I were very pleased to see their nice fresh faces, I'm referring to the fact that the 'early turn' had arrived. The suspects were all then cuffed up and taken to Kettering Police Station. Dave and I then had the pleasure of recovering and exhibiting all of the stolen goods. What a great result. This left Dave and I working, an extra five hours at the end of our seven night tour.

On another 'night car' tour of duty, my partner and I were sent to a Wellingborough night club disco in the early hours of the morning. A young girl had been attacked by another girl and had been struck fully in the face with a broken bottle. On arrival we found the victim in the back of the ambulance, being treated by paramedics. She had lost most of her nose in the attack and the paramedics asked my colleague and I to search for her nose, on the disco floor.

We spoke to the head doorman who was of the opinion that this was an impossible request. I said 'watch this space'. I then went up onto the stage and told the DJ to turn off the music. I then borrowed the microphone and apologised for stopping the music. I then instructed everyone on the dance floor to move back to allow a search to take place, for the victim's nose. Everyone moved back in an orderly fashion and together with the bouncers we searched for the missing nose. I'm very sorry to say that we couldn't find it, and in truth, it was probably stuck under someone's shoe. We reported back to the paramedics who then took the young lady to the local A and E for treatment.

On another occasion, we visited a pub disco at the *Royal Hotel* in Kettering where another person had been attacked with a bottle. A young man had lost the sight in one eye when another man pushed the broken bottle in his face. The offender had run off, but witnesses identified a young lady who had ordered the attack after arguing with the victim. I spoke to the young lady who of course denied any knowledge of her involvement in the assault. She in fact used some rather bad language when telling me to go away.

She was with a large group of quite well spoken people who didn't seem to understand, when I told her I was arresting her for incitement to inflict a wound on another. The suspect then tried to make off, assisted by her friends. I grabbed hold of the suspect who then started to resist arrest. As a result of the crowd intervention I started to lose my grip on the prisoner. In the turmoil that followed I found myself pulling her along the floor by her long auburn hair. This was a very serious crime in my opinion and I was determined not to lose my prisoner. Having exited the premises, I managed with uniformed help to regain order and my prisoner was conveyed to the station by colleagues.

I returned to the disco to continue recovering any necessary evidence, including witness details. I was still there when I received a call from the duty Inspector who wished to speak to me at the police station. I completed my work at the disco and then went to the police station, where I found the Inspector looking rather concerned. He said that he was not happy with the arrest of the young lady and furthermore that he was considering releasing her. I explained that she had unlawfully incited her boyfriend to inflict a wound on another, with drastic consequences. Furthermore that she was drunk, and in my opinion needed interviewing the following day, by which time she would have sobered up.

The Inspector pointed out that she was making a complaint about the arresting officer. I said that her complaint against police could be investigated as and when appropriate. I'm pleased to say that the Inspector eventually agreed to keep the young lady in for the night, with a view to a proper interview the following day. I resumed duty the next night when I learned that she had identified her boyfriend during her interview and that he had been arrested for the offence. He had admitted his

273

part in the matter, and was charged with 'wounding with intent, to cause grievous bodily harm'.

I was never called to give evidence, and later heard that he had pleaded guilty to the offence. No official complaint was ever made against me by his girlfriend, who had realised the error of her ways.

I continued working the 'night car' for five years before it was disbanded. It was an interesting part of my career, where I learnt what it was like to work in the towns of Kettering and Corby. Corby proved to be a very tough town to work, and I recall getting knocked about a bit whilst working there. I dealt with many serious and interesting cases on the 'night car'. I wouldn't have missed the experience for the world. I should add that I did quite a few of those duties with my old friend Detective Constable 'Reg' Timpson.

The new Chief Constable

I remember during this period that Northamptonshire Police had a new Chief Constable who joined us from the West Midlands Police. He was Mr Maurice Buck who had worked for many years in the Metropolitan Police, before going to the West Midlands Force. I was quite excited about his arrival and attended a quarterly training day at Wellingborough Police Station, to hear his initial address to The Wellingborough Sub Division. The meeting seemed well attended with approximately one hundred and twenty officers present.

The new Chief covered a number of interesting matters, including his future vision of the force. He then touched upon a raw nerve for me when he started saying that we were all very well paid and that he expected money for money's worth. He was basically referring to the Edmund Davis Report which had increased our pay considerably overnight, during the 1970s. I found this comment a little upsetting and decided to raise my

274

hand, with a view to reply. As I stood up Mr Buck said 'yes, what can I do for you officer?'

I told Mr Buck that many of the police officers gathered before him had worked very hard indeed prior to any pay increases and that their loyalty to the force should not be questioned. I then realised that I was on a complete looser when he replied 'sit down sonny, when I joined we never had any pay'. I sat down wondering whether I had blotted my copy book and fully expected to be returned to uniformed policing the next day. I'm pleased to report that I managed to stay in the CID for many more years, despite my outburst. Perhaps Mr Buck was more flexible than I had imagined.

In hindsight, my remark that day probably related to PC Terry Hancock, who you may recall, joined with me in 1972 but resigned three weeks later, because of the limited income. My point was simply that those of us, who did not resign, did so out of complete loyalty to our badge of office, and as such, had nothing to do with our pay. I lost touch with Terry all those years ago, and often wonder how his life panned out.

I'm going to mention a very puzzling case now which occurred in Wellingborough and turned out to be a very sensitive attempted suicide. It occurred on a lovely sunny day on a residential estate in one of the nicer parts of Wellingborough. The control room sent me to the scene, indicating that a woman had been found seriously stabbed in her home and appeared to have life threatening injuries. I arrived at the scene at the same time as the police surgeon and was both shocked at what we were confronted with.

We had arrived at a large well-kept four bedroom detached house, which oozed success. The street door was open and we made our way into the house where we found the victim lying on a double bed, in an upstairs bedroom. The women aged about thirty five years was laying on her back with a long bladed bread-type knife sticking in her chest. The whole length of the blade had penetrated her chest near to her heart and the handle of the knife was pulsating in time with her heart beats.

The police surgeon quickly diagnosed that the slightest movement of the victim could result in a severed artery, and subsequent death of the patient. He began to reassure the patient who in fact seemed incredibly calm. My role as the detective was to establish quickly who had inflicted the wound on the women. I quietly introduced myself to her and asked who had attacked her.

She immediately said that she had stabbed herself and that no one else was involved. The uniformed duty Sergeant had also arrived on scene and confirmed that a very young baby had been found fit and well in a cot near to the double bed. It was confirmed that the patient was the mother of the baby who had been born only two weeks earlier. We could see that the baby had been well cared for and was wrapped up warm and snug in the cot.

The paramedics were now on scene and on closer examination of the wound, found that the point of the blade had passed all the way through to the victim's back. The police surgeon then led the assembled medical team in the method to be adopted for moving the patient safely from scene to the ambulance. It was agreed that she would be placed on a stretcher with extreme care. We would then negotiate the galleried stair case to remove the patient from the house. A total of eight people were needed to carry out this extraction from the house, which took over an hour.

I'm very pleased to be able to say that on arrival at hospital the patient had a successful operation to remove the knife and made a miraculous recovery. The blade of the knife was found to be within a millimetre of her heart and the careful extraction from the house had fortunately helped to save her life. The mother was diagnosed to be suffering post natal depression and after successful treatment was happily reunited with her baby.

The whole team involved in this case were delighted with the results, as of course were the family of the lady concerned. I felt that the police surgeon deserved recognition for his life saving work that day, but knowing him as I do, this idea would not even enter his mind. The good news of course from a CID perspective, would be that we had no need to set up an incident room on this occasion.

Some people (hopefully one day reading my book) would wonder how certain police officers manage to keep their sanity. Well in my case, I can tell you very briefly that annual holidays with my wife and children played a big part. I particularly enjoyed camping under canvas, walking, and fishing. Both of my sons enjoyed fishing, Steven admittedly more so than Ian. We particularly liked camping in the New Forest, where we would fish a couple of lovely tranquil lakes for small carp and tench.

Another fondly remembered family holiday would be on the canal system on narrow boats. As a family we used the Grand Union Canal, the Oxford Canal and the Ashby Canal. For a busy detective officer these were the most relaxing holidays I ever had. You could enjoy the idyllic side by cruising at no more than four miles per hour along the beautiful canals, which were simply full of history and beautiful wildlife. This would be coupled with good exercise when working your way through the many canal locks.

I may have already mentioned this, but on one occasion I got it completely wrong whilst manoeuvring the boat through a lock. Basically, you need to keep the boat forward whilst in the locks, but as I drained the water from the lock, I'm afraid I allowed the boat to drift backwards in the lock. The result of this lapse of concentration left the back of the boat sitting on a sill and as the water drained out, the boat nearly sank. Nicola and Ian were on the boat at the time and didn't thank me for putting them in such danger. Fortunately we were all saved when people ran from the pub and re-floated our boat. The only trouble with those holidays was the well-known fact that they all come to an end.

I was soon back at work and found myself dealing with a police stabbing which had occurred at Wellingborough. Basically, a colleague of mine PC Griffiths, had made an arrest of a young man on the town centre, late at night. As the officer took hold of the offender he lunged out at him with a flick knife, the long blade of which then passed straight through the officer's upper arm. The officer suffered considerable pain as a result of the attack, but very bravely manage to restrain the prisoner who was taken into custody.

The officer had suffered a serious wound to his arm and was in some respects quite lucky because the lunge with the knife was only six inches from his heart. Clearly this could have been far more serious, and in truth, I don't think the offender cared where the blow landed. The offender had been drinking heavily and was held overnight in the cells to be dealt with the following morning. I had the privilege to deal with the case which culminated with a five year prison sentence. With the passing of time I can't recall the specifics of the arrest, but it was probably for being drunk and disorderly, knowing the individual concerned.

PC Griffiths spent a short time in hospital and had surgery to repair the damage to his arm. This officer incidentally was a real grafter and was known to notch up many arrests of active criminals. The officer later joined the traffic department where he worked for many years and became very specialised.

A murder on the train

Returning to the subject of CID work, I soon found myself being called up to Northampton, on yet another murder. A train had arrived at Birmingham New Street Railway Station with a carriage floor completely blood sodden. This had been a complete mystery at the outset, with no report of assault on the train. British Transport Police had taken up the initial enquiry and had established that the train had travelled from London to Birmingham via Milton Keynes, Northampton and Rugby. There was some evidence to show that someone may have been thrown from the train.

An incident room had been set up at Northampton, and the investigating team were given a briefing at Wootton Hall, Northampton by the Detective Superintendent. He informed us that he had travelled to Birmingham to examine the passenger carriage involved in the case and had been shocked at the amount of blood he saw on the floor of the carriage. In his opinion someone must have been murdered in the carriage and a body was likely to be found on the track.

A thorough search of the track between London and Birmingham subsequently resulted in a body being found beside the track between Milton Keynes and Rugby. The body was that of a women who was thought to be between twenty and forty years of age. The victim had sustained numerous stab wounds prior to being thrown from the train. As a result of a thorough forensic examination of the scene and the body, the victim was identified as a social worker, who had been travelling home from work on the day of the murder.

The body had in fact been found within the county of Northamptonshire, giving Northamptonshire Police the lead role in the enquiry. However, a two pronged attack was mounted by the combined investigation team. Northamptonshire officers visited the relative railway stations in an effort to trace potential witnesses, who had used the train in question. The British Transport Police tasked themselves with the recovery of all tickets issued to users of the train that day. Amazingly they recovered approximately two thousand tickets, all of which were then examined for evidential purposes.

As a result of these examinations, a blood sodden ticket was found and exhibited for forensic examination. A major breakthrough was then made in relation to the ticket. It had been issued to a youth named Jack Roy from Scotland, who had travelled to Milton Keynes that day, to appear as a defendant at the Juvenile Court. The blood group found on the ticket matched that of our victim. This was good evidence to link the juvenile to the victim.

In addition to the ticket, a footprint of a training shoe was also found in blood, on the vinyl floor of the railway carriage. A warrant was issued for the arrest of Jack Roy in Scotland and officers from Northamptonshire Police travelled to Scotland to assist in the arrest. The arrest team were successful in effecting the arrest of Jack Roy and also found his blood sodden trainers. A perfect match was later made between his training shoes and the shoe impression left in the blood, on the train.

Jack Roy was brought back to the county and interviewed at length for the murder. He eventually admitted the offence claiming that the victim had poked fun at him on the train. The police were of a different view believing that this evil individual had set out to rob the victim. Clearly that initial objective had gone badly wrong, and he went on to murder his victim very brutally. Again my thoughts are with the victim's family and I can only hope that the passing of time may have helped them in their sorrow.

The train carriage concerned in this case was not compartmented and as such the victim was very unfortunate to find herself alone with the assailant. Roy was kept in custody until his trial, later receiving what amounted to a life sentence for the murder. Clearly the fact that the train tickets had not been discarded in this case, proved vital in the detection of a very brutal murder.

Acting Detective Sergeant

I've probably bored you with this fact already, but I'm going to remind you anyway, what the heck. I sat the Sergeants' exam every year for a total of ten years and, yes you've guessed it, I failed ten times. Anyway, the management found themselves short of a Detective Sergeant for a five week period, and rightly or wrongly, decided that I would fill the gap. I was duly appointed as Acting Detective Sergeant for the whole five weeks. 'Bingo', yes, you've guessed it, I was absolutely delighted with my new role.

I was now required to arrive at the CID office a little earlier each shift, in order to brief the officers on duty. I would also allocate the work to my colleagues and brief senior management in relation to the crime status. In addition to that I would direct enquiries into more serious incoming crimes, as and when received. I was actually stationed back at Wellingborough at the time and I'll refer to two cases of particular interest.

The first was one of suspected child abuse, when we were informed that a ten day old baby boy had arrived at Kettering General Hospital, with a suspected fractured skull. The parents from Wellingborough were at the casualty department waiting for results of the X-rays. I visited the hospital together with other detectives and briefly spoke to the medical staff who confirmed that the baby had a fractured skull. The consultant confirmed that the fractures appeared to be non-accidental and probably were caused by means of an assault on the child.

In the interim, the child had been moved to a paediatric ward for observation and on-going treatment. I then spoke to the parents of the little boy who confirmed that no one else had been present, when the injury to their son had been discovered. In the circumstances I decided to arrest both parents on suspicion of causing grievous bodily harm to their son. Having made the arrests I arranged for the husband to be detained at Kettering Police Station and his wife to be detained at Wellingborough. The parents were both shocked by my decision, but I explained as duty Detective Sergeant, I had no other option in that, the safety of the baby was my only priority.

The mother had her other son with her, who I confirmed was only three years of age. On arrival at Wellingborough Police Station, I lodged the mother with the custody officer and organised for a social worker to visit the station. The social worker arrived and agreed to look after the three year old child, in the confines of the police station front office. I then interviewed the mother of the baby under caution, who maintained that she had no knowledge of the likely cause of her baby's fractures. Similarly, the father was interviewed under caution at Kettering Police Station and also denied any knowledge of his son's fractures.

I was now reaching a point where I was hoping for divine intervention. Wait for it, because that's exactly what happened next. Jill Cooper, the social worker had requested to see me, with a development in the case. I went to the front office where Jill explained that she had established who had caused the fractures. I stood with baited breath as she explained that the three year old brother had inflicted the injuries. Initially, I couldn't believe what I was being told, but I knew that Jill Cooper was a very experienced social worker. I listened intently as Jill explained that the little boy had been showing aggression and had hit her repeatedly with his shoe.

I pushed Jill for more details and she confirmed that the little boy had become irritable whilst playing with toys and had then struck her several times with his shoe. When asked how firmly he had struck her, Jill said firmly enough possibly, to fracture an infant's skull. I thanked Jill for her observations and decided to pass the information to the Consultant at Kettering General Hospital. The consultant confirmed that such injuries had previously been inflicted by a sibling.

I decided that further enquiries needed to be made at the family home and those enquiries proved to be satisfactory, in that the parents kept a very clean and well organised home for their children. Both parents were again independently interviewed under caution with the theory put to them, that their older son may have caused the fractures. On reflection both stated that they had noted certain jealousies creeping in, on the part of their three year old son. They confirmed that he had previously shown aggression towards his baby brother.

I explained to them both what had happened to the social worker, at which point it really hit home, that their three year old son had probably caused the injuries. After further discussions with the custody officer and Jill Cooper, it was decided to give the parents the benefit of the doubt and release them on 'delayed charge bail'. The social worker would put a package in place to monitor the situation jointly with the parents and children, with a view to safe progress for the baby, when discharged from the hospital.

I'm pleased to say that the baby made a full recovery and that social services monitored the situation, with a successful conclusion all round. The 'delayed charge bail' in respect of the parents was later rescinded and we parted on good terms. The parents had no hard feelings with the police, and said that they fully understood the police action taken in their case. I accept that being cruel to be kind came into play in this case. The priority must of course be the child's absolute safety, in all of these types of cases.

The second case of interest was one held very close to my heart, namely one of drug abuse and associated crime in the local community. A drug den had been set up in a council house on the Hemmingwell Estate, Wellingborough. Problems had been occurring in and around this den for many months. Reports of injuries being inflicted amongst dealers and users were becoming common place. All the indications were that they were now resorting to the use of weapons such as knives and sabres. A pronounced increase in house burglary and street robbery around the den had remained unchecked.

With my new found authority, I decided that resolving these issues would be my next project. I approached The Detective Inspector and informed him that I intended to bust the drug den. He was rather concerned and reminded me that the majority of the players were of an ethnic minority background. That fact was of no interest to me and I pointed out to the DI that all the normal considerations would be met. As we parted he said he would monitor the 'bust' with interest. I then prepared an operational order and obtained a search warrant under The Misuse of Drugs Act from a local magistrate.

Intelligence showed that knives and sabres were kept at both the front and back doors of the den, to warn off unwanted guests. I decided that I would use two police dogs and handlers to gain entry to the den. These would be placed at front and back door when the operation was carried out. I liaised with the dog section who requested that long shield units also be deployed to support the dog section. I then arranged for a unit of uniformed Support Group officers with long shields to attend the bust.

A large team of Drug Squad officers were also rallied together with plain clothes and more uniformed officers. I held a briefing at Wellingborough Police Station at 5am with all the relative teams present. I made it very clear indeed that no police officers were to be injured and that the whole team were to act as one. Both doors, back and front, were to be forced open on entry to the den, and all occupants were to be detained or fully monitored during the searches. Any resistance was to be repelled by the long shield team and any persons deemed to be obstructing police would be arrested for obstruction.

After the briefing, we visited the den and executed the warrant. The initial officers were met by some resistance at the front door, but this was quickly subdued by the dog handlers. The shield units then stood to the side allowing the main group of arrest officers into the premises. All occupants were detained pending the detailed drugs search, which was very successful, with cocaine and cannabis being recovered. A number of knives and a sabre were also seized. Four of the occupants were arrested on suspicion of dealing in 'Class A' drugs, namely cocaine.

All of the recovered drugs, drugs paraphernalia and a large quantity of cash, were all appropriately bagged and exhibited for court purposes. All four suspects were later interviewed after caution and charged with dealing in 'Class A' drugs. After liaison with the local council, it was decided to evict all of the occupants and board the house up, thereby preventing further use as a drug den. House burglary and street robbery soon dropped back to normal levels, making the whole operation an overwhelming success.

Good convictions were later achieved in the courts and appropriate sentences were given to the dealers. Even the DI was pleased with the overall results and of course there were no complaints against police in this case. The local council were pleased with the results and the Hemmingwell Estate settled back down to reasonable levels of normality. It was never going to be Heaven on Earth, but definitely a better place for the wider community to live. I don't know about the other officers but I thoroughly enjoyed the day out.

I can confidently say that I enjoyed a lot of proactive policing during my five weeks as Acting Detective Sergeant, but sadly the opportunity was not to be repeated. Before you could say 'boo to a goose', I was back in the office, resuming normal duties as a Detective Constable. Time to mention a couple of cases involving sawn off shotguns, one in Rushden and the other in Wellingborough.

The case in Rushden, involved a man referred to as a biker, who according to police intelligence was dealing in various illegal drugs. A search warrant was again obtained under the Dangerous Drugs Act and this was executed by a team from the Drug Squad and local CID officers. We carried out the early morning knock by forcing entry to the front and rear of the house, thereby maintaining the element of complete surprise. We were very relieved to capture our suspect in his bed in the upstairs bedroom and were very shocked to find his sawn off shotgun sitting beside the bed, on the bedside cabinet The gun was a double barrelled ·410 gauge shotgun and alarmingly had two cartridges in the breach position.

It will not come as a surprise for me to tell you, that the biker was arrested and secured at break neck speed. The premises were searched thoroughly, and an assortment of hard and soft drugs were found to be in the biker's possession. He was taken into custody and admitted to shortening the barrel of the gun illegally, and admitted to loading it for his own protection. To add to his troubles he had never had a shotgun licence, which may have authorised his possession of the gun.

He was later charged and convicted of several serious offences for which he received two years imprisonment. I shudder to think about what may have occurred that day, had we not used the element of surprise. At that close range the officers present could easily have sustained fatal gunshot wounds. The old sayings 'there but for the grace of God, go I' immediately springs to mind. I'm afraid to say that sawn off shotguns are known to cause devastating wounds when used at close range. When discharged in that way the result is often a fatality. I'm pleased that we all went home safely to our loved ones that day.

The case in Wellingborough was another one of those 'night car' jobs on the good old Hemmingwell Estate. Wait for it, information came in to say a man on the estate had no less than six sawn-off shotguns in his house, and had threatened neighbours with one of them. I put in a request for a firearms team to assist us with the 'bust', but they were otherwise engaged, somewhere else in the county. I managed to muster two uniformed officers to cover the rear of the house, leaving my 'night car' buddy and I to knock the front door. Prior to this we carried out checks on the occupants, only to establish that they were of Polish descent.

On occasions, there is little time to obtain a search warrant and we decided that this was one of those occasions. We knocked the door which was answered by the male Polish occupant. He was immediately taken to the floor of his own entrance porch and secured with handcuffs. I'm pleased to be able to say that he was in complete shock, as indeed we were, when we sighted a sawn-off shotgun lying on a shelf in the porch. Having secured the suspect, my colleague then checked the shotgun, a double barrelled twelve bore, and found two cartridges in the breach. Once again this unlawful weapon was loaded and ready to be used. It could have again caused huge injury to a victim, if and when discharged.

We next quickly checked the rest of the house, finding his wife and two children at home. To our amazement we found five replica twelve bore double barrelled sawn-off shotguns, hidden around the premises. The good news was, that they were all made of wood and were therefore imitation firearms. The prisoner chose to give no explanation about his possession of the weapons, and was soon under lock and key at Wellingborough Police Station. I wish to point out that the

286

replicas were very convincing and had been shaped to match the twelve bore guns perfectly.

My colleague and I carefully packaged the exhibits, and were satisfied that none of the remaining occupants was involved in the offences. The prisoner had no shotgun licence and no lawful authority to possess any of the recovered items. This was clearly a very good result and had removed a very dangerous individual from the estate. He was later interviewed by the daytime CID and admitted that he had possessed the real shotgun illegally. He further admitted reducing the length of the barrels on the gun, in the knowledge that it was an offence under The Firearms Act.

He would give no proper account for the making of the wooden replicas, other than to say they were for playing with. We did not believe his story and felt that he may have planned carrying out a robbery. This, of course, is only an opinion, and could never be proven in a court of law. He was nevertheless pleased to sign a disclaimer for all of the guns which were later destroyed under The Police and Criminal Evidence Act. In all honesty, with the passing of time I am unable to recall the length of the offender's prison sentence. Having seen people with severe shotgun injuries in my service, I hope this individual received a long sentence. The courts certainly need to give a very clear message to people who possess such weapons illegally.

Rape

Yes, you'll be pleased to hear that I'm now moving away from stories about firearms, but not for long! One of the Detective Sergeants approached me one morning and asked me to liaise with a police woman called Caroline, who was working on the rural area. He went on to say that she had received a report of a very old rape and that I had been handpicked to assist her with the case. I was actually quite intrigued, because I had never been involved in a rape case that had occurred many years ago. I knew the police woman quite well and knew that she was a very experienced officer, who I looked forward to working with.

I contacted Caroline on the phone and after the normal 'hellos', she agreed to pop in to the CID office later that day. We met up as arranged and I was stunned when she explained that the offences of rape had taken place twenty two years ago, in Finedon. The complainant, a thirty eight year old female, had decided to come forward because the pressure of her secret, had become too much to bear. Caroline said that the victim had allegedly been raped by her father over a three year period, when she was aged between thirteen and sixteen years.

Faced with such a complaint, Caroline and I realised that we needed to plan our enquiries very carefully indeed. It was decided that Caroline needed to sit down with the complainant, in an appropriate environment and obtain a very detailed written witness statement from her. We hoped that the statement might contain a detail which would help us to date the year of the offence accurately. Also we needed some evidence of what, in legal terms, is called 'evidence of early complaint'. Details of the scene of the offences also needed to be described in the statement, in great detail.

Caroline arranged to meet the woman with a view to obtaining a very detailed statement. The victim's memory of the events was exceptional, detailing the fact that her father had raped her every Sunday afternoon for a three year period. The offences had occurred in an upstairs bedroom at the family home, after the family had returned each Sunday from a lunch time drinking session at the local Working Men's Club. It was her mother's habit to fall asleep in a fireside chair on returning from the club. Dad would then take his daughter upstairs to the bedroom and enjoy intercourse with her. There was a threat of violence to her and her family if she didn't go along with Dad's wishes.

When she became sixteen years of age, she realised that her Dad's threats were unlikely to be carried out, and refused his

288

sexual advances. The victim recalled having a fracture to her ankle at the outset of the attacks, which she had sustained at her school. We managed to trace the injury and the relevant dates from her school records. She also recalled telling her mother at the time that Dad had been assaulting her, but Mother had dismissed it at the time, probably because of the excess consumption of alcohol. The couple had in fact later split up, and when approached by police, Mum remembered her daughter's complaint of assault, and provided a detailed witness statement. We now had evidence of early complaint, and the relevant dates, which I described earlier.

Caroline and I explained to the victim that she would be put through the mill at court, mainly because of the passing of so much time. She told us that she needed to put an end to her story, whatever the cost in court, and needed very much to move on with her life. Her father was now in his early sixties, and lived in Irthlingborough. I assumed with the passing of twenty two years, he had long forgotten his horrendous rapes on his defenceless young daughter. The time was quickly arriving for Caroline and I to rattle his cage.

Yes, we gave him the early morning knock, and boy was he surprised to see us standing on his doorstep. I explained the reason for our visit and he immediately denied any knowledge of the offences. He was clearly quite confident that the passing of so much time was on his side. We shall see about that, because his facial expression changed somewhat when I told him he was under arrest for the repeated rapes of his daughter. I cautioned him and he said something like 'absolute rubbish'. A thorough search was made of his home, but no additional evidence could be found.

He was conveyed to Wellingborough Police Station, where he was seen by the custody officer and placed where he belonged, in a cell. He was interviewed at length on tape and admitted that he and his family had used the club regularly during the relative years. He accepted the family's practise of having a nap after returning home from the club, but insisted that his daughter was lying about the rapes. I would say that he

289

was in fact quite smug about the whole interview procedure. Although he denied the offences, his body language during the interviews told me a different story. I was confident that his daughter had told the truth about these sexual attacks on her. and I made my thoughts known to the suspect.

Despite the protracted nature of my interviews, the father would not budge an inch and gave us no quarter. He continued to deny the offences and clearly believed that the passing of time was on his side. He was a little rattled when I told him that his daughter had confided in his wife at the time, but he stuck to his denials. Throughout the case we had taken advice from the Crown Prosecution Service and on concluding the interviews it was decided he should be charged with the offences of rape of his daughter. Caroline and I were delighted because we were convinced that he had committed the offences as described by his daughter.

After further discussion with the custody officer, it was decided that the offences were grave enough for him to appear before the next available court. At court we opposed bail, and asked that he be kept in custody pending trial. The grounds for opposing bail were based on the safety of the victim and other witnesses. Also we had fears for the safety of the suspect, as is the case with many persons charged with serious sexual offences. The court agreed with Prosecution submissions and the father was declined bail. He was remanded in custody effectively until his trial began some months later at the Crown Court.

I seem to recall that the trial lasted about a week and I for one was delighted when the jury returned a 'Guilty' verdict. Rape of course can carry a life sentence but I knew a man of the father's age was not likely to receive such a sentence. I was though, nevertheless pleased when he received eight years imprisonment. Caroline and I spoke to the victim who was satisfied with the sentence handed down to her father, and pointed out that she could now move on with her life. We both congratulated her for her bravery in seeing the case through to a successful end. I watched the father as he was taken down the stairs from the dock and he no longer had that smug look on his face.

Police officers are not often applauded for their good work, but I wish to applaud Caroline for exceptional police work and understanding in this case. Well done you, wherever you are now.

I felt it very important to tell this story and show others that offenders can be brought to justice, despite long periods of time passing between offence and detection. I also wish to say, that I admire the courage of the victim in this case. Having come forward after such a long period of time she must have been devastated when her father declined to admit the offences. I feel that I met a very brave woman indeed whilst dealing with this complaint, and I hope that she has enjoyed a happy existence since the conclusion of the trial.

Gold Finger

I now want to tell you about a case that my colleague Derek Griffiths and I dealt with, whilst we worked at Wellingborough together, as Detective Constables. It revolved around the good old Hemmingwell Estate, although we weren't aware of that fact at the outset. Reports started coming in to the effect that people around the county, were losing their debit cards whilst trying to withdraw cash from cash point machines. The people concerned were then reporting the card loss to their banks, only to find that large amounts of cash had been taken from their accounts overnight.

Derek and I started making enquiries, and soon established that cash was being obtained from cash point machines in five counties. £200 cash was being taken on every withdrawal and initially the Modus Operandi was not fully understood. The victims of these thefts thought that the debit cards were being snatched by the cash point machines, but this was not the case. The machines were checked by the banks and none of the cards was found inside. Many thousands of pounds were now being stolen, and we decided to start looking at video footage in the area of the various thefts.

The video footage proved useful when on two occasions we saw a male aged in his twenties, approach the relevant cash point machine shortly before debit cards were snatched by the machines. The male appeared to place a small object above the cash point screen and also pushed something into the card slot. The young man then walked off and was seen to return after a customer had used the cash point. The young man then removed the object from the top of the screen and also retrieved something from the card slot. Further intelligence indicated that the suspect was placing a magnetic video camera above the cash point screen, in order to record people's Personal Identification Numbers. He was also using a coil device to trap and retrieve the victims' debit cards from the cash point machine.

Unfortunately, the video of the suspect was of poor quality, and we were unable to identify him. However we were about to have a break through when information came in stating that a young man on the Hemmingwell Estate had started to put bars up his windows. The locals had noted that the young man concerned had begun to flash the cash and he had been given the nickname of 'Gold Finger'. An informant was tasked to find out why this everyday council house was now being barred up like Fort Knox.

We didn't have to wait long before our informant came in with a wonderful piece of information. He had managed to access the target house, and had seen a full size cash point machine standing in the main bedroom. Derek and I couldn't believe what the informant was telling us, I mean how on earth would he manage to acquire such a thing? The informant went on to do rough sketches of what he had seen and we were then convinced that the suspect did in fact have a cash point machine. We acquired a search warrant from one of our wonderful magistrates and we were knocking the door in very quick time.

292

As the street door was opened I immediately recognised the occupant as the young man from the video footage. I introduced myself and then arrested the young man on suspicion of theft. After caution he replied 'all good things come to an end'. Derek and I then executed the search warrant and immediately found the cash point machine in the main bedroom. It was in fact a full size, made-to-measure, balsa wood replica. We could not believe our eyes, it was simply incredible, and we formed the view that the maker could only be a genius. As we examined the replica cash point machine, the prisoner proudly stated that he had made it at his home.

The search of the house continued and a number of very interesting items were found. These included a miniature video camera which had magnetic feet for fixing to the cash point machine. This was enclosed in a thin metal skin which had been shaped to look like part of the cash point machine. A large number of stolen debit cards and a large quantity of cash were also found. There were numerous pipe cleaners, which had been specially shaped, to retain and later retrieve debit cards from the cash point machines. A large quantity of balsa wood off-cuts remained after the production of the replica machine.

In another room we found an electronic device which had been assembled in a wooden box, measuring eighteen inches square and four inches deep. We also found a number of large plastic trays. I briefly spoke to the prisoner who said that he had made the electronic device and had hoped to use it to steal large amounts of cash from cash point machines. He intended to position the trays beneath the ATM and programme the electronic device to empty the machine throughout the night. He estimated that each machine would contain a very large amount of cash and it would take him two hours to remove the money in the manner described.

I arranged for all of the recovered exhibits to be photographed in the situation we had discovered them. With assistance from our uniformed colleagues we then took our prisoner into custody and recovered all of the exhibits found at the house. The suspect was booked in at Wellingborough Police

Station and placed in the cells. Considering the reasons for his arrest, I found the suspect to be incredibly co-operative throughout the period of dealing with him. Whilst he was in custody, Derek and I spent a couple of hours recording all of the items that had been recovered from the house. Considerable time was also spent counting and recounting the large amount of cash that had been recovered.

Derek and I then carried out a tape recorded interview of the suspect, during which he admitted using his miniature video recorder on ATMs to record people's Personal Identification Numbers. He further admitted using the specially shaped pipe cleaners to retain, and then retrieve, their debit cards, from the card slot of the machine. Armed with the cards and the PINs, he would then spend the night travelling around various counties stealing £200 from each ATM visited. Of course on occasions there were insufficient funds in the account to meet his demands and on other occasions the cards were snatched, having been reported stolen.

He went on to say that he had been very successful in his venture, and had been enjoying life to the full. He stated that no one else had been involved and that he was aware that people on the estate had nicknamed him as 'Gold Finger'. I asked him about his electronic device, and he confirmed that it would have been ready for use within a matter of weeks. On a jovial note, he said he hoped to retire early, once the electronic device was up and running. I further questioned him about the replica ATM and he confirmed that he had made it to practice his techniques.

On a serious note, he now regretted the pain and anguish that he had caused to so many people. Derek and I later charged the suspect, who was in his mid-twenties, and he was detained overnight for a court appearance, the next morning. He was then remanded in custody to appear at Northampton Crown Court at a later date. Subsequently at the Crown Court he pleaded guilty to all charges and received a six year prison sentence. The good news was that he was likely to serve four years of that sentence, with good behaviour.

Despite the serious nature of the offences committed, this was one of those cases where I felt that industry was losing out, with regard to the engineering ability of this young man! Derek and I spoke together often over the subsequent years about the 'Gold Finger' case, and often had what we would call, a good chuckle about it. Unfortunately Derek suffered a serious illness in later years and now no longer remembers the case. I on the other hand, remember all of the details, and wish to place on the record what a great detective I had the good fortune to work with that day. I'm sure Jane won't mind me saying that Derek's now in a home, and unfortunately no longer knows my name.

I'm pleased to say that the banks fully supported their account holders in this case, and returned all of their losses to their accounts. I of course eventually lost touch with the offender and I hope that he never managed to patent any of his designs.

Why not build a house?

In 1988 Danusia and I decided to design and build our own house in our spare time. The design stage took three months and before we knew it the plans were approved and we began the work. Basically we had quite a large garden to which we added a small piece of land purchased from our neighbours Winnie and Joan. As a family we did a lot of the work ourselves, but also had a digger driver, bricklayers, plumber, and electrician and, of course last but not least, my brother David who was a carpenter.

The property consisted of four bedrooms, two bathrooms, kitchen, dining room, lounge, study and a double garage. My son Ian was brilliant and helped Danusia and me with a great deal of the work. One day we nearly lost our main helper when he fell through the first floor joists. The good news however was that I managed to extract him from the timbers with a few cuts and bruises and of course some dented pride. Fortunately Ian was soon back on site working his butt off. Steven on the other hand, was now of an age where girls were more important, and to get him on site, he would admit, was like pulling teeth. Nicola had moved out of the family home and wasn't able to assist us. Had she been local, I'm sure she would have been a tower of strength.

At an early stage of the building we suffered an enormous problem on site, and I must admit that the project would have been doomed had it not been for the help of both my sons. My friend Chris had just finished digging out the footings for the house with his JCB. That evening I actually ordered eight lorry loads of ready mixed concrete to be delivered the next day. In the middle of the night we suffered a heavy thunderstorm which completely flooded the footings. Worst still was to follow when the weight of water in the footings caused them all to collapse.

I managed to contact the concrete supplier just in time and cancelled the order. When we examined the site it was found to be so water logged that the digger could not be used to reinstate the footings. Steven, Ian and I then spent three weeks digging the footings out by hand, with shovels. I believe I still have the photos of the three of us completely caked in mud. I have very fond memories of that task, which were even better when the concrete eventually went in.

Not everything went entirely to plan, for example, the mortgage rate soared from 9% to 15% in one year and that alone nearly broke our will to build. I will not bore you with the finer details other than to say it all got very painful. We managed to move into the property one year after we started the project - not bad, hey? However it took a further five years to complete the interior and gardens. It was simply a great family home and I can tell you that we had a few parties, which were great fun - you know, shaking your booties and all that.

The house nearing completion

❀ ❀

Tally Ho!

CID officers were always going on courses, and someone in their wisdom decided I was due for another one. This time it was a CID refresher course to be held at the Training Centre of the West Midlands Police, the wonderfully named Tally Ho, Edgbaston, Birmingham. Tally Ho was a well-established CID training school, situated close to the famous Edgbaston Cricket Ground. I was told by my force that I was going on an interviewing skills course. Well I was in a state of shock, because I had been interviewing suspects of crime for at least fifteen years and thought I knew it all. In any event I attended the course and found it a great experience.

The class consisted of about twenty detectives, all of long standing and the course lasted for three weeks. The majority of the class were from northern police forces, and all spoke with what I refer to as 'interesting' accents. To assist us in the

297

learning process, West Midlands Police had engaged a psychologist, who had considerable experience in the art of body language. For the uninitiated, body language is a very useful way of accessing people, when police are dealing with them for a variety of reasons.

It relates in the main to signs that a suspect is lying or telling the truth. These signs can be either visual or verbal, but they are not an exact science. In other words, the fact that a suspect does not look you in the eye may or may not indicate guilty knowledge. To deploy body language an officer must observe the suspect discreetly, whether it during an interview or when dealing with him in the street. By doing this, the officer should be able to build a picture of the individual's body language and establish whether he is lying or not.

In order to complete the course, a large number of volunteers had been invited into the training school to play the part of the suspect. The volunteers came from many different walks of life, consisting of managers, builders, teachers, soldiers and factory workers. Each of them would be given a script to read which outlined a particular crime, which they were alleged to have committed. Some would be responsible for the crime and others not. It was explained to the volunteers that a number of detectives on the course would be interviewing them about their alleged crime.

For the purpose of the interviews a room had been set up with both audio and video recording, for later analysis of the interview. The detectives formed pairs to conduct the interviews and a minimum of five pairs would be used to interview the same suspect five times about the same crime. The psychologist would also observe and listen to the interviews with a view to marking and advising each detective on his interviewing skills. This was quite a testing time for all concerned, as we were all under the spotlight.

I only really remember one of my interviews on the course, at which time I was paired with a lady detective. The man under interview was a manager from a large local company and he played out the part of a would-be arsonist. He had entered a

298

well known store which sold leather and fur coats. A security officer had seen him acting suspiciously on the store's video cameras. He had been seen trying to ignite matches and set fire to a batch of fur coats. Fortunately he had been unsuccessful and the security guard had made an arrest. The guard provided us with the matches and some singed jackets. The scene was set and the interviews were now underway.

The first four interviews were conducted by detectives from the north. The lady detective and I were not allowed to see or hear those interviews. I recall going into the interview and finding the manager somewhat drained. My colleague arranged for refreshments and made sure he was both refreshed and comfortable. I then conducted the interview finding out firstly about his life style and family life. I also told him a little about our careers in the police force. He seemed to be very interested and was keen to listen to our stories.

I felt that he had been traumatised by the previous interviews and adopted the 'softly-softly' approach. He seemed to warm to us until I mentioned the Animal Rights movement, at which point he became rather agitated and said he had absolutely no involvement with them at all. I told him that I believed him, and that that subject was now history. He gave a look of relief and then opened up to us saying his young son had been very ill. I said 'go on Peter, tell us about your little boy'.

Peter then confided in us saying that his little boy suffered with serious asthma, and had been in and out of hospital for most of his childhood. Looking at Peter, I could see that his young son was the answer to his current predicament. I asked Peter if he had ever taken his son to the store in question. Peter didn't rush to reply and after a very long pause he said, 'yes it's all about my son. My son and I visited the store a few days before and those ruddy furs gave him an awful asthmatic attack'. He then said that he was very angry and decided to set fire to the fur coats. Shortly after Peter's admission, the interview was suspended and the recording equipment was turned off.

On conclusion of the interviews the class resumed and the interviews were assessed by the psychologist. He started by asking the manager about all of the interviewing officers. He said that he found all of the northern officers too aggressive in their interviewing technique, but had warmed to the last interviewers. The psychologist agreed with the manager and said he had been impressed with the last pair of interviewers. He said he admired our patience and pointed out that he had timed us waiting seventeen seconds for a reply, which he thought was key to getting the admission to the crime. He also felt that we had kept an open mind as to the reason for committing the offence.

The lesson concluded with the relevant body language points being picked up from the video footage and being explained by the psychologist. The main point made was that this suspect had facially shown concern for his family during the interview. Also he had become angry when pressed in relation to animal rights matters. He clearly needed some refreshment after four intense interviews. He needed a shoulder to cry on. I would add that my colleague allowed me to speak to the manager and never once intervened, this is a skill in itself. Knowing when to remain silent in an interview is very important indeed. A big 'well done' to my colleague that day.

The manager was then thanked for donating his valuable time to improving police officers' interviewing skills. He was asked if he had enjoyed the experience and he replied in the positive. These methods continued for a whole week and we all learnt an enormous amount by taking part. I will admit that I was wrong to think I knew it all, the course was a real eye opener. I will speak later about a murder case where the suspect only uttered five words to me during four days of interviews. Obviously the interviewing skills course can only help you in certain types of cases and the murder case was not one of them.

I have one very fond memory of this particular course, yes you've guessed it - curry. The officers from Birmingham on the course soon introduced us to the Balti House. You only had to walk out of Tally Ho's front door and turn immediately left, before you soon smelt delicious curries. We had numerous Balti Houses to choose from as we progressed on foot along the street. Obviously tradition made us consume some beer before we reached the curry houses.

The Balti Houses were very good at Birmingham, but the instructors were never too pleased to be teaching us the following morning, with the smell of garlic and cumin wafting around the classroom. Another aspect of the course was to visit Pebble Mill, where the BBC did the *Pebble Mill at One* programme. We referred to this as part of our media studies, but to be entirely honest it was entertainment all the way, because we met some interesting people. Well the three week course soon came to an end and we were on our way back to the good old police stations, to resume our day to day work.

Overleaf

The CID course at Tally Ho, where my taste in curry was honed. I am in the middle row, second from right

❀ ❀

Robbery

Soon after returning to divisional work, I received a report of a serious armed robbery at Rushden. A jeweller had been attacked in his home at Wellingborough Road, Rushden, and had sustained serious injuries, during the incident. I visited the scene and commenced enquiries, but have to report that this heinous crime has not been detected to date. In view of the fact that the crime remains undetected I will not be naming the victim. The victim had left his house via his back door to feed a stray cat in his rear garden. It was there that he was attacked by two masked men, one of whom was holding a sawn off double barrel shot gun.

Despite the victim's compliance with the robbers' demands, the barrels of the shotgun were forced into his mouth, resulting in bleeding and chipped front teeth. The victim was then dragged back into his house and knocked to the floor. The man wielding the gun was very heavily built and very powerful, manhandling the victim with ease. He spoke with a deep voice, but uttered very few words. The other offender was tall and slim, well spoken, with a good command of the Queen's English. The victim was of the opinion that this offender may have had a military background. He seemed to be the one in charge.

Two safes were found in the house by the robbers, who then demanded the security numbers from the victim. The victim had few options and provided the numbers, but not at the drop of a hat. It took him some time to recall the relevant numbers, this was of course due to the shock, pain and suffering, he had suffered. The victim had a wonderful jeweller's shop at Higham Ferrers, a small town just north of Rushden. The robbers were aware that he had another safe at the shop and demanded that he give them the security numbers.

Again the victim struggled to recall the numbers and was then thrown to the floor by the more aggressive of the two men.

303

He hit the floor with a heavy thud and this had the effect of completely winding him. The strong man then produced two lengths of heavily linked steel chain, which he used to wrap around the victim. Having wrapped the chains tight around him he then padlocked the chains securely. The chains were so tight that the victim could only just manage to breathe and whilst gasping for breath, the robbers continued to press him for the numbers.

Again due to the stress of the situation he was struggling to recall the numbers. After further prompting he managed to recall the numbers and whispered them to the bully boy. The victim was hoping that his ordeal might now be over, but it was about to get a lot worse. The man running the show told bully boy to wrap the victim in the lounge carpet. His orders were quickly obeyed culminating in the victim being rolled up in the carpet, directly in front of an open fire. The victim recalled the well-spoken man saying 'get rid of him', at which point he was convinced he was about to be shot.

This was of course an additional agony for the victim who noted at the time that they had turned the volume up on his TV. The victim's temperature was now rising rapidly and he had been left, unable to take a proper intake of breath. Although now in a semi-conscious state the victim realised that apart from the TV noise, the room had otherwise become silent. He somehow realised that he had been abandoned by his attackers. On the one hand he was relieved, but on the other he was convinced that he would now suffocate. His wife had gone to the theatre and was not due home for at least two hours.

Fortunately the attackers made one mistake, by leaving the street door half open. An eagle eyed neighbour known as Mick observed that the door was open and went to investigate. He noted that the interior lights were on in the house but could not raise anyone. He sensed that something was wrong and decided to enter the house to investigate. He soon found the rolled up carpet and could hear muffled shouts for help. Mick then unrolled the carpet and found his neighbour shackled inside. Mick later said that he could not believe the sight that met his eyes, with his neighbour appearing to be unconscious and at death's door.

Mick wrestled with the chains but could not budge them. He then ran home and returned grasping a pair of pliers, which he then positioned on a link of the chain. To this day Mick doesn't know where the strength came from, when he managed cut the chain link, with his pliers. This link was followed by a second and Mick had managed to release his neighbour from his bonds. Mick then pulled the victim away from the fire and worked on reducing his temperature. The victim was slowly revived by Mick and began to tell the story. He was battered and bruised but relieved to have been rescued by his amazing neighbour.

The victim reluctantly agreed to go to hospital by ambulance for a proper check-up. He was found to be in shock, but I'm pleased to say slowly made a full recovery. In fact he was determined to make a lengthy written victim statement, in the hope that the offenders would be apprehended quickly. The jeweller's shop at Higham Ferrers had been entered and the safe had been emptied by the offenders. In excess of £200,000 worth of diamond jewellery and cash had been stolen in total, as a result of this awful cowardly crime. Despite a very lengthy enquiry neither the stolen goods nor the offenders were ever traced. As the main investigating officer, I consider this case to be my biggest ever failure.

Detectives must always keep an open mind, but in this case I believe the offenders came from a major city, most probably London. I base my thoughts on the brutality of the crime and the fact that the victim regularly visited Hatton Garden, in London, to order or purchase diamond jewellery. In my humble opinion, it's likely that the offenders followed him from Hatton Garden, to his home in Rushden. It is also likely that they carried out many similar robberies, throughout the country.

Several years later, the National Serious Crime Squad was set up to deal with national crimes of this type and I for one wish them many successes.

I'm sorry to say, that soon after the commission of the robbery, the victim closed his jeweller's shop. He was not prepared for his family to suffer such an ordeal again. No one could blame him for the closure, when there is little doubt that he narrowly escaped with his life that night.

The sad deaths of police colleagues

I had now been in the police for over twenty years, and sad news was on the horizon. Two officers that I had joined with were now to be deprived the privilege of long life. I'm sure their families won't mind me mentioning them both because I viewed them both as very good friends and of course, police colleagues. The first of the two was John Kendall who had been promoted to Sergeant. He had just finished a night shift at Wellingborough Police Station at six in the morning and had walked home. Sadly, John collapsed and died of a heart attack as he reached the back door of his home. To this day, my heart goes out to his lovely wife and children. Just to remind you, that John was the officer interviewed to join the police just before me, back in 1972. We were all in great shock at the time of John's death and all remember him dearly.

The second of the two officers, was Inspector John Askew who went to Ryton-on-Dunsmore with me and others in June 1972. He also was a great guy, full of fun and always had an infectious smile on his face. He died far too young after a long illness and I again wish to say that my thoughts, as I write this, are very much with his wife and family. After initial training, our paths rarely crossed, with him being at Northampton and me being at Wellingborough.

Again with complete respect to his family, I also wish to mention another colleague who was taken from us all during an act of crime. I have fond memories of this officer, namely Sergeant Simon Lilley, who you may recall, travelled with me to Hawick in Scotland many years before to bring back a prisoner. He of course was a young probationer Constable at that time who shared a wonderful day out with me.

Simon's untimely death came at night when he was on duty in full uniform, carrying out a traffic check. Simon was standing in the road when he signalled to a motor cyclist to stop. The motor cycle then increased in speed and the rider rode straight at Simon, colliding into him at high speed. Simon died instantly as a result of the impact. He stood no chance of recovery because of the manner in which the rider had accelerated into him. I'm pleased to be able to say that the offender was given an appropriate prison sentence.

I attended Simon's funeral at Kettering, and would not be exaggerating if I said that there were over a thousand people present. Over five hundred of the police officers present were all dressed in their very best uniforms, to show their respect. It was a fitting tribute to a very nice young police officer, who had been mown down by a mindless thug. Prior to Simon's death, he lived with his wife and two young children in a police house at Wootton Hall Park, near to Police Headquarters. At the time, I was working on a job with the 'rubber heel' brigade and used an office overlooking Simon's garden. It was great fun for me to watch Simon playing with his very young children. In fact I would say that Simon spent more time with the toys, than the children did. I was doing some very tedious work at the time and found the occasional sight of him and his children very uplifting indeed. On hearing the news about Simon, I can honestly say that I just could not and have not got my head around it.

If I were granted a wish, it would be that all three officers were standing with me at my eventual retirement from the force. However, I know that we are not in fairyland and I have a few more stories to tell, before retirement arrives. I know one thing for sure and that is, that it was great to share experiences with my three colleagues who passed away so early.

Completely pointless stabbings

I want to now tell you about another awful incident which occurred in my town of Rushden. It was about 10pm when two young friends from Raunds parked their car in the High Street, Rushden, and were sat passing the time of day. The driver Paul was eighteen years of age, and the friend Gary was aged thirteen. Two local Rushden men approached the car and requested that they be allowed to sit in the back of the vehicle. Paul being a quiet reserved individual agreed to their request, not wishing to upset the two men.

After a few minutes of conversation in the car, the men instructed Paul to take them for a spin in his car. Both of the men who were in their twenties, then directed Paul to drive them around various parts of Rushden and Higham Ferrers. Paul did as he was told, although starting to fear for his personal safety and that of his young friend Gary. Paul was next told to drive to Wellingborough, which was a further five miles from Rushden. On arrival at Wellingborough, Paul was told to drive the car to a number of street corner locations. The whole trip didn't make much sense to Paul and he continued to feel unsafe, in their company.

The men in the back now instructed Paul to drive back to Rushden, via an isolated road, known as Ditchford Lane. On arrival at the Lane, Paul was instructed to park the car at a remote unlit car park. It was now midnight, and the Lane was now devoid of other vehicles. Suddenly one of the men named Terry, who was sitting behind Paul, produced a long bladed Bowie-type knife. He immediately lunged forward with the knife stabbing Paul four times in the back. The blows were very determined and all caused deep wounds to Paul's back. Two of the stab wounds punctured Paul's lungs and he immediately suffered breathing difficulty and shock. His wounds began bleeding quite heavily.

Gary in the meantime, was in deep shock, having witnessed the stabbings. He looked at Terry in the back of the car and said 'don't hurt me, I won't say anything about this to anyone'.

308

Terry then plunged the same knife deeply into Gary's stomach, which punctured his pancreas. Gary suffered terrible pain as a result and was also left bleeding heavily from his stomach wound. The cowardly pair in the back of the car then ran off and left both victims to their suffering. The victims managed to flag down a passing vehicle and soon received emergency treatment from paramedics. They were both taken by ambulance to Kettering General Hospital for on-going treatment, in intensive care.

Paul had both lungs drained of blood, and needed a lot of stitches to the four stab wounds. He remained in hospital for over a week before being discharged, and took many more weeks before making a good recovery. I took his witness statement at the hospital and found him to be a very nice pleasant law abiding young man. Gary had emergency surgery on his spleen and pancreas, having suffered a potentially life threatening injury. He made a good recovery but has undergone long term treatment because of the damage to his pancreas. He again was a nice young teenager who was enjoying an evening out. Unfortunately. he bumped into one of Rushden's worst thugs.

I was soon on the trail of the two men involved and both were arrested very soon after the offences of wounding. Terry admitted what he had done to the two victims and put it down to having too much alcohol. He could give no other reason for his conduct that night, and maintained that he had no real motive for the offences. He insisted that his mate in the back of the car had no involvement in the wounding offences. The other man in the back of the car was interviewed at length and denied any involvement in the offences committed by Terry. He insisted that he was unaware that Terry even had a knife with him that night. He said that he had consumed a lot of alcohol that night prior to taking the lift in Paul's car and meant him no harm, at any time. Paul knew the identity of this individual but could place no blame on him. He was unable to say that the two men acted as one.

I was of the opinion that Terry should be charged with 'attempted murder', but was instructed to charge 'grievous bodily harm' instead. He later pleaded guilty to that offence at Northampton Crown Court and received five years imprisonment. Again on advice, no charges were brought against the second man in the rear of the car. I feel that Terry's sentence was inadequate when considering the degree of damage he inflicted on two innocent young men. Despite my feelings in this case, I must concede that Terry admitted what he had done and pleaded guilty to the charges.

I quite recently saw Paul fishing quietly on a river bank and he remembered me. He said he had recovered well from his ordeal, had since married with two young children and was enjoying life. I say good luck to him and thank God for our wonderful medical profession.

❀ ❀

Murder of a Mother-to-be

I worked on many other murder cases, many of a domestic nature, but I must confess that these cases have now faded from my poor old memory banks. However I wish to tell you a little about the last murder case which I worked on in my long CID career. This was during the 1990s when a young lady's body was found in a car, in the middle of a residential close, in Wellingborough. The body was in the driver's part of the car and was found in a very contorted state. The victim had died of asphyxiation with her head and feet positioned by the floor well and her buttocks positioned up at the driver's window.

An incident room was immediately set up at Rushden Police Station. It was soon established that this poor lady had remained at the location in the car, undiscovered for many hours. The car was situated in the middle of the close, where both pedestrians and other vehicles had made their way past it, not noticing the victim's body. She had in fact been murdered the day before she had been discovered. It was soon confirmed that she resided in the Close and was making her way home at the time of the attack. This poor lady was in fact eight weeks pregnant, at the time of her demise.

The victim resided alone at the house and had a boyfriend who lived in Rushden. Initial suspicions fell on him and I visited Rushden together with a colleague to trace him. We found him at the flat and informed him as tactfully as one could about the finding of his girlfriend's body. He seemed genuinely shocked but could not provide us with any form of alibi. I decided in all the circumstances that he should be arrested and taken into custody. On telling him that I was arresting him on suspicion of murder he became somewhat aggressive towards me. Without going into chapter and verse, I spent some time explaining the need for his arrest, pointing out that it was very necessary to assist in proving, or disproving, his involvement in the case.

He calmed down, and thanked me for explaining the situation in detail. He was then handcuffed and a search of his flat was carried out. Again as a matter of routine I took possession of his clothing which was placed in forensic brown paper bags, which were then sealed and labelled. Nothing else of an evidential nature could be found and we secured the premises on leaving. This, of course, left us the option of conducting a forensic examination subsequently, should the need arise. I interviewed the boyfriend on tape at Wellingborough Police Station, and formed the view that he loved his girlfriend dearly and probably had not been responsible for her murder. He was clearly absolutely distraught and broke down several times during the interview.

The boyfriend did eventually give an alibi which was checked out and confirmed to be bona fide. A lengthy witness statement was then taken from him, which gave us all the necessary background information about his girlfriend. Shortly after that, he was released on bail, pending further enquiries. I would like to point out that it's always difficult to interview a friend or relative who has just received such awful news. You have to treat them as a suspect, but at the same time show them

311

respect, not knowing of course whether they committed the murder or not.

Again, out of respect for the families in this case, I will not be naming the victim or the suspects. A full scene of crime examination was carried out in the vehicle and also the home of the victim. The body was then moved to the mortuary where a *post mortem* was carried out by a pathologist. The victim had sustained numerous blows to the face and head, probably with a clenched fist. It was thought that the assault had taken place in the car, as the victim approached her driveway. It was thought that the offender entered the vehicle, with the intention of either stealing money or sexually assaulting the driver. It was likely that the victim resisted or refused to give money and then sustained a continuous beating with clenched fists.

This theory would be consistent with the ultimate contorted position of her body. In other words, her feet were operating the foot pedals, at the same time that she was attacked. We believe that she lowered her head more and more as the blows rained down on her. Despite her valiant resistance, the victim's head ended up right down beside her feet, at which point it would be impossible to breath. In medical terms the victim died of asphyxiation.

Very little evidence was found of a forensic nature, relating to the car and the house. However a crucial piece of evidence was found on the body by the pathologist. Two small dark coloured human hairs were found on the stomach area of the deceased. This news of course was viewed as a major breakthrough by the enquiry team. The hairs were appropriately packaged and taken directly to the Forensic Science Laboratory for analysis.

Information was then received from a confidential source indicating that a local man of Afro-Caribbean descent had been in the general area at the time of the murder. Alarm bells started to ring when enquiries revealed that he had once had a girlfriend living at the same address as the victim of the murder. His girlfriend had in fact been the previous occupier of the property. Further enquiries were made which showed that he had visited a nearby medical centre the same afternoon, for treatment by a doctor. The Medical Centre was within one mile of the scene of the crime.

On leaving the Medical Centre, the suspect would need to walk along two specific roads to reach the scene. I had in fact known this individual for most of my service at Wellingborough, I had actually watched him grow from a small boy. He had a troublesome upbringing and had been dealt with by both the Juvenile Court and the Magistrates' Court, for a number of fairly minor breaches of the law. He also had a propensity to violence and was a frequent user of cannabis.

The suspect was arrested on suspicion of the murder and taken into custody at Wellingborough Police Station. Another Detective Constable and I were told that we would be the interviewing officers. On receiving that news I felt honoured to be selected by the senior investigating officer, to carry out such an important task. My colleague and I started our preparations immediately and were very much aware that the preparations would be very time consuming. I would say it took eight hours for our preparations, but we then went into the interviews with a very detailed knowledge of the case.

The suspect was represented by a highly respected local solicitor who had many years of local case work to her credit. The interview was of course tape recorded and it was decided that I would conduct the interview for the duration of the first two tapes. This proved to be far from straight forward with the accused electing to make no comment throughout the first two tapes. Putting it very simply indeed, it becomes a war of attrition when a suspect declines to speak to you during the interview. You certainly have a moment where you wish that the room would just swallow you up.

Obviously with many years of experience to fall back on, I soldiered on regardless. Each tape lasted for forty five minutes and I must admit that you can become fed up with the sound of your own voice. Occasionally the solicitor would interject in relation to matters of concern and I must admit I found that quite refreshing. The sound of another voice can in fact help the interviewing officer, in that it gives him what we call, breathing space.

A suspect is of course entitled to remain silent during an interview, but it remains to be very important that an interviewing officer discloses all the relevant information, to him during the interview. You could easily be put off when a suspect makes no replies to your questions. It is crucial that the interviewing officer remains focused and properly discloses all of the relevant information. On completion of the first two tapes it was agreed by all concerned that a break was now due. The tapes were then signed and sealed by all persons present, allowing the accused to take time out with his legal representative.

I recall asking my colleague how he thought the first interview went, and admit that I am unable to tell you his reply. I would sum it up by saying he found my interview somewhat boring. It was at that point that I decided that he could carry out the next two tapes of interview. He was not impressed, and said he was happy for me to continue. I declined his offer and was sure that he would find it very interesting to interview a murder suspect, who didn't wish to speak to you.

We resumed the interview, and continued to outline the case against the suspect. The interviews continued for three days during which time numerous tapes were used. The suspect uttered five words only during the entire interview, namely 'it is a birth mark'. As an interviewing officer, I considered those five words to be quite an achievement. I later spoke to the senior investigating officer who said he had listened to the entire interview and found it very interesting. He was satisfied that my colleague and I had carried out a very thorough interview in somewhat difficult circumstances.

The hairs found on the deceased, were found to be similar to those of the suspect. It was decided in all the circumstances that the suspect should be charged with the murder. After charging him, he appeared at Wellingborough Magistrates' Court where he was remanded in custody. I must confess that I lost track of this case when the accused appeared at

314

Northampton Crown Court, to face the charge. I believe he was found unfit to plead on the grounds of diminished responsibly, being diagnosed with paranoid schizophrenia. He was then held under lock and key at Her Majesty's pleasure. I for one hope that this individual is still held under lock and key.

For the uninformed, I should point out that, in the old days, senior officers always carried out the interviews of murder suspects. It was then realised that Detective Constables had a wealth of experience in this particular area of policing, resulting in us being handed the baton. Detective Constables were of course interviewing suspects for serious crime on a fairly regular basis.

❀ ❀

The loss of Tony

March 1995 had now arrived and this was a very sad time for my family, with my father-in-law, Tony, dying after a long period of illness. In many ways it was a blessing in disguise, because he had suffered considerably with heart problems and had also had one leg amputated. The surgeons wanted to amputate Tony's other leg in an effort to save his life, but he declined their offer. He had suffered considerably in his last year of life, mainly because of the ulceration of his remaining leg. I will always remember his fight for life, which was quite lengthy and well fought. He eventually died on the 15 March 1995, with his family at his bedside, at Wellingborough Hospital. After a well-attended funeral he was buried at Higham Ferrers Cemetery, beneath the branches of a beautiful pine tree. This was a fitting place for a man whom had always loved gardening.

He had kept many birds during his lifetime, including chickens, pigeons, budgerigars, cockatiels, and canaries to name but a few. His final resting place was full of mature trees which I'm pleased to say attract many different birds. My dear old

315

friend was at last at peace and our family began the grieving process.

My two eldest children, Nicola and Steven, had long since moved away from the family home. Nicola was living at Romford in Essex with her partner Jason, and Steven had a flat in Irthlingborough, where he was living alone. Nicola and Jason had a son Jake, who was nearly two years old. Nicola was also expecting her second child, Ben. Steven had packed a lot into his early life, by successfully completing two apprenticeships, one in carpentry and the other in shoe making. He had also obtained two mortgages for houses in Glassbrook Road, Rushden and Pemberton Street, Rushden.

My
father-in-law,
Tony

❀ ❀

Our worst nightmare

Danusia and I were both very proud of our children's achievements. It was now Friday 12 May 1995, and we had retired to bed about 11pm. Danusia and I were fast asleep, when we were suddenly awoken by our front door bell ringing. Danusia turned the lights on and made a somewhat startled exit from the bedroom. I glanced at the bedroom clock and was a little concerned to see it was now 3am. I then heard a male voice in my hallway and realised it was Fred Mills a police colleague of mine.

I was rather concerned when I realised that he was in uniform and accompanied by the duty Inspector. I heard Fred say 'it's about your boys'. Danusia was now downstairs in the hallway and I could see that she was very upset. I went downstairs and said 'what's happened Fred?' He asked me if my son owned a Maroon Mini Metro. I said 'yes, that will be Steven's car'. Fred then said that we should all take a seat in the lounge. I remember feeling very relieved for a moment when my younger son Ian walked into the room, wearing his boxer shorts. He looked sleepy eyed and had clearly only just awoken, from his bed.

The Inspector then said that there had been an accident in Irchester involving the Maroon Mini Metro and that the driver had been killed instantly. Danusia and I completely broke down on hearing any parent's worst nightmare. I tried to put my arm around Danusia to give her some comfort, but she left the room at pace shouting 'not my Steven, not my Steven'. The officers said that Steve had lost control of the car on the bend at the junction of Wollaston Road with Irchester Road, and had hit a tree. He had been declared dead at the scene by the police surgeon.

Despite being in complete shock I told the officers that we needed to be with our son as soon as possible. We were then driven to Kettering General Hospital where we were shown into a small room in the casualty department. Steven was lying on his back and had sustained a small laceration to his lower right cheek. Outwardly, he looked otherwise uninjured. Danusia and I gained some comfort from the fact that our son Steven was still warm to the touch. We sat together holding his hands, conveying our love to him. I'm fairly sure that Ian came with us to the hospital, but in all honesty my mind was in turmoil and I can't remember to this day.

I formally identified my son to PC Mills, who then offered to take Danusia and I to the scene of the accident. As parents, we wanted a better understanding as to what had happened. Fred drove us to the scene where Danusia and I stood in stunned silence. The early explanation was that Steve's car had clipped the kerbstone on his nearside, causing his car to be propelled across the road into the well-established tree on the other side of the road. He had been evidently thrown around inside the car at high speed, resulting in fatal brain damage. Steve's car had been written off and I could see that the tree had lost a lot of bark in the impact.

Danusia and I then learned that Steve had spent the night at a town centre night club in Wellingborough, leaving in the early hours of the morning. He had been drinking quite heavily and had been in an argument with his on/off girlfriend in the club. As Steve left the club, a police officer spoke to him and asked him how he was getting home. He ascertained that Steve was going to drive his car home and advised him not to drive the car as he had been drinking. Steve took his car keys and threw them in a bush. Somehow, Steven managed to obtain the car keys and was seen to drive off the wrong way up a 'one-way' street. This then resulted in Steven being followed by two police officers in a marked police car. It was further explained that Steven had crashed his car at Irchester whilst the two officers were following him. It transpired that he had hit the tree at seventy miles per hour. I had worked with both officers during my career and had no concerns as to their integrity, at the time of the incident. However, I obviously found the whole event very difficult to come to terms with. I learned that both

318

officers were still on duty and found it necessary to contact them, to inform them that I held no malice against them. Knowing them both to be very professional police officers, it actually comforted me to know that they always patrolled by the book. I remember phoning Wellingborough Police Station early that morning but I can't recall whether I spoke to the officers personally or not.

That same day, Danusia and I drove to Romford in Essex to carry out the awful task of informing our daughter Nicola, about Steven's death. That was definitely the most difficult thing we have ever done together. Nicola loves her Mum to bits, but on giving her the news about Steven, she struck Danusia several times. The shock was just too much for Nicola to bear. We then travelled back to Northamptonshire with Nicola, and carried out the awful task of emptying Steve's apartment. We took his entire belongings home to our house and allocated a bedroom for his belongings, which remained untouched for a very long time. It just broke your heart to go in that room.

I was later invited to listen to the audio tape recordings of the whole incident. I actually found it very helpful in coming to terms with my loss and felt that I was actually with Steven at the time of his passing. The tapes clearly confirmed my thoughts about the complete integrity of the officers, and the proper way that they had conducted themselves that morning. Danusia didn't wish to listen to the tapes and I fully understand why not, it would have been far too painful for her.

Danusia and I were informed that a traffic officer would investigate the accident and that an inquest would be held on conclusion of his enquiry. Steven's body was released for his funeral and the service took place at St Peter's Church in Rushden. I prepared a fitting eulogy but could not bring myself to utter the words at the funeral. It would just simply be too difficult for me. My brother John stepped up to the plate and kindly read out Steven's eulogy. Steven was then buried at Higham Ferrers Cemetery in a plot close to his grandfather Tony.

319

Part of his eulogy had referred to our fishing days together and to continue that theme, I designed a fishing scene to be engraved on Steven's headstone. When delivered by the stone masons, the whole family were pleased with the fishing scene, which shows our son sitting with his rod catching yet another fine fish.

I was off work for two weeks, and spent a lot of that time drinking whisky in the house and listening to Steve's favourite music. When I resumed work, I found it very difficult and struggled for a couple weeks. I don't know exactly why, but I had lost my normal confidence and needed others to take the lead at work. I remember a prisoner needed dealing with in the cells and a particular colleague being picked to interview him with me. I asked my so-called colleague to conduct the taped interview, because of my lack of confidence. He made it abundantly clear that he was unimpressed with my request, but reluctantly did the interview. I suppose a better detective would have read my body language, resulting in no need for a request in the first place.

I soon became absorbed in my work and found that to be the best medicine to help me through an extremely difficult period of my life. Danusia remained off work for four months, and found that period of time very difficult to cope with. We managed however to spend a couple of weeks away from home, camping in our favourite county Suffolk. We were alone in the peace and quiet of the beautiful Suffolk countryside. We both enjoy walking, and spent many hours talking about Steve as we walked. I feel that we both found the walks very therapeutic at the time.

A whole year passed by before we were called to the Inquest at Kettering and I again found it a very difficult experience indeed. However, the Coroner gave me the opportunity to question witnesses. Even though a year had passed since my son's demise, no one had established who had handed him the car keys at the time. Several of Steven's fellow 'clubbers' were present at the Inquest and I questioned the one whom I had always suspected. I said to him 'why did you give Steve the car keys?' The young man burst into tears and replied 'I ask myself the same question every day since and I don't know why I gave them to him'. I said to the coroner 'I have no other questions'.

My son Steven, on the right, at a Christmas celebration

One of the conclusions at the Inquest was that Steven had been using cannabis. This came as quite a surprise to Danusia and I, especially when it was pointed out that a mixture of cannabis and alcohol made individuals feel indestructible when at the wheel of a car. Although surprised that he used cannabis, it helped me to understand why Steven drove in the unusual manner that he did that night. My point would be, that he would normally comply with any request from the police. I decided to make a press statement after the Inquest, in relation to the effect on youngsters using both alcohol and cannabis. This feeling of being indestructible was obviously a very serious one.

I didn't want other youngsters going down this same path to destruction. The press officer kindly wrote the story and it appeared in all of the local papers.

I want to make it very clear to anyone reading my story that our Steven was a wonderful son, who had been very successful in everything he did. He lived life admittedly in the fast lane, but packed an awful lot of life into the few years that he had. He was a lovely boy and we have very fond memories of him, which will remain with us forever. I feel that my son Steven was also denied the privilege of long life, when he was handed the car keys. I suppose anyone reading this part of the story will need to draw their conclusions, as to why he drove the car that morning.

A 'Tenure' policy

It was soon after Steve's untimely demise, that rumours were circulating, relating to the introduction of a force 'Tenure' policy. Someone at Headquarters had decided that police officers should only stay in a specialised role for a set period of time. The example that pricked up my ears was that CID officers should not remain in the CID for more than seven years. As you can imagine, on hearing this rumour, I was in a state of shock. I had been in the CID for twenty years and, yes you've guessed it, the uniform had rotted away in the fullness of time. At this time in my career I only had one goal, and that kind sirs, was to become the longest serving detective in Northamptonshire. I took the first opportunity to speak to my Superintendent and whilst doing so reminded him of my goal. Wait for it. He said not to worry, because things were bound to revert back to normal within three years of the policy being introduced.

Well, I managed to cling onto my beloved role until June of 1997, at which point I was tenured out of the CID and back into a uniform, yes, a new uniform. I was now forty eight years of age and I must confess that my second uniform was a couple of sizes bigger than the first. I remember speaking to my Detective Sergeant who was tenured out of the CID the same day as me. He was also a little shocked but said that we should look forward to the new challenges. It was decided that I would resume my uniformed role, on the rural area. I was actually quite up for it, because I had never before worked on the rural area.

Part Five

Back to uniform - and Retirement

It was decided that I would become a beat officer at the town of Raunds, where considerable problems were being experienced. To name but a few of those problems, the town and its surrounding villages had a total of fifty heroin addicts. To support their heroin habits, a house burglary was being committed every day in the Raunds area. Occasionally residents were also being robbed in the street. At weekends, the market square in Raunds had become a battle ground for drunken yobs. All of this needed to be stopped by an officer with twenty year's experience in another world.

The rural area was managed from Finedon Police Station by John Wright my former Detective Sergeant. Initially, I found myself dealing with prisoners relating to several different towns on the rural area. I didn't mind, because for the more serious crimes committed, I was using all my experience when dealing with these characters. However, after about six months and a discussion with Sergeant Wright, it was decided that I needed to be spending all my time on the beat at Raunds. From that time onwards, I started walking the beat in full uniform with my helmet raised aloft.

325

My new uniform 1997

I particularly recall working my first 6pm to 2am 'half night shift' on my first Friday evening in Raunds. I must confess that the first four hours related to paperwork, which I did in my new office at Raunds Police Station. The police station had in past years been manned by two Sergeants and six Constables. Although backup was never far away, the police station was now manned by me. I will admit that the backup didn't always arrive as, quickly as I would have liked.

On that Friday evening, I decided I would walk down to the market square at 10.30pm and introduce myself to those previously referred to as yobs. The police station was situated in Marshalls Road, some four hundred yards from the market square. As I left the station, I could immediately hear an almighty din emanating from the Market Square. Frankly it sounded like drunken jobs running amock on the square. I walked down to the square and could see that my ears had not deceived me.

I was confronted with over a hundred people milling around drinking from beer glasses and beer bottles. They were spread out across the entire Market Square area. Many of them were actually standing in the roads, causing an impasse for traffic. They had all clearly emanated from the local pub on the square, namely *The George and Dragon*. I made my way through the mayhem and entered the pub via the front door. The landlord of the pub asked me if he could be of assistance. I said that he could, adding that I would give him ten minutes to clear the streets of his customers.

He then said that he would struggle to carry out my request in ten minutes. I explained that failure would result in me closing his pub for good. Together with a posse, the landlord then herded his flock back into his pub. I then introduced myself to the landlord explaining that I was the new Raunds beat officer and pointed out that drunken yobs would no longer be permitted on the streets. The landlord welcomed me and said he was sure we could work well together in the future. I assured him that we could. Of course I was happy for his customers to enjoy a beer in the front or back beer gardens of the premises.

The landlord of the pub was actually a very nice chap, who needed a bit of support from the local police. Having seen the disorder that evening I decided that insufficient beat work had been carried out in the town, and that I would walk my beat at every opportunity. In doing so, I intended to regain order on the streets of Raunds. I certainly had the expectation that local residents would be able to walk the streets without being harassed.

Walking the beat sounds rather idyllic, but I can assure all of you that it's actually hard work. Raunds beat consisted of a series of hills which impacted on me considerably after completing an eight hour shift. It was necessary to carry a number of items including a stab proof vest, baton, radio, handcuffs, a torch, pocket book and assorted papers. I was very determined to walk being a firm believer that old fashioned policing with a modern twist was the proper way to police.

I should perhaps explain what I mean by 'a modern twist'. I decided that I would confront all heroin addicts and dealers head on. My message would be simple, co-operate with me or go to prison. Many of them were responsible for the house burglaries and the 'muggings' in my area. I simply told them that such offences would no longer be tolerated on my beat. Furthermore they would not be allowed to congregate in groups of more than three persons at any one time. Intelligence showed that the offences were occurring in areas where the addicts congregated.

I told all of them that house burglary was my pet hate, and as such would be stopped. The street term for robbery was 'mugging', and I again told the addicts that these offences needed to stop. I had a number of uniform colleagues working on other parts of the rural area, who often came to Raunds to assist me, if and when need arose. The house burglary rate for such a small town was simply appalling and became my main target for reduction in numbers.

328

Shop lifting was also rife, and again the heroin addicts were the main players in this area. I started by visiting the shops regularly in the town and removing known addicts from the premises. I then started looking at intelligence relating to which addicts were carrying out the dwelling burglaries. I started to build up my own informant base and, with the assistance of colleagues, locked up the offenders. It felt great to be able to recover some of the stolen property and return it to householders on completion of the court cases. Slowly but surely the offenders started being sent to prison and word began to spread, that house burglary would not be tolerated.

Deaths of Heroin addicts

Sadly, two heroin addicts died in Raunds as a result of heroin abuse during my time working in the town. One was only eighteen years of age and the other twenty one. Another well-known addict also died at Ringstead, a nearby village, which formed a part of my beat.

Some of the addicts managed on a £10 bag of heroin a day, others had more serious habits, and used up to £120 per day. Various programmes were introduced to help the addicts, but I rarely saw any good long-lasting results on my area. Prison was proving to be the best cure and to my way of thinking helped both them and the community. A good number of the addicts managed to kick their heroin habits whilst serving time, but others would be back on it within a week or two of release.

The management at the police station could see the results stemming from being allowed to walk the beat, and in the main, allowed me to continue walking whenever possible. Over the five years that I walked the Raunds beat, we managed to reduce the house burglary rate to only one a month. In my book of course, this was still one too many. A number of 'muggers' were also caught and sent to prison. Another very good result whilst working at Raunds was the fact that the heroin addict population was reduced from fifty to fifteen during my five years working the beat. Again I wish to make it very clear indeed that these are team results and not the results of the beat officer alone.

Whilst working closely with the community of Raunds, it became apparent that street disorder was a major concern, resulting in a lot of my time being spent regaining peace on the streets. This was achieved by simply walking the hot spots and dealing with the individuals firmly, but fairly. As a result of my hands-on approach, the street disorder was reduced considerably. I helped to set up a Residents' Association, and had regular meetings with the residents. As a result of the meetings, we had a good exchange of information which had mutual benefits, for both the community and the police.

It was nice to be able also to attend the local meetings and update the council with regard to monthly results relating to policing. I found Raunds Town Council to be very supportive during my five years on the Raunds beat. During my time there, I dealt with a large number of very interesting cases, but you will be pleased to hear that I'm not about to expand on them all.

I must also mention Special Constables, who work alongside police in their spare time, and without any form of payment. I have the utmost respect for them and found them to be very supportive when working with me on my beat. Several of them deserve to be mentioned for the outstanding work they did, but they would not thank me for doing so. Nevertheless I wish to thank them all for the very supportive work they did with me over the years, and I'm sure they will know who they are.

Assault on police

One of the Specials was working with me at Raunds one night when I made a bit of a mistake. We were called to a domestic dispute where it was alleged that the male occupant of the house had assaulted his wife, after he had been drinking heavily. On arrival we were invited into the house and found the victim had a blooded and battered face. The victim and her children were very upset by what they had experienced in the house that evening. I spoke to the suspect who had obviously been drinking and informed him that I was arresting him on suspicion of causing 'actual bodily harm' (ABH) to his wife. I then led him to the police car in the street outside and placed him in the rear seat of the vehicle.

The suspect was quite short in stature with a rather stocky build. He appeared to be co-operating fully with me, despite the obvious amount of alcohol he had consumed. The Special Constable then sat in the driver's seat, with me sitting in the front passenger seat. I explained to the prisoner that we were taking him to Wellingborough Police Station for the purpose of conducting an interview with him. He seemed outwardly happy with the situation, and was speaking to us with a quiet Scots accent.

All was well until we were approaching a roundabout at Rushden on the A45 dual carriageway. This was when the prisoner lunged forward and placed his forearm around my neck, from behind. He then locked his strangle hold on my neck with the use of his other forearm. I was now being strangled from behind by a man who had a vice like grip on my neck. The resulting pain in my neck was unbearable and I was now completely unable to breath. I managed to force my fingers between his forearms and my neck in an attempt to break his hold on me. The cowardly individual then increased his grip on my neck, making it even more difficult for me to breath.

During a period of time which seemed to be an age at the time, the Special Constable brought the police car to a stop. By this time I was feeling rather faint to say the least. I simply had to break this man's hold on me. With all the strength I could muster I managed to force his forearms away from my neck, and then over my head. I jumped out of the car and piled into my assailant in the back seat of the car. I landed directly on top of him and it took all my remaining strength to hold him down on the back seat. I found him to be a very strong man indeed and later learned that he was a stonemason. I now understood why he had such strong forearms.

My colleague called for back-up, which eventually came from Wellingborough. A Sergeant and a PC arrived and took over with the detention of the offender. I was feeling quite poorly, although much relieved that order had been restored. Clearly the actions of the individual had created a very dangerous situation on dual carriageway. I was looking for words of reassurance from the Sergeant. How wrong could one be, as the Sergeant admonished me for failing to handcuff my prisoner.

I must confess that I was officially in the wrong, and had clearly misread the situation with this particular prisoner. I'm afraid that my laid-back approach to my beat work had let me down on this one occasion. Maybe it was a price worth paying because generally I treated people 'softly-softly' on my beat, resulting in many good results. The price paid by me consisted of a very badly bruised neck, and badly bruised fingers on both hands.

The offender later pleaded 'Guilty' to ABH on his wife and Assault on Police. I believe he agreed to be bound over to keep the peace. He was made to pay me a small amount in compensation. I felt that he was treated too leniently. As time passed, I changed my opinion over the case when the offender resumed a normal position in our community and settled back down.

❀ ❀

A close encounter

I was working with Fiona, another rural officer, one evening, when we dealt with an accident in Marshalls Road, Raunds. This one was absolutely shocking, involving a fully grown horse and a small hatchback type car. The car was being driven by a lady whose daughter was the front seat passenger. It was dark at the time, and the lady was driving up Marshalls Road towards the junction with London Road. She suddenly became aware that a horse was galloping down the middle of the road towards her. The driver had no time to take avoiding action, and the horse collided with her car head on.

On arrival at the scene, Fiona and I could not believe the scene that met our eyes. The horse had been killed by the impact and had smashed head-on through the car windscreen. We found mother and daughter in a state of shock, still seated in the car, with the horse's head between them. The rest of the horse was spread-eagled across the bonnet of the car. Miraculously, although showered in fragments of windscreen glass, the mother and daughter were uninjured.

Paramedics were now on scene, and they assisted the mother and daughter from the wreckage. The front end of the vehicle had been flattened by the impact, and the horse needed hoisting to remove it from the scene. I must confess that this type of incident wasn't exactly my cup of tea and I'm pleased to say that Fiona took details and directed the enquiry.

This accident could easily have produced human fatalities that evening, when you consider the sheer weight of the horse, combined with speed it was galloping. All persons attending were pleased with the outcome, apart from the loss of the horse. Fiona kept horses herself and proved to be the best person for breaking the news to the owner. If my memory serves me correctly, I believe someone had been unseated by the horse just prior to the incident occurring.

Another interesting case

I now want to tell you another short story about a police colleague of mine, who became damaged somewhat, as a result of rough handling. I was walking my beat alone one evening, when I stopped outside a resident's house to admire the front garden. It was about midnight and rather dark ,when I noticed a new item in the front garden. Well you're not going to believe it, but I now had a fellow 'officer' standing to attention amongst the gnomes.

I was actually a little shocked, because although only made of stone, he was in a state of undress. He stood about two feet tall, wearing full uniform, including accompaniments and wore a fine looking police helmet. The shocking thing was that his trousers were dropped to his knees and he was taking a leak! I had concerns because he was on full view to passers-by in the street. On a bright note I must say it was great to have company, on my sometimes lonely beat.

I decided to speak to the occupants the following day, with a view to my colleague moving to a more appropriate part of the garden. The occupants were actually very pro-police and agreed to move him accordingly. I was actually less than delighted to find when next passing, that they had merely turned the officer around. On reflection I decided that his buttocks were in fact more appropriate. I resumed walking my beat again and admit that I now had a smile on my face, thinking there's nothing as funny as folk.

A few weeks later, I received a worrying phone call, my stone colleague had been stolen. I visited the scene and found the occupants very upset indeed. I assured them that the theft would be given top priority, despite me not having a single clue I decided not to go to press, but notified my best informants. I was of the opinion that this particular theft would be much talked about in the criminal fraternity. Several more weeks passed before I learned from my source, that the 'officer' had walked all the way to Stanwick.

He had been dishonestly received by a well-known handler of stolen goods, who had given the 'officer' pride of place in his lounge. I visited the address with a colleague and recall peering through the lounge window to confirm my information. I was shocked to see the stolen goods lying down beside the lounge fireplace, with a broken foot. I then gained entry to the house and spoke to the male occupant, who on this occasion was merely looking after the goods. I was satisfied with his story and recovered both the 'officer' and his broken foot.

On examining the damage, I could see that it was a clean break, which could be easily repaired with masonry glue. I then visited the thief who resided in Raunds and arrested him on suspicion of theft. After caution, he fully admitted the offence, stating that he was drunk at the time. He explained that the damage to the gnome was caused accidentally when he dropped it onto the pavement. I reminded him that it was a small statue of a policeman, at which point he laughed. He was not so amused, when I further informed him that he was also under arrest for 'assault on police'. In fact he was quite shocked, until I explained that I was having a joke with him. This youth was a first time offender and accepted a police caution for the offence of theft.

It was with much pride that I later returned the 'officer' to its rightful owners. They in turn quickly reset his leg, and gave him a completely new coat of paint, bringing him back to his former glory. They again gave him pride of place in their garden and I continued my beat work in the knowledge that support was just around the corner. No before you ask, I'm not mad, it's cases like this that keep one sane.

I was saddened when in my twenty ninth year of policing, the powers that be decided to sell Raunds Police Station. I of course objected, stating that the community of Raunds and the surrounding villages needed the police station. My views were waved to one side and of course the station was sold. I fully realise that cuts have to be made, but feel that more consultation should take place, particularly with beat officers.

Although mortally wounded, I managed to pick myself up and found myself an office at the local Co-operative supermarket. I was made most welcomed at the Co-op, and recall regularly using their canteen for my lunch breaks. After five very enjoyable years working the beat in Raunds, retirement was now looming. I recall stopping late on my last day, clearing a backlog of paperwork.

❀ ❀

Retirement

My official finish date was 2 June 2002, but with outstanding leave I managed to finish on 13 May. Prior to leaving, Danusia and I were invited up to force Headquarters at Wootton Hall for an audience with the Chief Constable. We were led into the same room where thirty years earlier I had been interviewed for the job. This was great for me because Danusia had previously only got as far as the lane leading to Wootton Hall. We were greeted by the Chief Constable, Chris Fox, and had a nice farewell chat over tea and biscuits. The Chief then shook my hand and handed me a retirement certificate which highlighted my thirty years exemplary service. I was simply delighted to receive the certificate, having never once received any form of commendation from my police force.

My wife Danusia and I decided to go out with a bang, and we invited over three hundred people to my retirement party at Raunds Town Football Club. Not everyone could attend of course due to the nature of policing, but we managed to muster in excess of one hundred and sixty guests. Many of my guests were persons who had been retired for many years, shall we say, some of which were my heroes.

I was also particularly pleased to see many from the civilian ranks also accepting my invitation. People who I had worked with closely from the public sector also attended.

We had a wonderful buffet, followed by speeches and a good old disco, where all our 'booties' were shaken. Five of my colleagues came along and told 'jolly-good' stories about me as a policeman. I of course replied, and thanked everyone for making the effort to attend. I was presented with a present from my colleagues by my dear friend PC Phil Saynor, and Danusia was presented with a bouquet of flowers.

My present consisted of golf vouchers which I later used to purchase some very nice golf clubs. I was also given the traditional caricature depicting me stood beside my station desk, putting a golf ball into my police helmet. The artist had done a very good job and I feel that the painting will fetch a good price at auction one day! Danusia and I, together with our family, had a marvellous time that night and I for one will never forget it.

Danusia and I at headquarters with the Chief Constable, Chris Fox, 2002.

Overleaf

A good likeness of the retired officer

Prior to my retirement, I was asked by my Inspector whether I would like to stop on as a beat officer for a couple of years. Although I felt honoured to be asked, I decided in very quick time, that on behalf of my family, it was time to go. Putting it simply, I had spent thirty years conscientiously working in the police force, and in doing so, had on many occasions failed to phone home. My wife Danusia had been an absolute rock, during those thirty years, and a man couldn't have wished for better support. Danusia knew how much I loved my job, and never put me under any domestic pressure to change the direction of my loyalty.

Many of my work colleague's marriages collapsed during my career, some I'm sure due to the pressures of policing. There were other reasons of course. I remember a Detective Inspector saying 'how come you managed to stay in the CID for so many years Mick?' I replied 'I avoid the pitfalls and have a great wife'. He said 'what pitfalls?' I said 'wine, women and crime'.

Unfortunately I'm unable to call upon the DI, who died quite recently. I was very fond of him, and sadly happened to be abroad on holiday, at the time of his demise.

Well I have many more stories but, I feel enough is enough.

Retirement was very strange for the first six months. I kept thinking that colleagues would be contacting me for one reason or another. Wrong - very little contact was had with them. My wife kept saying 'you're retired now, and the others are working'. She was right. I suddenly realised that when I was working at the police station, I didn't spend any time contacting retired colleagues. It's shameful but true.

Left speechless

Nine months into my retirement, I received an invitation to dress formally together with my wife and attend a function which was taking place at Force Headquarters. On arrival we discovered that the evening consisted of an awards ceremony, on behalf of deserving people in the overall community of Northamptonshire. The Chief Constable chaired the event, together with the members of the Police Authority and the High Sheriff of Northamptonshire, and congratulated individuals and presented the awards.

Danusia and I sat enjoying the evening, assuming that we had been invited to make up the numbers. How wrong could one be when I heard my name called out and I was invited to join the High Sheriff on the stage. I simply had no prior knowledge of what was about to happen. The High Sheriff then announced that the community, in which I had served as a beat officer, had nominated me for an 'Unsung Hero's' award. He then congratulated me, stating that I had won the award which was supported by the Raunds Town Council and East Northamptonshire District Council. He then shook my hand and handed me a framed certificate, which marked the occasion.

For the first time in my life I found myself completely unable to speak. I was in complete shock and suddenly realised that Raunds Town Council and many residents known to me were in the audience, applauding me. I found the occasion to be very emotional and just about managed to thank the High Sheriff for the award. For me personally this was simply the icing on the cake at the end of a long and enjoyable career. On completion of the awards ceremony, I did manage to thank all those concerned and thanked them also for attending. Apparently I was the first county policeman to be nominated for this award and for that fact alone, I am very proud to have won it.

Anyway, I've moved on and got on with being retired. I've loved every minute of retirement. I do DIY whenever I want. I've realised that flowers have scent. I've played some golf, done some fishing, moved house and done plenty of gardening. To mark my retirement, Danusia and I spent four weeks in Australia, with my brother and sister in law, namely Bob and

Bernie. We had a great time and I wrote a lengthy poem about the trip.

Danusia and I also spent a lot of time camping in Suffolk and in the New Forest. We also bought a small house in Spain, where we spend a lot of time walking and bird watching. Danusia also retired in 2011, allowing us much more time together, for our walking both here and in Spain. My daughter Nicola provided us with four grandsons prior to my retirement, and I can tell you that we have been blessed to be able to spend a considerable amount of time with them.

I'm writing these final paragraphs eleven years after retiring from the police, and can tell you that those eleven years have just flown by. If you were to ask me, had I got any regrets, I would say 'yes, I wish I had devoted more time to my family during my CID career'. I did become a bit of a workaholic, but without doing so, I would not have experienced all of the cases and people mentioned in my story. I hope you enjoyed my journey through what I consider to be a very interesting life - thus far!

Acknowledgements

Special thanks to my wife Danusia for her support and assistance whilst I wrote my book.

Thanks also to my sister-in-law Bernie Johnson for her enthusiasm when reading my material at an early stage of writing.

Thanks to my dear friend Jane Griffiths who was the first person to read my finished manuscript, and stated that she enjoyed it and found it difficult to put down. Although Jane has been quite ill over the last little while, I feel that Jane was the person who inspired me the most, and encouraged me to go on to publication. Many thanks to you Jane, for your very special support.

Many thanks also to my special friend Christine Stone who read the initial manuscript and among other things assisted me with my spelling! Christine said she enjoyed the read, particularly the stories relating to Rushden, where she had lived for many years. I very much appreciated Christine's efforts because she also had suffered an illness at about the same time.

I wish to thank all of the members of *We loved Aspland Grove.* They will know who they are. Many of the photographs in my book were produced by members of the group, and I send them very special thanks. In the knowledge that Aspland Grove was demolished many years ago, I wish to point out that your pictures were a God send.

Many thanks also to my friend and colleague Richard Cowley who has kindly read my manuscript and assisted in the preparation of my book with the printers. Special thanks to you Dick for liaising with me on 13 March 2014, whilst suffering the effects of jet lag. I should add that Dick enjoyed the read and will no longer be referring to Rushden as 'Sleepy Hollow'.

Also of course, special thanks also to my Mum, Rose, for bringing me into this wonderful world.